AutoCAD Essentials

AutoCAD Essentials

Melton M. Miller
Department of Civil Engineering
University of Massachusetts at Amherst

The Benjamin/Cummings Publishing Company, Inc.

Redwood City, California · Menlo Park, California
Reading, Massachusetts · New York · Don Mills, Ontario
Wokingham, U.K. · Amsterdam · Bonn · Sydney
Singapore · Tokyo · Madrid · San Juan

This is a module in *The Engineer's Toolkit*, a Benjamin/Cummings SELECT edition. Contact your sales representative for more information.

Photo Credits:
Chapter 1: Courtesy of Autodesk, Inc.
Chapter 2: ©Peter Menzel
Chapter 3: Courtesy of 3M
Chapter 4: ©Walter Urie/Westlight
Chapter 5: ©Jeff Greenberg/Photo Researchers, Inc.
Chapter 6: ©Tim Davis/Photo Researchers, Inc.

ISBN 0-8053-6420-X

The Benjamin/Cummings Publishing Company, Inc.
390 Bridge Parkway
Redwood City, CA 94065

Contents

1

Tackling Design Problems with AutoCAD

Computer-Aided Design

Drawings are a critical medium of communication for professionals in fields as diverse as engineering, landscape architecture, and the theater. Engineers, landscape architects, and theatrical set designers all rely on graphic presentations to communicate their designs to those who bring the designs to life. As relatively new arrivals in the field of engineering, computer-aided design (CAD) programs aid immeasurably in the design process. Using CAD programs, you can design and view your models on the screen, easily making modifications and then printing or plotting your design only when it is just right. CAD programs simplify the design of projects as straightforward as a bird house and as complex as a space shuttle. Even a sophisticated CAD program won't do all your work for you, however. You still need to plan ahead and hone your problem-solving skills. This chapter introduces you to a five-step problem-solving strategy to help you do just that.

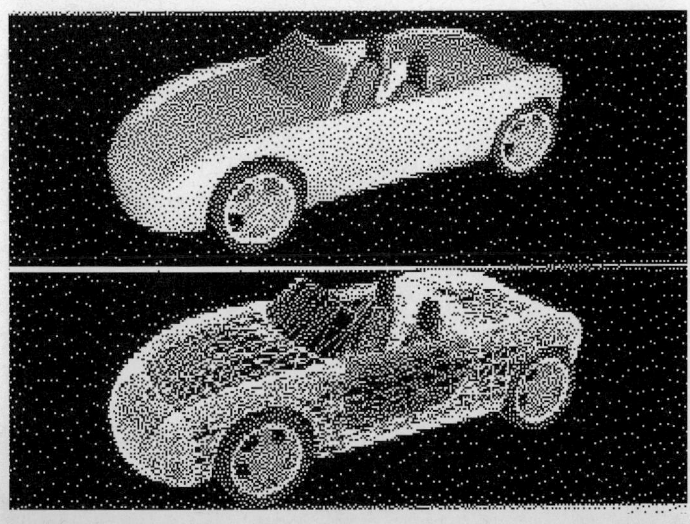

INTRODUCTION

This chapter introduces the AutoCAD program, explains the types of design problems it is equipped to solve, and lays out a five-step approach for solving a wide range of design problems. It also illustrates this five-step process by describing how to draw a bolt-and-nut assembly.

1-1 CAD SYSTEMS AND AUTOCAD

Simply put, *computer-aided design (CAD)* programs enable you to draw objects using your computer and view them on the screen. Before the advent of computers and CAD programs, design calculations were done with what now seem to be very primitive tools, including slide rules, triangles, T-squares, and pencils. Creating drawings was a labor-intensive process, and making modifications was time-consuming. Fortunately, these old tools have been replaced with hand-held calculators and personal computers (PCs). Now that PCs are relatively inexpensive, you can generate your designs with an easy-to-use program. CAD programs enable you to draw with extreme accuracy. Furthermore, drawings created with a CAD package can be saved in files, and later retrieved and modified as needed. You no longer need an eraser. The process of making changes to a drawing has become as straightforward as the drawing process itself. When you have finalized the design and completed the drawings, you can plot or print the finished drawings.

AutoCAD is one of the foremost CAD software packages. It provides you with commands in a menu format and supplies prompts to guide you through the drawing process. The prompts will ask you for the specific information needed to execute the command. AutoCAD doesn't do your thinking for you, however. Regardless of how easy and powerful the program may be, you still must have a plan of action before launching into a drawing. As mentioned, this chapter introduces a five-step process that will help you plan your drawings. An intelligent programmer does not begin writing code for a program in FORTRAN or Pascal without first developing an algorithm. Neither should an AutoCAD user begin a drawing without a plan.

You may have heard about the *AutoSketch* program, and you might be curious about how it differs from AutoCAD. Although AutoCAD and AutoSketch have many common features, AutoSketch is limited to two-dimensional views. In contrast, with AutoCAD you can draw objects in three dimensions and view those objects from any angle.

Most schools or colleges have set up *local area networks (LANs)* that support a number of PCs. These personal computers are actually *workstations* connected to a *fileserver,* which functions as one large hard drive for all the workstations. When you turn on the PC and connect to the fileserver through a login process, you have gained access to the software on the fileserver. (Depending on your privileges as a network user, you may not have access to everything on the fileserver.) The PCs are "intelligent" workstations because they have *central processing units (CPUs)* of their own. In contrast, terminals connected to a *mainframe* computer are "dumb" because they have no CPUs and rely on the mainframe for their processing power.

In most situations, AutoCAD will have been installed and will be ready for use without any special action on your part. However, if you have purchased AutoCAD for use on your own PC, you must follow the installation directions carefully before you can use the program. This text assumes that the program is installed and it is ready to run.

1-2 A FIVE-STEP PROBLEM-SOLVING STRATEGY

Solving problems is not something that you should do haphazardly. The problems that engineers must grapple with are often very complex, involving many levels of decision making. Essential to a successful design process is a well-defined strategy. Among other things, this strategy must involve determining what the object being designed is for and how it works. Above all, the design process should be methodical. Following a clearly mapped-out strategy often means the difference between success and failure.

This text describes the details of drawing with AutoCAD. As you draw, however, keep in mind that you will draw more effectively if you have a plan of attack. This text employs the following five-step process to solve problems using AutoCAD:

General Problem-Solving Procedure	AutoCAD Problem-Solving Procedure
1. Define the problem.	Identify the object and its function.
2. Gather information.	Research models and determine dimensions.
3. Generate and evaluate potential solutions.	Make a hand-drawn sketch.
4. Refine and implement a solution.	Make proper screen adjustments.
5. Verify and test a solution.	Draw, print, or plot, and save the file.

These five steps could be implemented to draw the bolt and nut shown in Figure 1-1.

Figure 1-1
Two Views of a Nut and Bolt

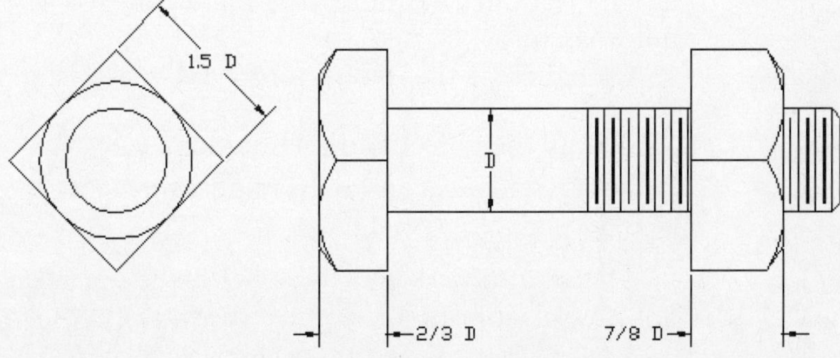

End view **Side view**

Step 1 is to define the problem at hand. With AutoCAD this means determining what the object is and what it will be used for. The object has been identified as a standard bolt and nut. Its function is to connect two parts together. Although these answers may seem self-evident, it is essential to take this step to avoid any possible misunderstanding. In this case the first step is: Draw a standard bolt with a nut.

Step 2 is to gather all of the information. With AutoCAD you will research possible models and determine the *dimensions* you will use to design the bolt. You or another engineer will have calculated how much load is to be carried by the bolt. You will have determined the length of the bolts by the thickness of the parts to be connected. The decision to use a square-headed rather than a hexagonal-headed bolt is a matter of choice.

Step 3 is to generate and evaluate possible solutions. At this stage you will produce a hand-drawn sketch. The drawing in Figure 1-1 shows the *symbolic dimensions* of the bolt head and the nut as multiples of the bolt diameter. This data is available from handbooks that list standard fasteners. Showing the dimensions in this fashion is convenient when you need to draw another bolt with a different diameter. The sketch will include the *actual dimensions* as well as the symbolic dimensions. Finally, as you are making the rough sketch, you should consider the order in which you will draw the elements in AutoCAD. In this case it's simplest to draw the end view first and then construct the side view. The end view of the square nut has four lines and two circles. The side view of the bolt head and nut shows that two arcs will have to be drawn. The arcs in the side view will be drawn using the standard style for square bolts and nuts. This data will be found in the handbook.

Step 4 is to refine and implement the solution. With AutoCAD this means setting up the drawing screen, including the units, the limits of the screen, and the precision with which dimensions are displayed. In this step you may use a custom-designed drawing template that has the units, the limits, and the precision already set up.

Step 5 is to verify and test the design by making the drawing in AutoCAD and then printing or plotting it. You should check the drawing for accuracy, and you should check the design against the parts that will be fastened together by the bolt. For example, a revision in any of the parts may require a change in the length. If a change is necessary, you will carry out another set of checks of the revised design. The design must be exactly right before the part is manufactured so that time and money are not wasted.

Again, here is the five-step process for solving problems with AutoCAD:

1. Identify the object and its function.
2. Research models and determine dimensions.
3. Make a hand-drawn sketch.
4. Make appropriate screen adjustments.
5. Draw, print or plot, and save the drawing file.

These five steps will be illustrated in the application problems presented in this module. The problems and the disciplines that they represent are as follows:

Applications	**Across the Disciplines**	
Discipline	**Application**	**Chapter**
Civil/Structural Engineering	Connecting Plate	2
Optical Engineering	Optical Disk Drive	3
Electrical and Electronics Engineering	Digital Electronics Circuit	4
Mechanical and Materials Engineering	High-Performance Bicycle Wheel	5
Civil and Structural Engineering	Hyperbolic Paraboloid Roof Structure	6

SUMMARY

With computers and application packages such as AutoCAD, engineers can make computations and design complex systems quickly and easily. To effectively use computers in general and AutoCAD in particular, however, it is important to have a problem-solving strategy.

AutoCAD is an excellent tool for creating the drawings that are part of any engineering design, as you will learn in the chapters that follow.

Key Words

actual dimensions
AutoCAD
AutoSketch
central processing unit (CPU)
computer-aided design (CAD)
fileserver
local area network (LAN)
symbolic dimensions
workstation

2 Getting Started with AutoCAD

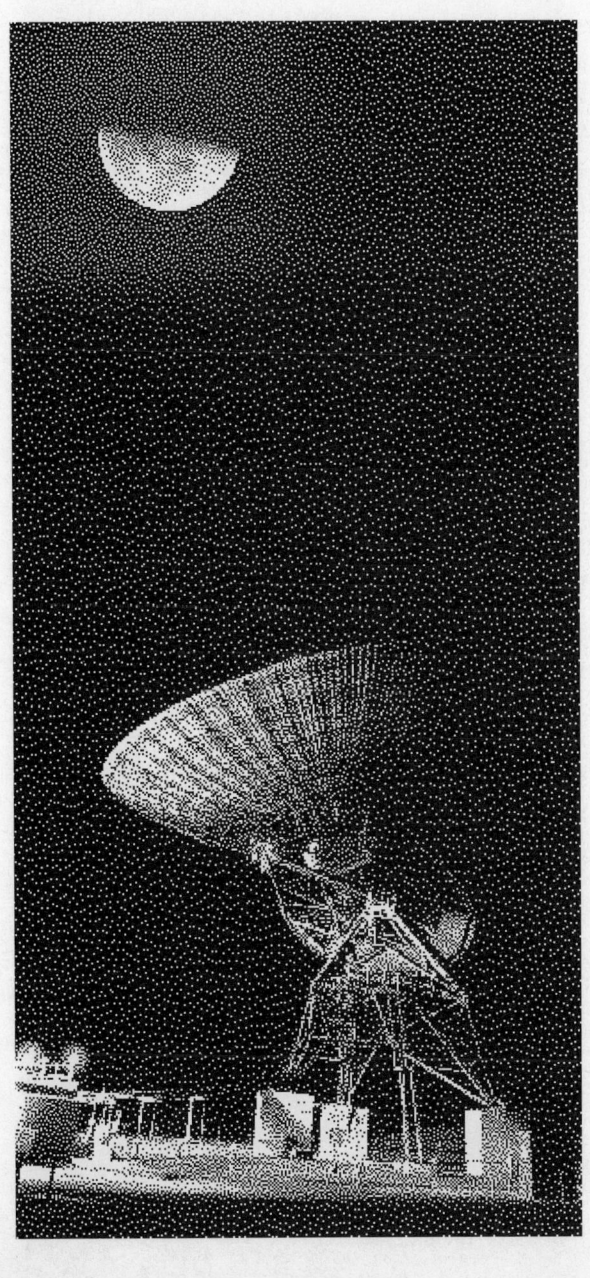

Application Satellites Application satellites relay information ranging from communication signals to weather information.

The data collected by application satellites is relayed to the earth and collected by satellite dishes. These dishes, in turn, transmit the data to a network of other receivers. The common satellite dish is often constructed as a network of structural ribs connected by plates. The geometry of the dish—the number of ribs and the angle between them—is used to design the connecting plate.

Buckminster Fuller's geodesic domes are another three-dimensional structure made up of ribs connected by plates. Geodesic domes are spherical in shape, but the surface is actually made up of a series of interconnected polygons rather than one sphere. Geodesic domes are used to protect satellite radio telescopes, satellite dishes, and other sensitive equipment. At the end of this chapter, you will draw a connecting plate for a geodesic dome.

INTRODUCTION

This chapter introduces some basic features of the AutoCAD program. You will learn how to start the program and how to identify and use the various elements of the screen. You will also learn some simple drawing techniques and a few easy editing tools. Throughout the text are "Try It!" exercises that permit you to test your understanding of what you have learned. It is best to read this module while you are sitting at a computer and trying these exercises. The more you experiment, the more quickly you will learn AutoCAD. It is assumed that you have no previous experience with AutoCAD but some experience with PCs.

2-1 STARTING THE AUTOCAD PROGRAM

To start the AutoCAD program, you simply type ACAD and press ENTER at the DOS prompt. You may enter commands in either upper or lower case. (If the ACAD command does not start the program, check your installation or check with the system administrator.) As it starts, AutoCAD displays a series of informational screens. Then the drawing area appears. After you have finished a drawing and saved it, you can exit AutoCAD by typing END and pressing ENTER.

Try It

Turn on the computer and start AutoCAD so you can follow along as you read this chapter.

2-2 EXPLORING THE AUTOCAD INTERFACE

This section explores various aspects of the AutoCAD interface. First you will learn a bit about the input devices you will use to communicate with AutoCAD. Next you will be introduced to the various components of the drawing screen. You will also learn how to use the two types of AutoCAD menus.

Using Input Devices

Communication with any applications package requires the use of input devices. The most common input device is the keyboard. In some situations when using AutoCAD, you must use the keyboard as the input device. For example, you may be required to supply the coordinates of a point in response to a command prompt. Remember that the computer cannot register the information until you press ENTER. You can also use special *function keys*—including F1, F6, F7, F8, and F9—to implement AutoCAD features. Function keys will be discussed as needed throughout the module.

The other common input device is the *mouse*. You use the mouse to select items from menus, to select specific points on the screen, and to select, or pick, objects. Moving the mouse changes the screen position of the pointer. When the pointer is in the correct location, you press the pick button on the mouse to choose a menu option or select an object or point on the screen. The *pick button* is usually the left mouse button. The right mouse button (on a three-button mouse) functions in the same way as the (ENTER) key. That is, if you press the right mouse button, AutoCAD will respond as if you had pressed the (ENTER) key.

Although some AutoCAD installations use another type of input device called a digitizing tablet, in this text you will use a mouse and keyboard.

Exploring the Drawing Screen

When you start AutoCAD you see a drawing screen like the one in Figure 2-1. The various parts of the screen are labeled in Figure 2-1 and described below.

Figure 2-1
Drawing Screen

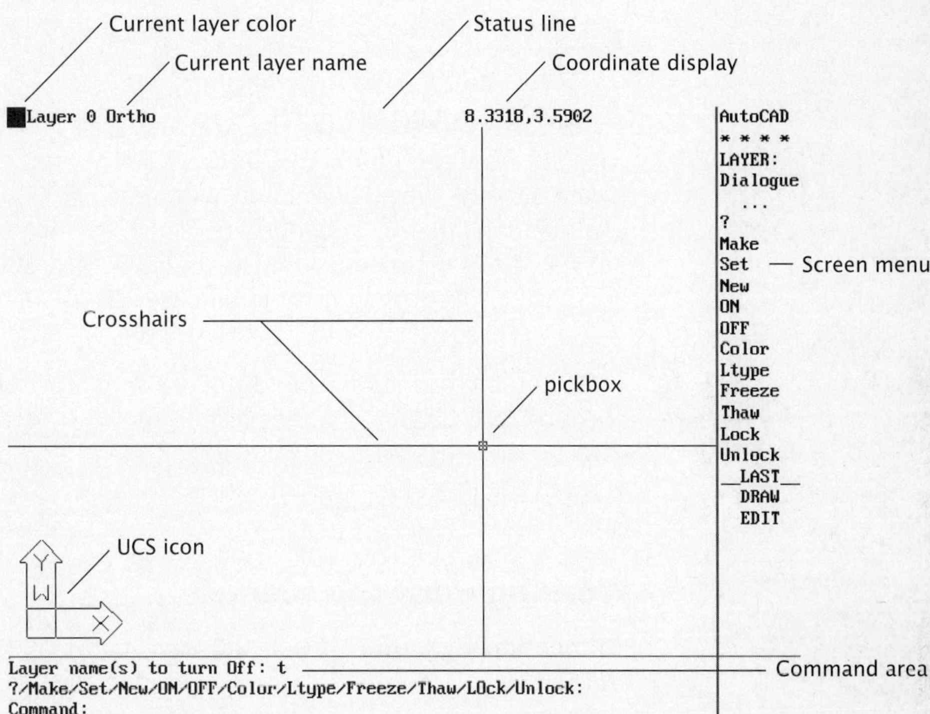

Drawing Area The actual *drawing area* is the blank area that occupies most of the screen. The lower-left corner of the drawing area is the origin (0,0) of the coordinate axes and is indicated by the User Coordinate System (UCS) icon. The icon displays a W to show that the current coordinate system is the World Coordinate System, which you will learn about in Chapter 6.

Crosshairs and Pickbox The *crosshairs* are the vertical and horizontal lines that extend across the entire drawing area. At their intersection is a small rectangle called the *pickbox*, which you use to select objects on the screen. You control the positions of the crosshairs and pickbox by moving the mouse. If you move the crosshairs to the far right side of the screen, they change into a highlighted bar in the screen menu. Likewise, if you move the crosshairs into the status line at the top of the screen, a menu bar appears. This menu bar is your means of access to a system of pull-down menus. Screen menus and pull-down menus will be discussed more fully later in this section.

Status Line The *status line* across the top of the screen displays certain items of useful information. Initially it lists the current layer name and color as well as the coordinates of the crosshairs. (If the coordinates at the right end of the status line don't change to reflect the current position of the crosshairs, try pressing F6. This function key should switch you between Cartesian coordinates, polar coordinates, and turning off the coordinate display so that it doesn't change to match the position of the crosshairs.) Layers are the equivalent of transparent overlays and are identified by an assigned name. AutoCAD starts with Layer 0. The status line may also display the status of certain drawing aids such as SNAP and ORTHO.

Command Area Below the drawing area is the *command area*, which consists of three command lines. When AutoCAD is ready to receive a command, the word Command will appear in this area. You can enter a command from the keyboard or select a command from a menu. The names of the commands that you choose are displayed in the command area. Any prompts requesting data are also displayed here.

Try It

- Move the crosshairs around the drawing area. Notice how the coordinate display changes as you move the crosshairs.
- Move the crosshairs into the screen menu and pick any item.
- Move the crosshairs up into the status line to display the menu bar.

Working with the Menus

As mentioned, AutoCAD provides two types of menus: the screen menu and pull-down menus. In some cases you can use either menu system to initiate commands. You should acquaint yourself with both types of menus and then use the ones you prefer. Often after you initiate a command a Dialog Box will appear. These boxes provide a direct way for you to enter values used in the execution of the command. Each dialog box is described in detail as it appears in the text.

Screen Menus The *screen menu* is organized in a hierarchical fashion; that is, selecting an item can cause another related submenu to appear. Some selections initiate commands directly. To select screen menu commands, move the crosshairs to the right side of the screen; the crosshairs change into a highlighted bar. Moving the mouse up or down moves this bar. When the command you want is highlighted, you select it by pressing the pick button on the mouse. To return to the first screen menu, choose the AutoCAD option at the top of any submenu.

Figure 2-2 shows the initial screen menu on the left and the submenu that appears after you select Draw on the right.

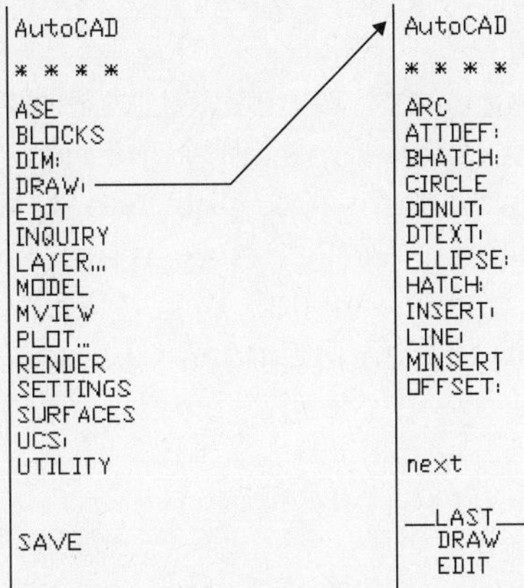

Figure 2-2
Screen Menu

Try It

- Select the DRAW command from the screen menu. Notice what happens to the menu and what appears in the command area.
- Select LINE: from the submenu again, observing the screen menu and the command line.
- Return to the first screen menu by selecting the AutoCAD item at the top of the submenu.

Pull-down Menus You can also initiate commands by activating a menu bar whose options lead to a series of *pull-down menus.* Although the pull-down menus are not as complete as the screen menus, some people find them easier to use. When you activate the menu bar, the crosshairs change into an arrow. You display a pull-down menu by placing the arrow on a menu item and pressing the pick button. You then select an item from the pull-down menu by clicking—moving the mouse up or down to highlight your choice and then pressing the pick button. The menu items marked by a triangle lead to another submenu that offers more options. Figure 2-3 shows the Draw pull-down menu with the Circle submenu displayed.

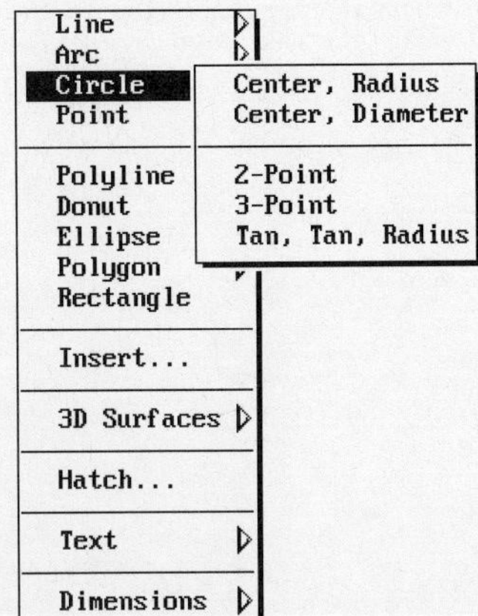

Figure 2-3
A Typical Pull-down Menu and Associated Submenu

Try It

- Select Draw from the menu bar, and then select the Line option.
- Select DRAW and LINE from the screen menu. Note that the two menus provide a different set of options.

Text Screen You can press (F1) to switch between the drawing area and the *text screen*. As you enter commands and responses into the command area, the lines of text scroll upward. Only two or three lines of text are visible at any time. To display the text screen and view the remainder of the text, press (F1). This screen is useful if you want to review a sequence of the most recent commands and responses.

2-3 USING THE HELP COMMAND

You can get information about AutoCAD commands by picking Assist from the menu bar and then Help from the pull-down menu that appears. The dialog box shown in Figure 2-4 appears. To obtain information about a particular command, type the name of the command in the Help Item box. If you do not know the name of the command, select Index to open the Help Index dialog box shown in Figure 2-5. This dialog box displays a full list of AutoCAD commands. Use the scroll bar on the right edge of the dialog box to move up or down the list. When you find the desired command, select it with the mouse and pick OK. The first page of help information about that command appears. Use the Next and Previous buttons to move forward or backward through the pages of information. Finally, exit the Help command by selecting OK.

Figure 2-4
Help Dialog Box

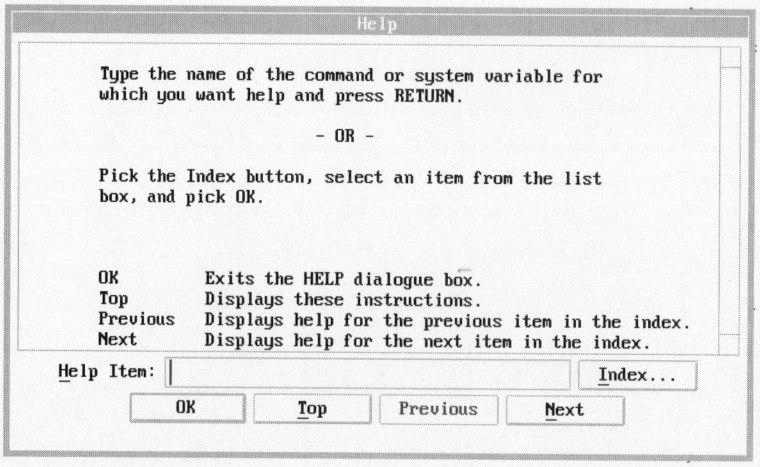

Help

Type the name of the command or system variable for
which you want help and press RETURN.

- OR -

Pick the Index button, select an item from the list
box, and pick OK.

OK Exits the HELP dialogue box.
Top Displays these instructions.
Previous Displays help for the previous item in the index.
Next Displays help for the next item in the index.

Help Item: Index...

OK Top Previous Next

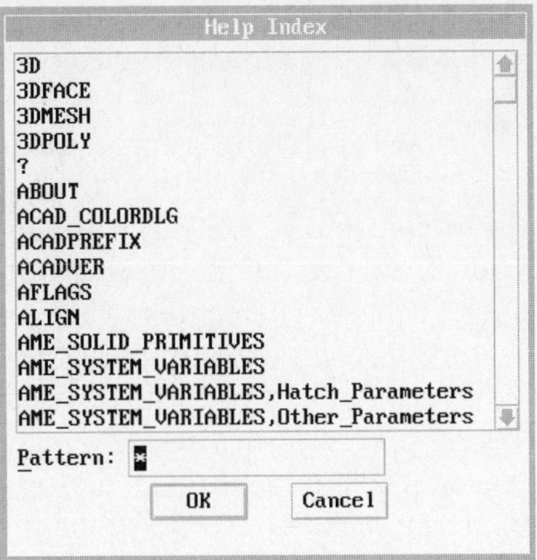

Figure 2-5
Help Index Dialog Box

Try It

- Open the Help dialog box and get help on the Line command.
- Open the Help Index dialog box to see the large number of items you can get help with.

2-4 SETTING UP YOUR AUTOCAD DRAWING

Before you begin to draw, you must take several crucial preparatory steps to set up your drawing. Among other things, you must select units and set the drawing limits.

Selecting Units of Measurement

Before you begin to draw you must choose the correct units for the drawing. If you are drawing a machine part, you may need to use decimal units. If you are drawing a house, you should use architectural units. In other words, you should select units that are appropriate to the type of drawing you will create. Examples of the units of measurement used by AutoCAD are shown in Table 2-1. The examples illustrate the precision of the unit as well as the appearance of the text that will eventually appear in the drawing dimensions. Dimensioning will be discussed in Chapter 4.

Table 2-1 AutoCAD Units of Measurement

Units	Example
Scientific	1.55E+01
Decimal	15.50
Engineering	1' - 3.50"
Architectural	1' - 3 1/2"
Fractional	15 1/2"

You can also control the direction of positive angles when setting the units. Positive angles are measured counterclockwise from the positive X axis.

The easiest way to select the units for your drawing is to choose Units Control from the Settings pull-down menu. The Units Control dialog box appears as shown in Figure 2-6. The choices for Units and Angles consist of columns of buttons. You click on the button associated with the desired units to select them. The center of the button becomes shaded to indicate that it is on. To select the number of decimal places, click on the down arrow under Precision and pick the desired precision. You select the angular measure and precision in the same way. When you are satisfied with your selections, click on OK. The dialog box disappears and the crosshairs return. If you decide to cancel the command, click on Cancel. (If you want to set the direction of the angles, click on the Direction... box.)

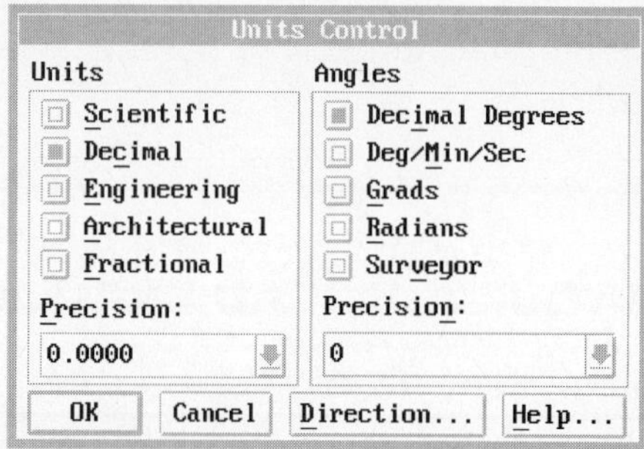

Figure 2-6
Units Control Dialog Box

Try It

- In the Units Control dialog box, select Architectural under Units and click on OK.
- Move the crosshairs around and notice how the coordinates appear.
- Restore the units to Decimal, and change the number of decimal places to 4.

Setting Drawing Limits

Before you begin a new drawing you should also set the *limits* of the screen. The limits are determined by the combination of the coordinates of the lower-left corner and upper-right corner of the screen. The default settings are 0,0 for the lower-left corner and 12,9 for the upper-right corner. The effect of the limits is easy to understand if you imagine drawing a simple rectangle using different units. A rectangle that is 6 units wide and 4.5 units high occupies one quarter of the screen area if the units are set to decimal. In other words, the screen represents an approximate 12-by-9 decimal-unit rectangle. Figure 2-7 shows the rectangle drawn with the default limits. If you change the units to Engineering—that is, change the upper limits to 3', 1.25' without redrawing the rectangle—its size becomes 6 by 4.5 inches, and it appears to be much smaller on the screen. Figure 2-8 shows the same rectangle using the new units and limits.

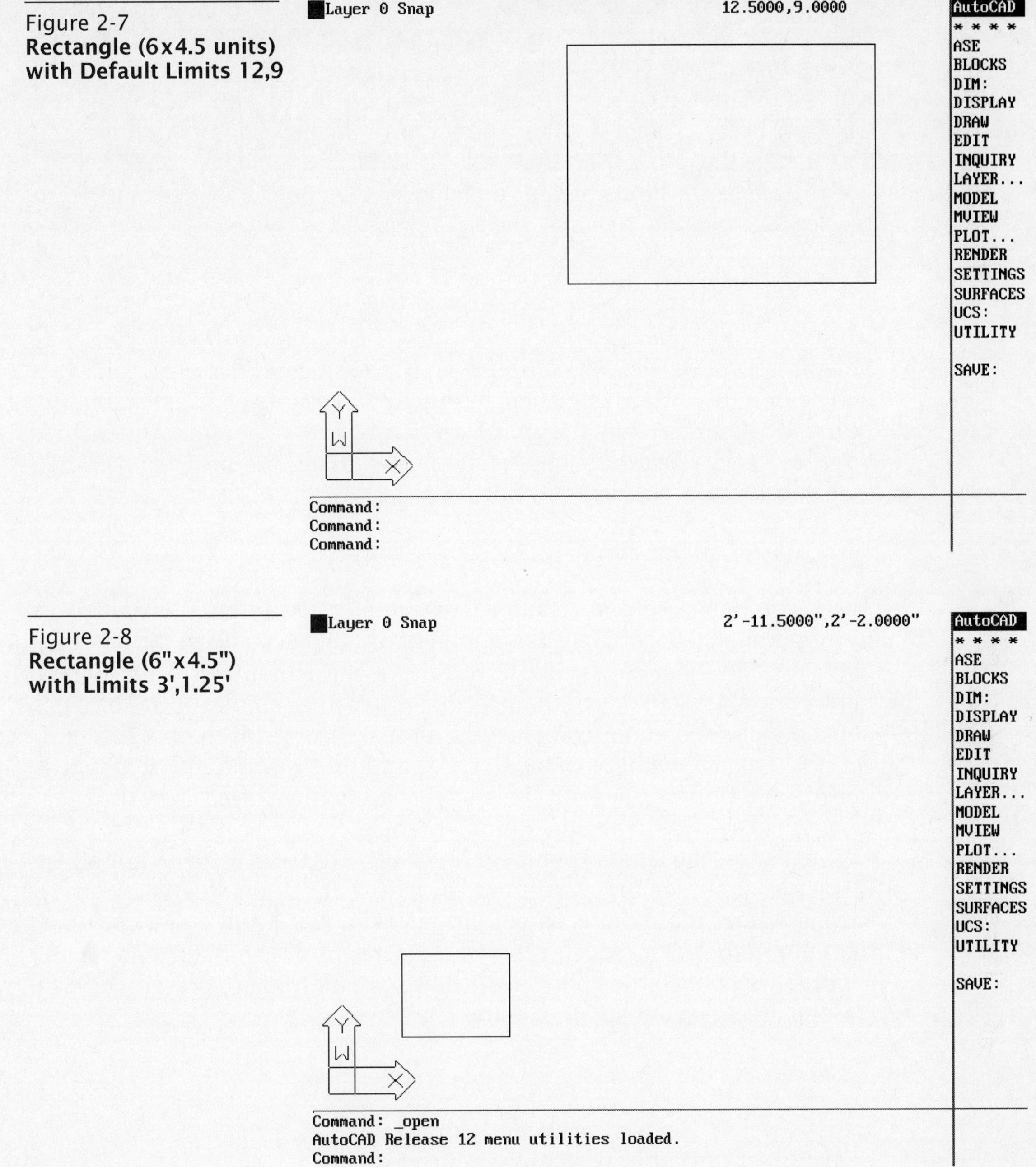

Figure 2-7
Rectangle (6x4.5 units) with Default Limits 12,9

Figure 2-8
Rectangle (6"x4.5") with Limits 3',1.25'

The drawing screen represents the space that you have available for your drawing. It is referred to as the *model space,* as opposed to the *paper space* on which the drawing will eventually be plotted. Objects drawn in the model space are always drawn full scale using the units selected for the drawing. When the drawings are plotted, the scale of the plot is adjusted so the drawing will fit on the paper. It is important that the model space (that is, the drawing area) be scaled to fit the size of your project.

If the rectangle is a drawing of a picture frame, you can use the default settings for the limits, and the image will fit on the screen easily. If, however, the rectangle is a drawing of the outline of a football stadium, you will need more model space to show the entire drawing on the screen. You will very likely change the drawing units to Engineering or Architectural and change the upper limit to 240,90 feet.

You change the limits of your drawing by selecting Drawing Limits from the Settings pull-down menu. The first prompt is

```
Reset Model Space limits
ON/OFF/<lower left corner>:<0.0000,0.0000>:
```

You can accept the default coordinates by pressing ENTER, or you can enter new values. (If you're using Engineering, Architectural, or Fractional units, AutoCAD assumes that the numbers you're entering represent inches. You can specify feet by entering the foot symbol, the apostrophe, after each coordinate.) The next prompt is

```
Upper right corner <12.0000,9.0000>:
```

Again, you can accept the default values or enter new values. If you expand the upper limits, the effect is not apparent until you extend to the new limits using the Zoom command. If you move the crosshairs to the upper-right corner of the screen, the coordinates of this point are the original upper limits. The Zoom command is discussed extensively in Chapter 3. For now type `Zoom` in the command area and press ENTER, and then type `A` (for All) and press ENTER to fit the model space to the screen. Now the coordinate display shows the upper limits correctly.

You can set the Limits command on or off. These settings do not affect the actual limits of the screen but provide a check on whether you are staying within those limits as you draw. When you begin a new drawing, the limits are off, in which case you can begin drawing an object with coordinates outside the limits. If the limits are on, you are prevented from starting an object outside the limits. The warning

```
**Outside limits
```

is displayed. If you are consistently drawing outside the limits, you have probably set the wrong limits for your drawing.

Try It

- Start the Limits command and enter `24,12` for the upper-right corner.
- Initiate the Zoom command and then move the crosshairs to the upper-right corner of the screen to see the effects of the change.
- Change the upper limit to 6,4.5, do the zoom routine again, and check the coordinates of the upper-right corner.
- Reset the upper limits to 12,9 and set the units to Engineering. Note that the coordinates of the upper-right corner are in inches.
- Reset the upper limit, this time typing `12',9'`. Now check the coordinates again.

Reviewing the Coordinate System

Another important step to take before you begin entering data for a drawing is to review the coordinate systems AutoCAD uses: the *Cartesian coordinate system.* AutoCAD uses this system to keep track of the data that you supply.

The UCS icon in the lower-left corner of the drawing area shows the directions of the positive X and Y coordinate axes. Initially in this text you will be drawing two-dimensional objects, so the Z coordinates of all points will be zero. Chapter 6, in which you will be drawing three-dimensional objects, introduces the Z axis.

As you begin to draw objects, you are prompted for the coordinates of various points. At that time you enter the X and Y coordinates for points in a drawing by typing the values or by picking the location on the screen with the mouse. If you know the exact coordinates of a point, you can enter them from the keyboard. However, if you do not know the exact coordinates, you have to use the mouse.

Angles are measured from the positive X axis. Positive angles are counterclockwise. This information is important when you use angles to describe the locations of points or when you rotate objects in the plane.

The coordinate system is illustrated in Figure 2-9.

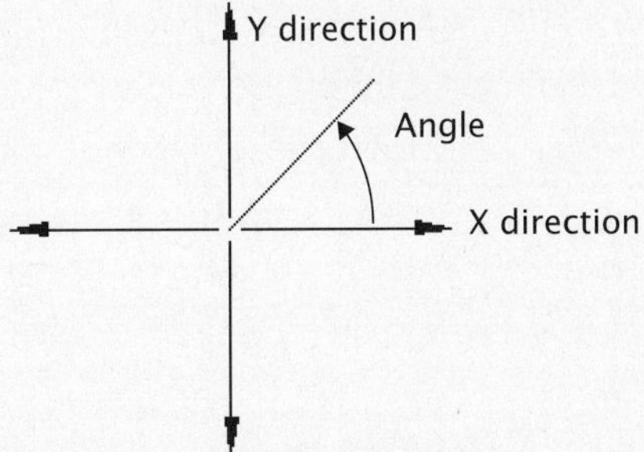

Figure 2-9
Cartesian Coordinates

2-5 MANAGING YOUR FILES

To work successfully with AutoCAD, you need to master a few easy file-management skills. You must know how to save a file, open an existing file, and create a new drawing (the electronic equivalent of getting a fresh sheet of paper).

Saving a Drawing File

You should make a habit of routinely saving your drawings so you can retrieve them later and to avoid the disaster of losing a large amount of work if the computer system goes down. Saving drawing files is a simple matter of specifying the name of the drawing and the drive or directory where the file is to be saved. To save a drawing, open the File pull-down menu, which is shown in Figure 2-10.

Figure 2-10
File Pull-down Menu

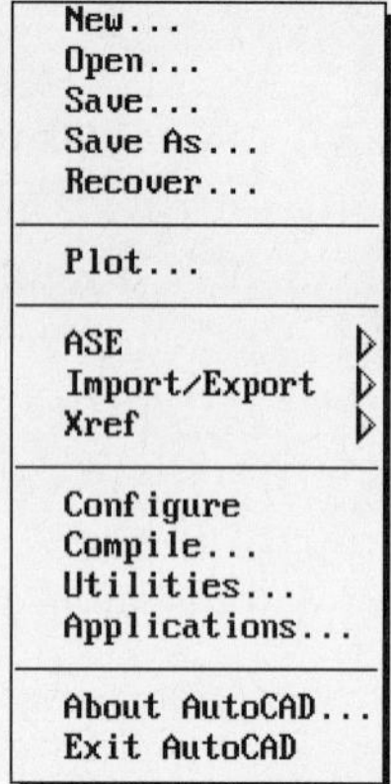

Click on the Save As option to display the Save Drawing As dialog box shown in Figure 2-11. At the flashing cursor in the File box, type the drive designation and then the name of the drawing. Click on OK to complete the task. AutoCAD names your files and automatically supplies the .DWG extension. It is easy to open drawing files because by default AutoCAD displays the names of only the drawing files. If you want to save the file subsequently without changing its name, choose Save from the File menu. If you want to save it under a new name, choose Save As from the File menu.

Figure 2-11
Save Drawing As Dialog Box

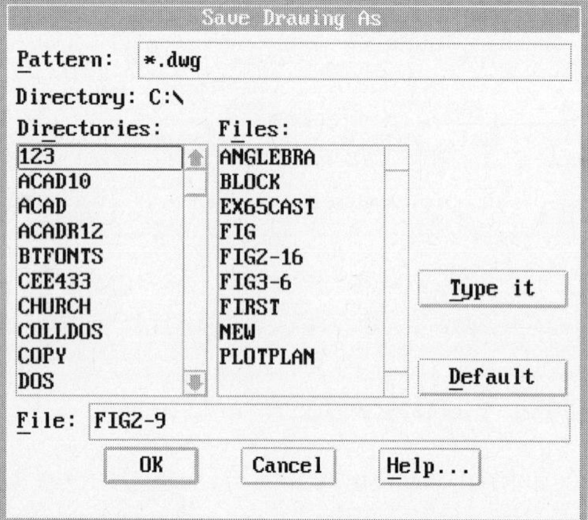

Try It

- Although you have not drawn anything yet, save your file as FIRST to save any settings you have changed. The file is saved to the default directory, which is probably C:\.
- Try saving your file to the A:\ directory. You need to have a formatted disk in drive A.

Opening a File

Once you have saved a drawing file, you can open it later to resume your work. Select the Open option on the File pull-down menu to open files that have been saved. The Open Drawing dialog box shown in Figure 2-12 appears; as you can see it is very similar to the Save Drawing As dialog box.

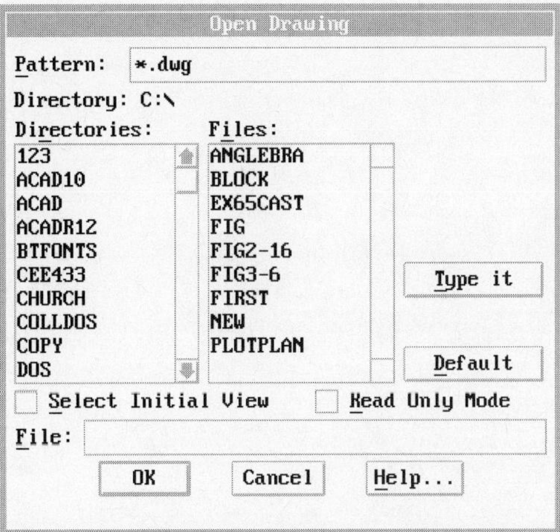

Figure 2-12
Open Drawing Dialog Box

In the left column of the Open Drawing dialog box is a list of directories. The current directory, which is most likely C:\, is where AutoCAD is searching for .DWG files. Any .DWG files in the current directory are listed in the right column. (You can use the scroll bar to scroll up and down the list as needed.) To open a drawing file, click on its name, and then click on OK. To see the contents of one of the other directories, use the scroll bar as needed until the directory name is in view, and then double click on the name. The name of the current directory displayed at the top of the column changes, and the list of files also changes. If you can remember a complete file name (file name plus directory), you can type the name directly into the File box and then click on OK to open the file.

Try It

- Open the FIRST.DWG drawing file in the C:\ directory.
- Try opening the file from the A:\ directory.

Creating a New Drawing

When you have completed a drawing, you may want to go directly to a new project. First you must clear the screen. You can do this by selecting New from the File pull-down menu. If you have not saved the current drawing, a dialog box appears with three options: Save Changes, Discard Changes, and Cancel Command. Choose Save Changes if you want to save the latest changes to your current drawing. Choose Discard Changes if you do not want to save the version of the drawing on the screen. Choose Cancel Command to continue with the current drawing.

The Save Changes and Discard Changes options lead to the Create New Drawing dialog box shown in Figure 2-13. Type the name of the new drawing in the New Drawing Name box, and AutoCAD clears the screen and puts the default settings of Units and Limits in effect as before. The other options in this dialog box will be discussed in detail in Chapter 4.

Figure 2-13
Create New Drawing Dialog Box

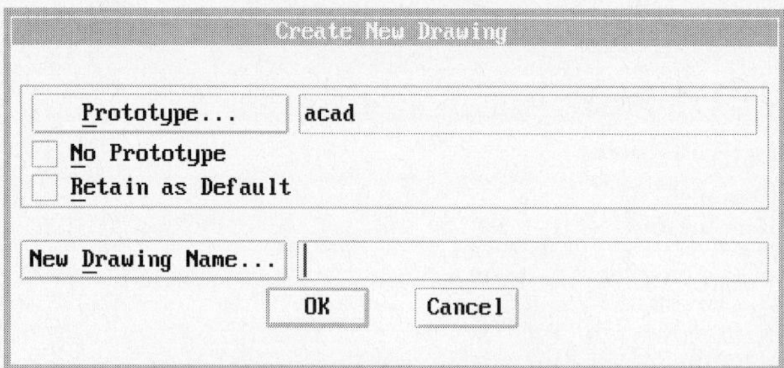

Try It

◆ Try creating a new drawing now.

Exiting AutoCAD

When you have finished with a drawing session, you can exit the AutoCAD program by clicking on the Exit AutoCAD option at the bottom of the File pull-down menu. If you have not saved the current drawing file, you are presented with three options: Save Changes, Discard Changes, and Cancel Command.

2-6 USING SIMPLE DRAWING TOOLS

Drawing with AutoCAD is a matter of drawing various geometric shapes on the screen (the drawing area) or editing existing shapes until the image you want is complete. This chapter demonstrates how to construct the easiest shapes: lines and circles. More complex shapes, such as arcs, ellipses, and polygons, are presented in later chapters. Most finished drawings are made up of some or all of these shapes. In this text the word *object* refers to a shape that has been drawn.

As important as drawing basic objects is the task of editing objects. Editing may include erasing all or part of an object, copying, moving, extending or trimming, and scaling or changing the size of an object. Later in this chapter you will learn some simple editing techniques.

Drawing Lines

The most common objects in drawings are *lines.* Lines can be combined to construct other objects such as triangles and rectangles.

Initiate the Line command by selecting Line from the Draw pull-down menu. The following prompt appears in the command area:

```
From point:
```

Type the coordinates of the first point on the line, or pick a point on the screen with the mouse. AutoCAD supplies the next prompt:

```
To point:
```

Respond by typing the coordinates of the next point or picking the next point with the mouse. AutoCAD continues supplying the "To point:" prompt until you press ENTER without choosing the coordinates of a point. If you move the mouse during the course of the command, you will see a line (called a rubber band) forming as the end of the line is dragged to a new position. This drag effect is common to many of the drawing commands.

Try It

- Initiate the Line command and start drawing the square shown in Figure 2-14.
- Start the square at point 5,1.
- Enter `9,1` as the second corner of the square.
- Complete the square by entering the coordinates of the other corners.

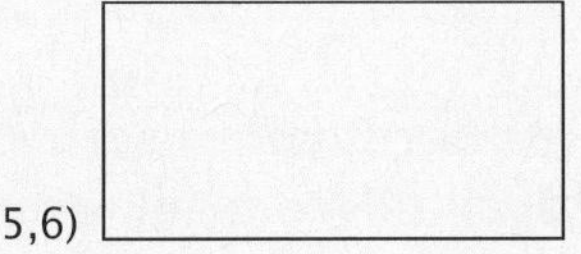

Figure 2-14
Drawing Lines

The Line command has a Close option for closing a figure of more than two sides—that is, drawing a line from the last selected point back to the first point. To issue the Close option, type C and press ENTER at the "To point:" prompt. For example, in this case, instead of entering the coordinates 5,1 to close the square, enter the coordinates of the fourth corner (5,5), and then use the Close option to both complete the square and terminate the Line command.

Drawing Lines with Relative Coordinates

Sometimes you cannot enter coordinates simply as X,Y values. Consider, for example, drawing a rectangle when the length of the sides is not an integer. You could use the length of the sides to calculate the coordinates of the corners and proceed as when drawing the previous square. It is more convenient, however, to let the computer do the arithmetic for you with the use of *relative coordinates.* Relative coordinates use the location of the last point that was entered as the origin for the next point. The @ symbol signals to AutoCAD that the coordinate values entered are to be added to that last location.

After you enter the starting point, type the @ symbol followed by the coordinates of the next point. The @ symbol tells AutoCAD to add the following values to the coordinates of the previous point. For example, @3,2 means add 3 to the X coordinate and add 2 to the Y coordinate of the previous point.

Try It

Use relative coordinates to draw the upper rectangle in Figure 2-14. The horizontal sides are 3.2 units long and the vertical sides are 1.6 units long.

- Start the Line command again, and start the rectangle at point 5,6.
- Enter the relative coordinates in response to the "To point:" prompt.
- Complete the rectangle by closing it rather than repeating the initial coordinates.
- Save the drawing using the same name.

Another form of relative coordinates uses the *polar coordinate* system, in which the location of a point from the origin is calculated using the length of a radius (R) and the angle (α) the radius makes with the X axis. The horizontal and vertical distances between the origin of the polar coordinates and the second point are R$\cos(\alpha)$ and R$\sin(\alpha)$, respectively.

For example, suppose the distance between two points is 3.7, and the second point lies on a line that makes an angle α of 153 degrees with the X axis. You can locate the second point by entering @3.7<153, which means "Enter a point relative to the last point, 3.7 units along a line making an angle of 153 degrees with the positive X axis." When AutoCAD sees this entry, it computes the horizontal and vertical distances to the second point and adds them to the X and Y coordinates of the first point. This is much more convenient than having to do the arithmetic yourself.

Draw the equilateral triangles shown in Figure 2-15. Line A–C is vertical, so line A–B must be 30 degrees with the X axis. Since the internal angles of equilateral triangles are 60 degrees, line B–C must make an angle of 150 degrees with the X axis.

Try It

- Open a new drawing called TRIANGLE.
- Start the Line command, type 6,4, and press ENTER in response to the "From point:" prompt.
- Type @3<30 and press ENTER in response to the first "To point:" prompt.
- Complete the triangle.
- Draw the mirror image of the triangle about the X axis by substituting negative values for each of the angles in the last drawing.

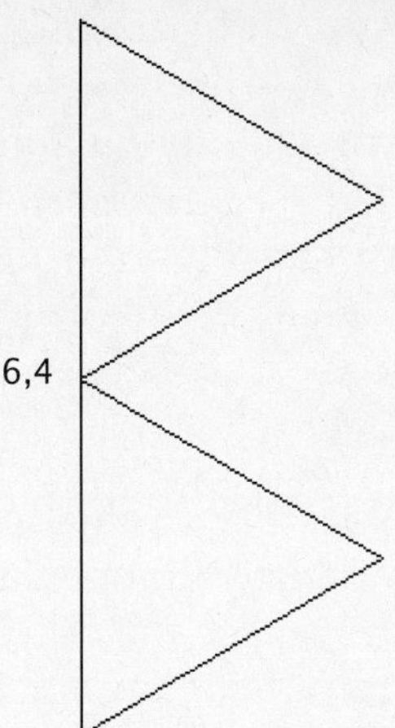

Figure 2-15
Using Relative Polar Coordinates

Drawing Circles

Circles are another commonly used object in engineering drawings. A circle may represent anything from a hole through an object to a flange, a screw head, or the end of a pipe. The size is usually given as a radius or diameter, while the location is defined by the coordinates of the center of the hole. In addition, circles can be drawn through two points that are the ends of the diameter, through three points, and tangent to two other objects on the screen.

Selecting Circle from the Draw pull-down menu displays these options for drawing circles:

Table 2-2 Circle Options

Option	User's Response
Center, Radius	Enter the coordinates of the center point and the length of the radius.
Center, Diameter	Enter the coordinates of the center point and the length of the diameter.
2-Point	Enter the coordinates of points on the ends of the diameter.
3-Point	Enter the coordinates of any three points on the circle.
Tan, Tan, Radius	Select any two objects on the screen, and enter the length of the radius of the circle. AutoCAD constructs a circle that is tangent to the two objects and has that radius.

To draw a circle using the Center, Radius option, select the option from the Draw, Circle pull-down menus. At the prompt

```
3P/2P/TTR/<Center point>:
```

pick any point on the screen or enter the coordinates of the center point from the keyboard. At the next prompt,

```
Diameter/<Radius>:
```

enter a value for the radius or move the crosshairs to select the radius. As you move the crosshairs you see the circle being formed. The circle appears and the command terminates automatically.

The Center, Diameter option is essentially the same as the Center, Radius option. Select Center, Diameter from the Draw, Circle pull-down menus and enter the center point as before. The next prompt is

```
Diameter/<Radius>: Diameter:
```

indicating that AutoCAD is expecting a value for the diameter. Enter the diameter from the keyboard or use the mouse to select the diameter. Again, as you move the mouse you see the circle being formed. This time the position of the crosshairs is outside the circle as it forms.

To draw a circle with the 2P option, select the option from the Draw, Circle pull-down menus. The prompt

```
First point on diameter:
```

appears. Enter a point on the end of the diameter of the circle from the keyboard or by picking a point with the mouse. At the next prompt

```
Second point on diameter:
```

enter a second point to complete the circle. Again, as you move the crosshairs you see the circle being formed.

If you select 3P from the Draw, Circle pull-down menu the prompt

```
First point:
```

appears. Select a point on the circumference of the circle and the next prompt

```
Second point:
```

appears. Select a second point. At the prompt

```
Third point:
```

select the third point on the circumference to complete the circle. The circle is formed as you move the crosshairs to locate the third point.

To draw a circle that is tangent to two objects in the drawing, select Tan, Tan, Radius from the Draw, Circle pull-down menus. At the prompt

```
Enter Tangent spec:
```

pick any object in the drawing using the pickbox. At the prompt

```
Enter Second Tangent spec:
```

pick a different object in the drawing. At the prompt

```
Radius:
```

enter a value from the keyboard. AutoCAD uses the value to construct a circle that is tangent to the two objects. If the circle cannot be constructed, the message

```
Circle does not exist.
```

appears in the Command area. This message usually means that the radius is too small.

Try It

- Open a new drawing called CIRCLES.
- Draw a circle with its center at 7,6 and a radius of 1.5.
- Draw a circle with its center at 7,6 and a diameter of 1.5. These are the two concentric circles shown in Figure 2-16.

Figure 2-16
Drawing Circles

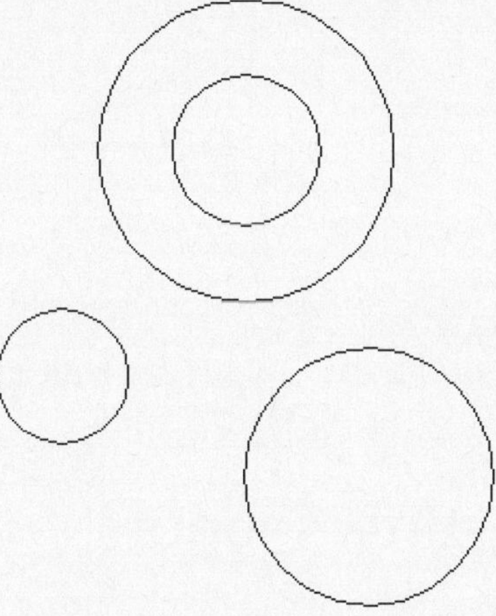

If you moved the mouse between typing the center coordinates and the radius, you may have noticed that a circular rubber band was formed as the crosshairs moved. This is the same thing that happened when you moved the cursor during the Line command.

Try It

- Draw a two-point circle with the coordinates of the ends of the diameter at 4.5,4 and 5.75,3.5.
- Draw a three-point circle with points at 8.5,1.5, 7,2.4, and 8,4. Notice that the rubber band did not begin to form until you entered the first two points
  These circles are shown in Figure 2-16.

Drawing circles that are tangent to two other objects is more complex. You need to pick two objects and supply the radius. To pick an object on the screen, you move the crosshairs until the object goes through the pickbox and then press the pick button on the mouse. Commonly two circles can be drawn tangent to two objects. AutoCAD calculates the location of the center of a new circle based on the radius and the two objects you selected. Which circle you get depends on where you pick the objects.

Try It

- Open a new drawing called TTRCIR.
- Draw two lines from 4,7 to 8,2 and from 4,3 to 9,7.
- Start the Circle command and select the Tan, Tan, Radius option.
- Pick the lines near their left ends as the first and second tangent specifications.
- Enter `1.5` as the radius.
- Repeat the task, selecting the lines near their right ends and using the same radius. Your screen should now resemble Figure 2-17. Notice that there is no rubber band because AutoCAD needs a specific radius before a circle can be completed.

Figure 2-17
Drawing Circles Using the Tan, Tan, Radius Option

2-7 USING SIMPLE EDITING TOOLS

This section presents some simple techniques for editing drawings. Before you can change objects in any way, however, you must learn how to select objects.

Selecting Objects for Editing

To begin editing your drawings, you can select the objects you want to change in two ways. The first approach is to choose the editing command that you want to use and then select the objects to be changed. The second approach, a feature of Release 12, is to select the objects and then choose the editing command. Both techniques are useful; it is up to you to decide which approach to use in any given situation.

Selecting Individual Objects When you select the editing command first, the command area displays the prompt

```
Select objects:
```

The crosshairs disappear, but a small square—called an *aperture*—remains. You can select objects one at a time by moving the mouse until the object goes through the aperture and then pressing the pick button on the mouse. When you select the object, it appears to be made up of short dashes, as shown in Figure 2-18. Two of the four lines making up the square in Figure 2-18 have been selected, and the aperture is visible on the right line in the square. AutoCAD responds by displaying the message

```
1 selected, 1 found.
```

in the command area for each object selected.

Figure 2-18
Selecting Individual Objects for Editing

Selecting Groups of Objects Using the aperture is not always the most efficient way to select a number of objects at once. AutoCAD provides four other options for selecting groups of objects. Two of the options use windows to select the objects. When you use either of the window options, you draw a rectangle around the objects that you want to select. You start one of these options by typing either `W` (for Window) or `C` (for Crossing Window) and pressing ENTER at the

```
Select objects:
```

prompt. AutoCAD prompts you for the

```
First corner:
```

of the rectangle. You then use the mouse to select some convenient point on the screen. Next you are prompted for the

```
Other corner:
```

which is on a diagonal of the rectangle from the first corner. As you move the mouse you can see the rectangle being formed.

If you type `W`, the W window is created and only those objects that are completely within the window are selected for editing. For example, the W window in Figure 2-19 selected only the left vertical line, because it is the only object entirely within the window. If you type `C`, a C window is created and all objects within the window and intersecting the boundaries of the window are selected. For instance, the C window in Figure 2-20 selected three lines: the two horizontal lines that intersect the boundary and the left vertical line.

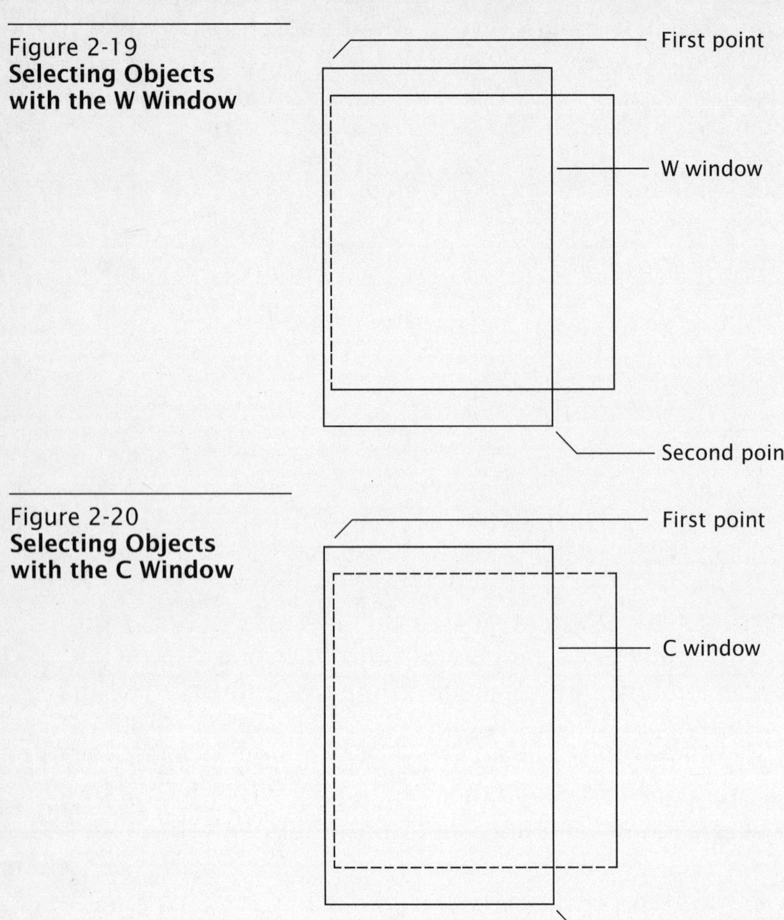

Figure 2-19
Selecting Objects with the W Window

Figure 2-20
Selecting Objects with the C Window

The third option is useful when you want to continue editing the group of objects used in the last editing command. AutoCAD remembers the last group of selected objects. If you respond to the

```
Select objects:
```

prompt by typing P (for Previous) and pressing ENTER, AutoCAD reselects the group of objects that was last selected and proceeds with the rest of the command. If you respond by typing L (for Last) and pressing ENTER, AutoCAD selects the last object that was drawn.

Selecting Objects Before Choosing an Editing Command To select an object before choosing the editing command, you use the pick-box. The selected object becomes dashed as before, and three small boxes appear on its ends and midpoint. These boxes, called *grips*, make certain editing commands easier to use. If you pick a point on the screen that is not on an object, you are prompted for the second corner. The second corner forms a W window, and all objects within the window are selected and equipped with grips. The grips in Figure 2-21 indicate which object has been selected. Once you have completed the selection process, you can select the editing command you want.

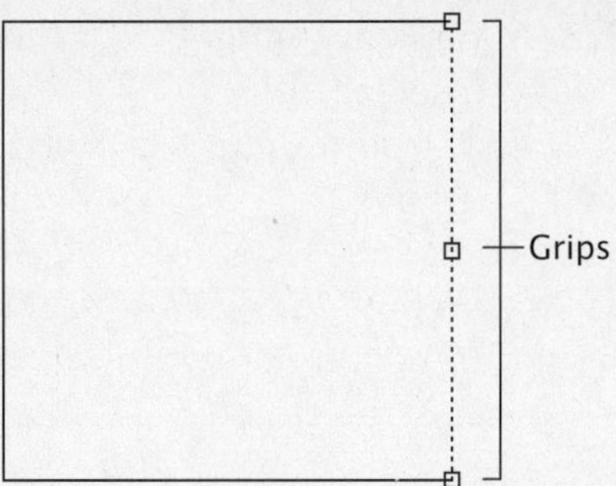

Figure 2-21
Selecting Objects Using Grips

Using ERASE and OOPS

ERASE is a commonly used editing command that does exactly what its name implies: It removes objects from the drawing. You can erase one or more objects with this command. If you change your mind, you can restore the erased objects with the Oops command. You initiate the Erase command by selecting Edit and then Erase from the screen menu. AutoCAD displays the prompt

```
Select objects:
```

Select one or more objects by using any of the techniques described earlier. When you have finished selecting objects, press (ENTER) at the last

```
Select objects:
```

prompt to complete the Erase command and delete the selected objects.

Try It

- Open the drawing file FIRST and initiate the Erase command.
- Select one of the lines in the small rectangle. Note the appearance of the line.
- Select another line in the small rectangle. Then complete the Erase command to erase the two lines.

Using OOPS to Retrieve Erased Objects You can recover erased objects by typing OOPS at the command line or choosing Oops from the ERASE screen menu. Only the last group of objects that were erased can be recovered.

Try It

- Use the OOPS command to recover the objects you erased a moment ago.

Erasing Groups of Objects You can use the Erase command to remove multiple objects at once. First you use the techniques you have already learned for selecting multiple objects. Then proceed with the Erase command as before.

Try It

- Initiate the Erase command and indicate to AutoCAD that you are going to use the C window to select objects.
- Pick any point as the first point, and move the crosshairs so that the rectangle crosses some lines.
- Complete the Erase command. Then restore the erased objects.
- Erase lines in the drawing using the W option instead of the Crossing window. Note the difference in the two options.

2-8 TAKING ADVANTAGE OF DRAWING AIDS

AutoCAD provides three drawing aids—Grid, Snap, and Ortho—that can assist you with the drawing process. Each feature helps you locate the position of the crosshairs quickly and with greater precision than is otherwise possible.

Using Grid

The Grid feature allows you to display a *grid* of dots on the screen. You can display or hide the grid by pressing F7. You can set the horizontal and vertical distances between the grid points by using the Drawing Aids dialog box shown in Figure 2-22. To display this dialog box, choose Drawing Aids... from the Settings pull-down menu. The default value for each grid distance is 0.0000. Change values by double-clicking on the X Spacing or Y Spacing box under Grid and then typing the new value. You can turn the grid on or off by clicking on the On box. When you are satisfied with your settings, click on OK. When Grid is on, the words <Grid on> appear in the command area, until they scroll out of view.

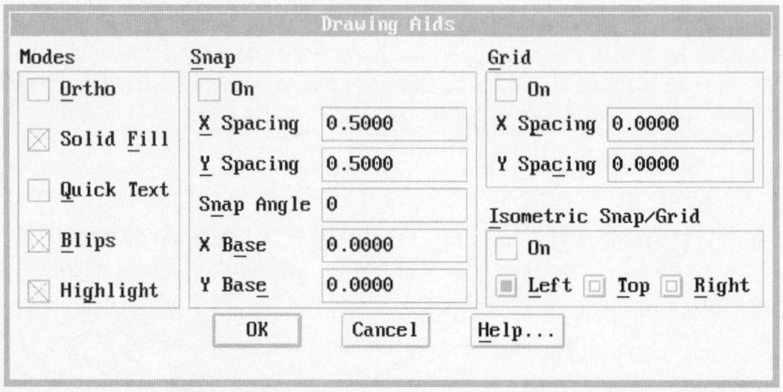

Figure 2-22
Drawing Aids Dialog Box

Using Snap

Closely associated with the Grid command is the Snap command. The Snap command sets up an invisible grid of snap points to which the crosshairs will snap when Snap is on. Press F9 to turn Snap on or off. When Snap is on you can select the snap points only by using the mouse. You set the Snap spacings by using either the Snap command or the Drawing Aids dialog box. You can change the snap settings by double-clicking on the existing setting and typing in a new one. Setting the Grid and Snap points to some common interval can be a great help in laying out the basic outlines of a drawing.

When Snap is on, the words <Snap on> appear, temporarily, in the command area, and the word Snap appears in the status line.

Using Ortho

The Ortho feature allows movement only in the horizontal or vertical direction. Turn Ortho on and off by pressing F8. For example, when Ortho is on you can draw lines only horizontally or vertically. Similarly, you can move or copy objects only in the horizontal or vertical direction. When Ortho is on the message <Ortho on> appears in the command area and the word Ortho appears in the status line.

Try It

- Make sure the coordinate display is on.
- Move the crosshairs from the lower-left corner to the upper-right corner of the drawing area, and watch the coordinate display.
- Turn on the Grid and Snap features, and note how the crosshairs jump as you move the mouse around slowly.
- Turn off the Snap feature, and note the smooth motion of the crosshairs.

Using Object Snap

The Snap drawing aid is useful when you are picking coordinate points that are on a regular rectangular pattern. However, you will often need to find a point that is established by one or more existing objects. For example, you may want to use the end of a line as the center of a circle. Or you may want to find the intersection of a line and a circle, or the intersection of two circles. In these cases you can use Object Snap (or Osnap).

In addition to finding intersections, AutoCAD can find midpoints and endpoints of objects, the centers of circles and arcs, points of tangency, and other types of points. You instruct AutoCAD to find one of these points by typing a code word that describes the nature of the point. You then pick the object, and AutoCAD finds, or snaps to, that feature.

Try It

- Start a new drawing and draw three circles similar to those in Figure 2-23.
- Start the Line command. At the "From point:" prompt type CEN and press ENTER to signal AutoCAD that you intend to use the center of a circle as the first point of the line. An aperture will replace the pickbox.
- At the "of" prompt use the aperture to pick any of the circles.
- Continue typing CEN after the "To point:" prompt until the three lines in Figure 2-23 are completed.

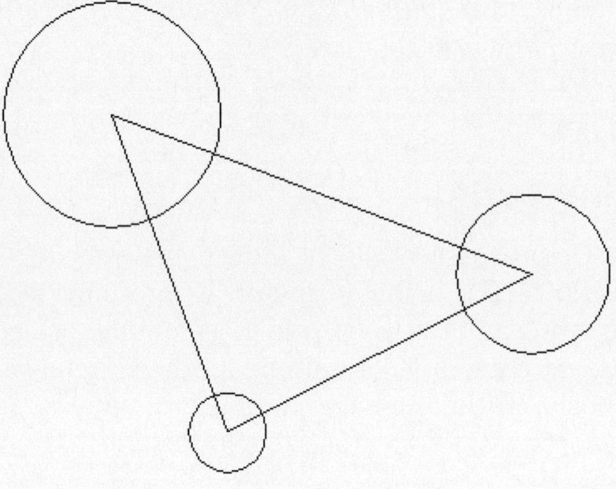

Figure 2-23
Drawing Lines with Object Snap

You enter an Osnap mode during the command sequence, when you would ordinarily enter a coordinate point. AutoCAD then prompts you with "of" or "to," depending on which Object Snap mode and command you are using. The "of" and "to" prompts tell you to select the object you want.

The code words, referred to as Object Snap *(Osnap) modes*, are described in Table 2-3. The abbreviation of each mode name is the capitalized part of the name.

Table 2-3 The Object Snap Modes

Mode	Action
CENter	Picks centers of arcs and circles.
ENDpoint	Picks the endpoint of objects nearest the end selected.
INSert	Picks insertion points of blocks and text.
INTersect	Picks intersections of objects.
MIDpoint	Picks midpoints of objects.
NEArest	Picks point on an object nearest to the crosshairs.
NODe	Picks a point object.
PERpend	Draws a line from the point perpendicular to the object.
QUAdrant	Picks the nearest cardinal point on an arc or circle. A *cardinal point* is the intersection of the X or Y axis and the object.
Quick	Allows AutoCAD to find the quickest point satisfying the Object Snap modes.
TANgent	Draws a line from the last point tangent to the object in the direction nearest the point selected.

Table 2-3 The Object Snap Modes

Mode	Action
NONE	Disables the current Osnap mode.

In this exercise you will draw several circles and a number of lines using various geometric points to be found by Object Snap modes. The result will be the lines and circles in Figure 2-24.

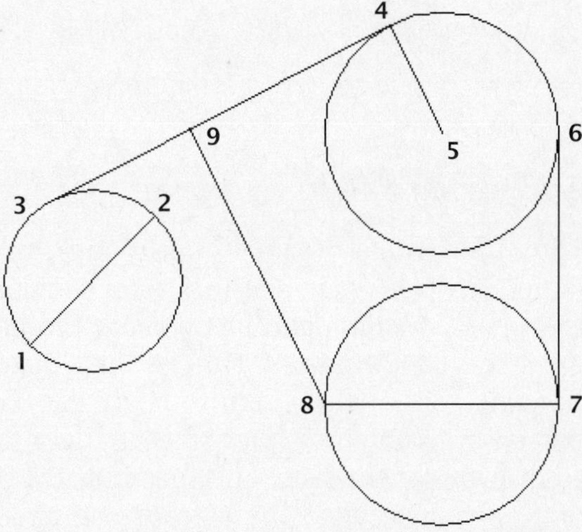

Figure 2-24
Drawing Lines and Circles with Object Snap

Try It

Start a new drawing. Draw Line 1–2 starting at 3.75,3.25. Make the line 1.50 units long at 45° with the X axis. Draw two circles, each with a radius of 1.0. Place the centers of the circles at 7.25,5 and 7.25,2.75. Draw the small circle with its center at the midpoint of Line 1–2 with a radius equal to 1/2 the length of the line. Use the MID and END modes.

Draw Line 3–4 tangent to the small circle just drawn and to the upper large circle. Use the TAN mode twice. Draw a Line 4–5 from the end of Line 3–4 to the center of the upper large circle. Use the INT (or END) and CEN modes. Draw Lines 6–7 and 7–8 using the QUA mode. Draw Line 8–9 using the END and PER modes.

Running Object Snap

In the previous section you had to enter the desired Osnap mode for each object that you drew. At times you will need to use the same Osnap mode repeatedly in a drawing, so you will want to keep the mode running while you draw. AutoCAD allows you to set one or more of the modes as running Osnap modes. After you have set the modes, AutoCAD uses them automatically without requiring you to type the codes individually.

To set running Osnap modes, click on Object Snap in the Settings pull-down menu to display the Running Object Snap dialog box shown in Figure 2-25. To choose the modes you want to use, click on the box to the left of the mode, and then click on OK to close the dialog box. You can turn off the running Osnap modes by returning to this dialog box and clicking on the boxes that you selected.

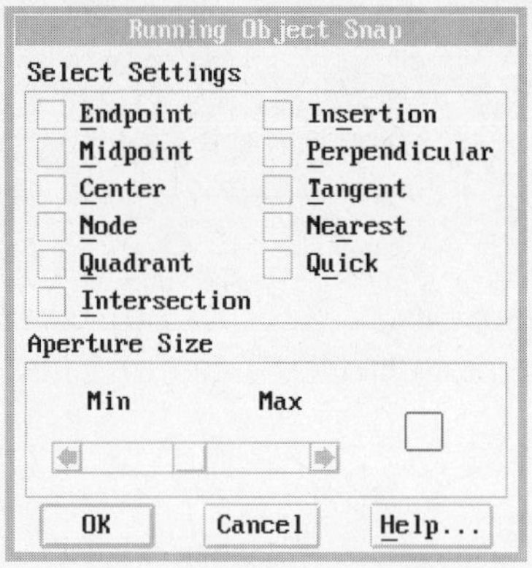

Figure 2-25
Running Object Snap Dialog Box

Running Object Snap
Select Settings
Endpoint | Insertion
Midpoint | Perpendicular
Center | Tangent
Node | Nearest
Quadrant | Quick
Intersection
Aperture Size
Min Max
OK Cancel Help...

Using Aperture Size

When you entered one of the Osnap modes, the pickbox changed into a much larger box called the aperture. You can control the aperture size by using the Aperture command or by using the horizontal scroll bar under Aperture Size in the Running Object Snap dialog box. As you move the scroll bar, the size of the aperture changes. The box to the right of the scroll bar shows you the actual size of the aperture. If you have a very crowded drawing, the normal aperture may overlap more than one object. If so, you need to reduce the size of the aperture to accurately select objects.

Try It

- Draw the large square and circle shown in Figure 2-26.
- Use running Osnap modes to draw the remaining lines in the drawing. Select the modes using the Running Object Snap dialog box.
- Increase the aperture to its maximum size, and observe the result.
- Return the aperture to an intermediate size.

Figure 2-26
Running Object Snap Exercise

Application 1: CONNECTING PLATE

Civil/Structural Engineering

The geodesic dome is used to shield people and equipment from the effects of the weather, wind, and earthquakes. The wind loads are transferred from the covering skin to the various rib elements. The ribs eventually transfer the loads to the foundation. All connections in a structural frame are extremely important to its safety. If only one of the connections in the structure fails, the entire structure may fail. The careful design of all connections is crucial to the integrity of the entire structure.

The drawing in Figure 2-27 shows the top and front views of a plate that is used to connect six ribs in the geodesic dome. The upper part of the figure shows the outline of the plate and the location of the ribs. The lower part of the figure shows the thickness of the plate and how the ribs are connected. In this application, only the plate will be drawn. The details of the bolt will be left for a later chapter.

We can now use the five-step problem-solving process to draw the connecting plate.

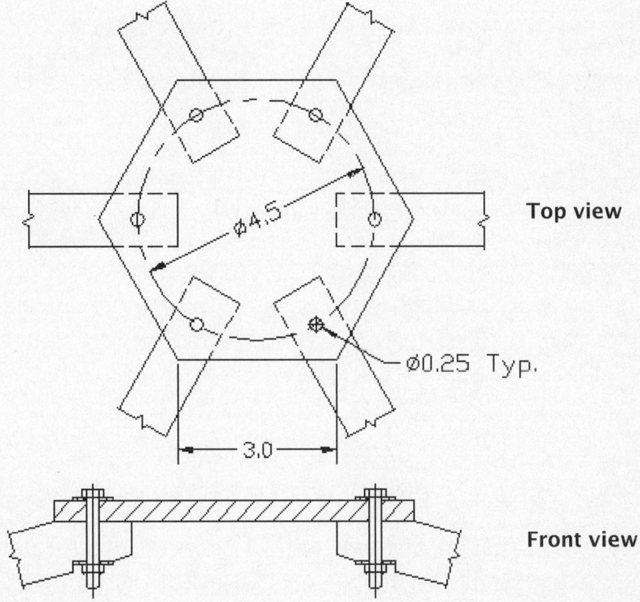

Figure 2-27
Connecting Plate with Connecting Members

1. Identify the Object and Its Function

The object is a hexagonal plate that will connect six ribs in a geodesic dome.

2. Research Models and Determine Dimensions

The thickness of the plate is based on the loads the ribs will carry and the quality of the material used in the plate. The hexagonal shape of the plate is determined by the number of ribs that are to be connected. The structural engineer determines the dimensions by drawing on previous experience and similar designs that have been used. It is important to note, however, that every new situation is unique and, therefore, each design must satisfy the specific load conditions of the structure.

3. Make a Hand-Drawn Sketch

You can use Figure 2-28 as the rough sketch. As you think about making the drawing, you have to decide on the order in which you will draw the lines and circles. In this project draw the polygon first. Draw radial lines connecting the opposite vertices of the polygon. Draw the circle around which the holes are located. Using the intersections of the radial lines and the circle as the centers, draw the small circles. Erase the extra lines and circle.

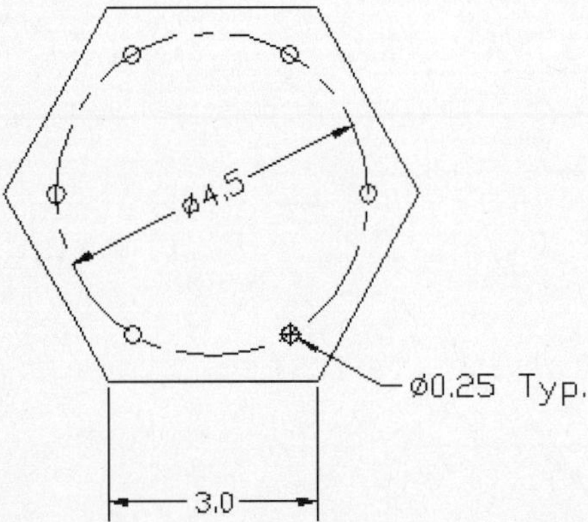

Figure 2-28
Connecting Plate

4. Make Appropriate Screen Adjustments

Set the units to decimal with a decimal place tolerance of 2. This accuracy is consistent with the precision of the fabrication accuracy. Use the default limits.

5. Draw, Print or Plot, and Save the Drawing File

Use the Line and Circle commands. When you have completed the drawing, save it as PLATE. (You will not plot drawings until later in the module.)

SUMMARY

This chapter introduced some of the basic features of AutoCAD. You gained some familiarity with the AutoCAD interface—the drawing screen, the menu systems, and various commands and dialog boxes. You also learned how to use on-line help. You discovered some of the essential steps you must take to set up your drawing, including selecting units and setting limits. You now know how to begin a new drawing, how to open an existing drawing, and how to save your drawing and exit AutoCAD. You learned the two most basic drawing commands: Line and Circle. You know how to select objects for editing and how to use the Erase and Oops commands. In addition, you learned about the SNAP, GRID, and ORTHO drawing aids.

Key Words

aperture
cardinal point
Cartesian coordinate system
circle
command area
crosshairs
dialog box
drawing area
function key
grid
grip
limit
line
model space
mouse
object
Osnap mode
paper space
pickbox
pick button
polar coordinate
pull-down menu
relative coordinates
screen menu
status line
text screen

Exercises

Draw the objects in each of the following exercises. Do not attempt to reproduce the text or the dimensions.

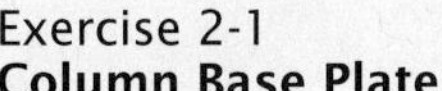
Exercise 2-1
Column Base Plate

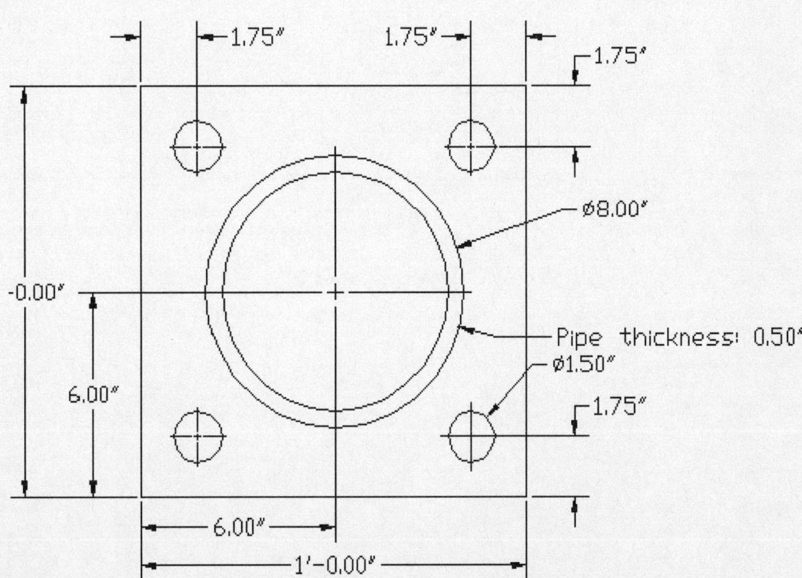

Exercise 2-2
Partial Site Plan

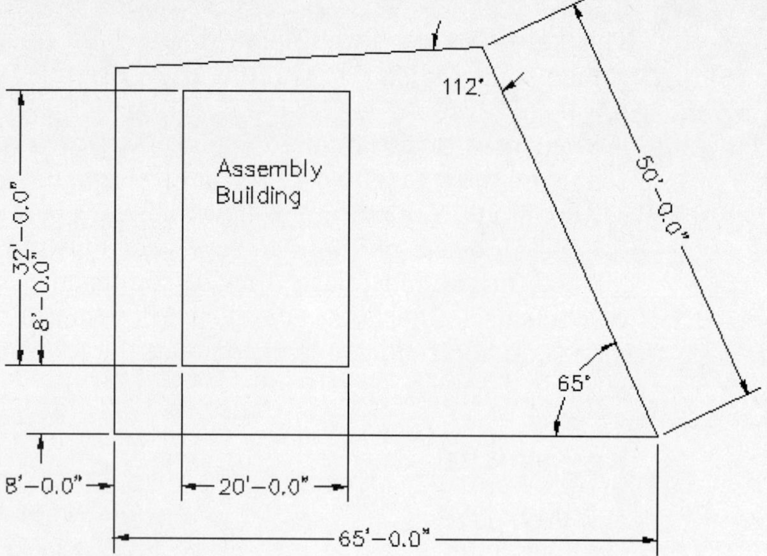

Units: Engineering
Limits: 0,0 to 80',60'

Draw the outline of the property boundaries.

Locate the lower-left corner of the building and draw the outline of the building.

Use the foot and inch symbols when you enter coordinates or distances.

Exercise 2-3A
Foundation Plan

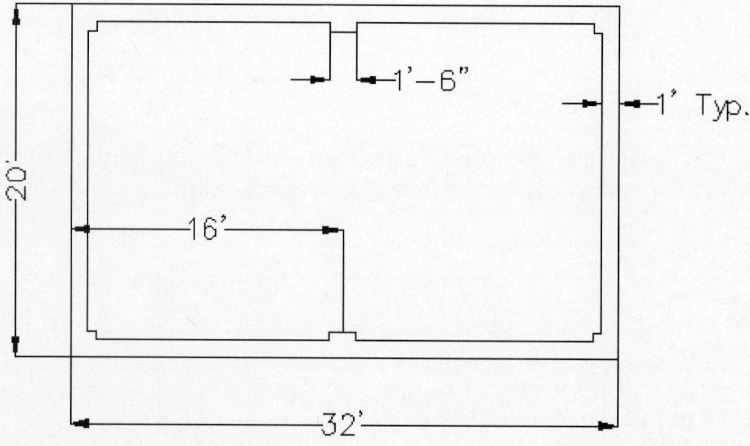

Units: Engineering
Limits: 0,0 to 36',27'

Exercise 2-3B
Corner Detail

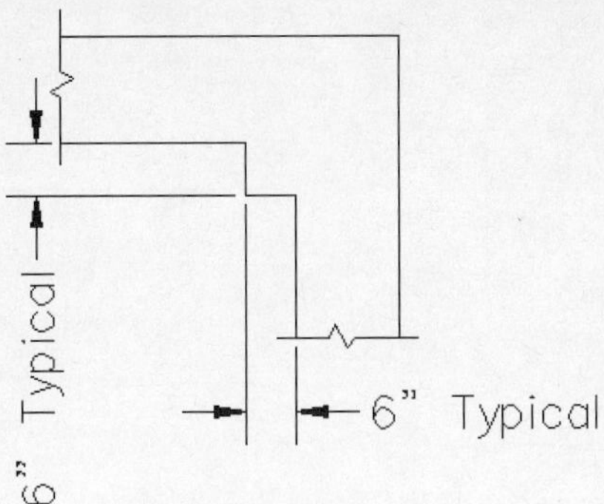

Exercise 2-4
Roof Framing Plan

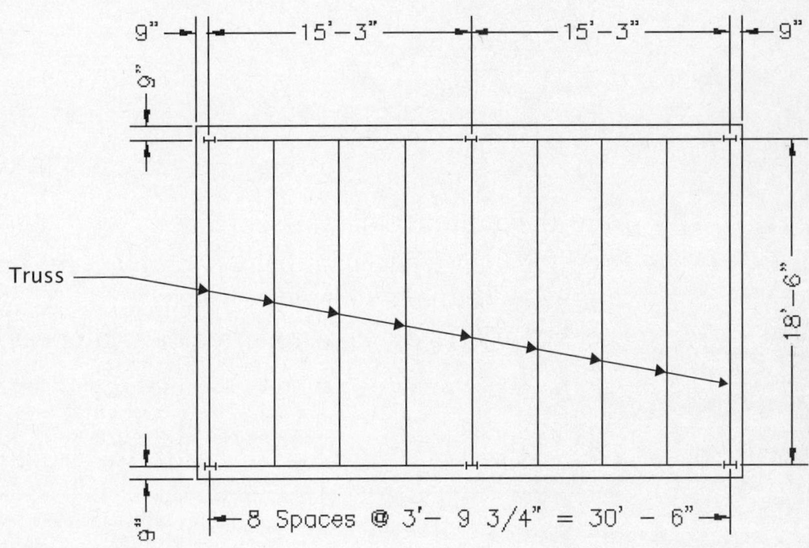

Units: Engineering
Limits: 0,0 to 36',27'

Exercise 2-5
Howe Roof Truss

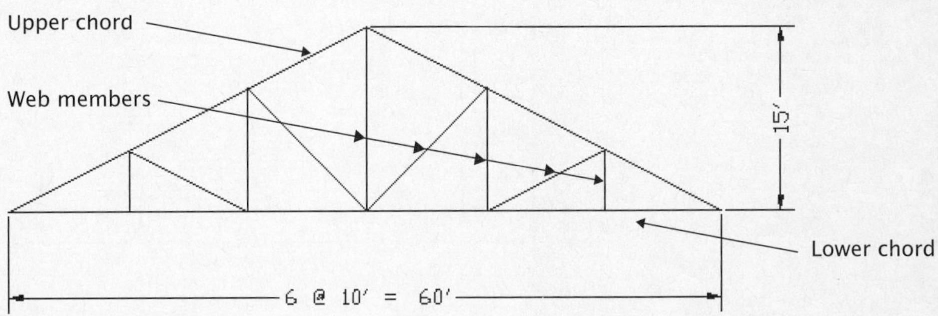

Draw the bottom chord as a series of 10-foot lines to provide endpoints for Object Snap.

Draw the upper chords next.

Turn on ORTHO and draw the vertical lines from the lower chord to the upper chord using the END and NEArest Osnap modes.

Complete the drawing.

Exercise 2-6
Gusset Plate

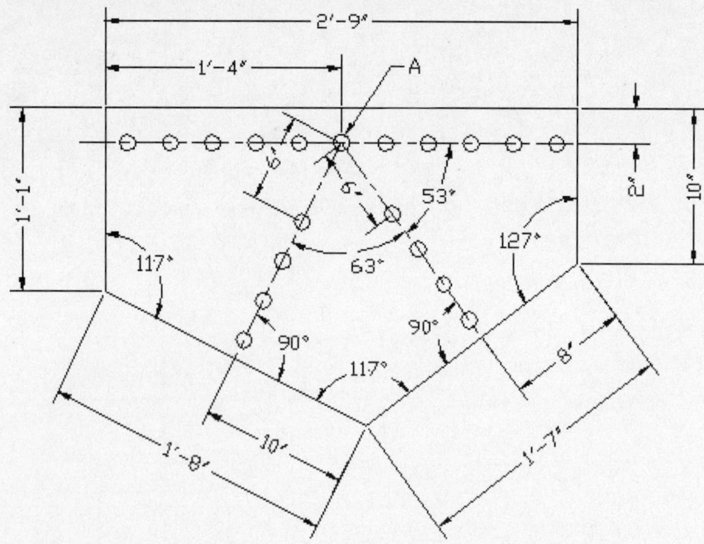

Draw the outline of the Gusset plate.

Draw the lines (starting at point A) through the holes as 3-inch segments to provide endpoints for Object Snap.

Use the END Osnap mode to locate the centers of the circles.

Exercise 2-7
Base Plate Detail

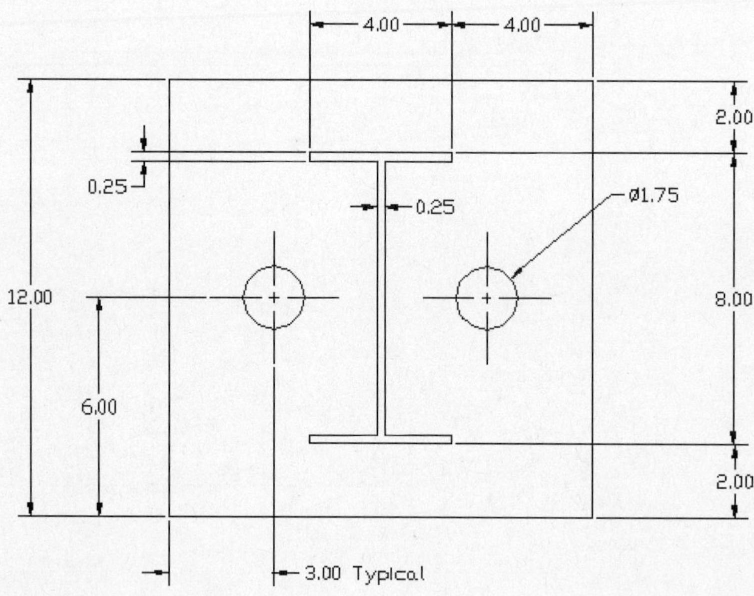

3 Learning Some Basic Editing Skills

Laser Technology

Since their discovery in the 1950s, lasers have been used to solve a wide range of problems—from medical to mechanical to musical. Surgical lasers remove cataracts, clear clogged arteries, remove brain tumors, and cauterize leaky blood vessels. Laser machine tools, controlled by computers, have increased the quality of manufactured products that require extensive and precise cutting of materials. Laser technology is also used to record and replay sounds and images. The quality of the sound and the images will not deteriorate with use because there is no physical contact between the recording and playing heads. At the end of this chapter, you will draw the schematic for an optical disk pick-up system.

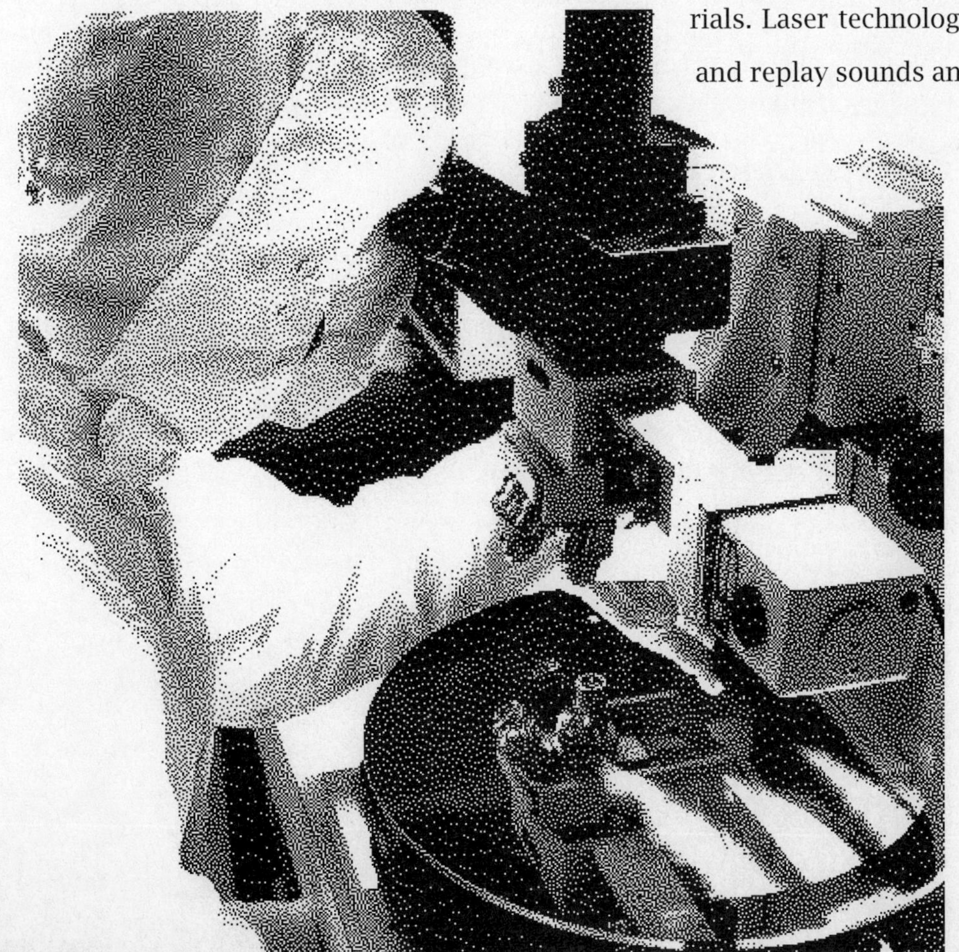

INTRODUCTION

You seldom complete a drawing by simply creating basic objects such as lines and circles. Usually, you need to use AutoCAD's editing features to refine the basic shapes in your drawing. So far ERASE is the only editing command that you have used. This chapter presents several additional editing commands. First you learn to use the Copy, Move, Mirror, Offset, Trim, and Extend commands, which allow you to modify existing objects. Another command, Layer, helps you organize your drawing, placing different elements on different layers as well as changing the linetypes and colors of the objects. The Chprop command is used to change the properties of objects. The third set of commands presented in this chapter—U, Undo, and Redo—is useful when you need to change the result of a series of commands without using Erase. Finally, you learn how to clean up the screen with the Redraw command, create a close up view of part of the drawing with the Zoom command, and see parts of the drawing that are outside the limits of the screen with the Pan command.

3-1 DUPLICATING AND RELOCATING OBJECTS

AutoCAD offers several commands that make copies of objects. The Copy command can copy one or more objects, leaving the original intact and placing the copy in a designated location. The Offset command also makes copies, but it can copy only one object at a time, and the new copy is always parallel to the old object. Like Copy, Mirror also makes copies of one or more objects. The Mirror command, however, makes a mirror image of the original object, while Copy makes an exact duplicate.

You use the Move command to relocate one or more objects. Moving an object is much like copying it, except Move deletes the object from its original location.

Copying Objects

The Copy command lets you copy one or more objects to a specified location. To carry out the command, you must select a *base point* on the object; you can think of this point as a handle. The base point is any convenient point, such as the center of a circle or the corner of a rectangle. Then you specify the new location of the base point, which determines where the new image will be located.

To issue the Copy command, choose Copy from the Construct pull-down menu, shown in Figure 3-1.

Figure 3-1
Construct Pull-down Menu

```
Array
Array 3D
Copy
Mirror
Mirror 3D
---------
Chamfer
Fillet
---------
Divide
Measure
Offset
---------
Block
```

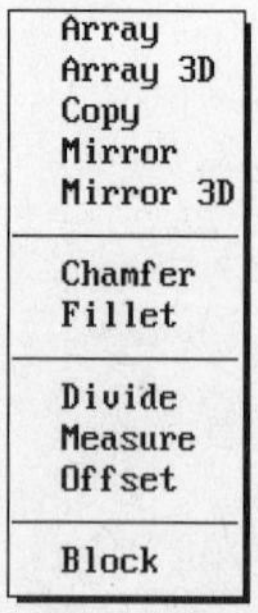

The first prompt is

```
Select objects:
```

Select one or more objects using any of the selection techniques from Chapter 2. After you complete the selection by pressing ENTER, this prompt appears:

```
<Base point or displacement>/Multiple:
```

To make a single copy of the selected object or objects, enter the base point now. You see the prompt

```
Second point of displacement:
```

Enter the new location of the base point. The command ends if you are making a single copy.

Try It

- Begin a new drawing, and draw a circle anywhere on the screen.
- Make a single copy of the circle using the center of the circle as the base point.
- Make a copy of the two circles.

Your drawing should look similar to Figure 3-2.

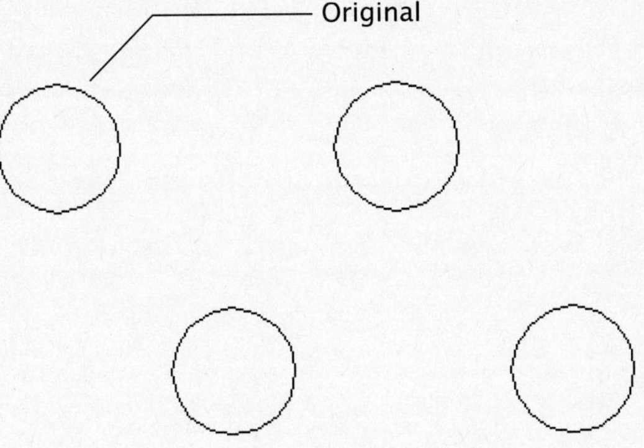

Figure 3-2
Single-Copy Exercise

You can use the Copy command to make multiple copies of one or more objects. Choose Copy from the Construct menu, as before, and select the object(s) you want copied. The prompt

```
<Base point or displacement>/Multiple:
```

provides the Multiple option. Type `M` and press ENTER to inform AutoCAD that you want to make multiple copies of the selected objects. AutoCAD responds with the prompt

```
Base point:
```

You supply a base point as before. AutoCAD continues to prompt you for base points until you press ENTER without entering a new point.

Try It

- Erase the circles that you copied in the last "Try It!"
- Use the Multiple option to create an image like the one shown in Figure 3-3.

Figure 3-3
Multiple-Copy Exercise

Moving Objects

You can use Move to move one or more objects to another location in the drawing. When you move a group of objects, all the objects are moved together—that is, each object maintains the same relative location with respect to the other objects. With the Move command, as with the Copy command, you select objects, select a base point, and specify the displacement. Unlike the Copy command, however, the Move command erases the original object(s).

To issue the Move command, choose Move from the Modify pull-down menu, which is shown in Figure 3-4.

Figure 3-4
Modify Pull-down Menu

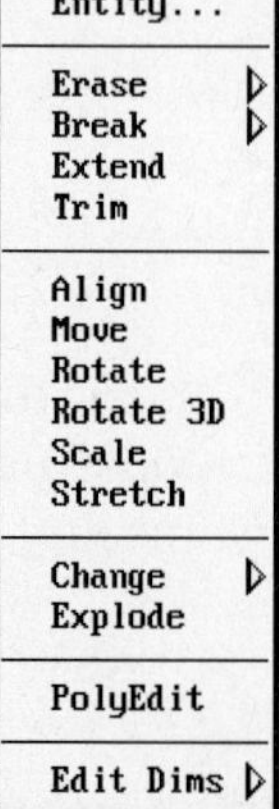

At the prompt

```
Select objects:
```

select the objects that you want to move. Again, use any of the selection techniques you learned in Chapter 2. The next prompt is

```
Base point or displacement:
```

Pick a convenient point as the base point, just as you do for the Copy command. (Note that this prompt does not provide the Multiple option, because such an option does not make sense for moving objects.) At the next prompt,

```
Second point of displacement:
```

pick the new location of the base point. The command terminates when the second point is picked.

Try It

- Draw a line and circle like those shown in the upper part of Figure 3-5.
- Move the circle from the left end to the right end of the line. Be sure that the center of the circle is at the end of the line. The result should resemble the "After" portion of Figure 3-5.
- Move the line so that the midpoint of the line is tangent to the top of the circle.

Figure 3-5
Moving a Circle

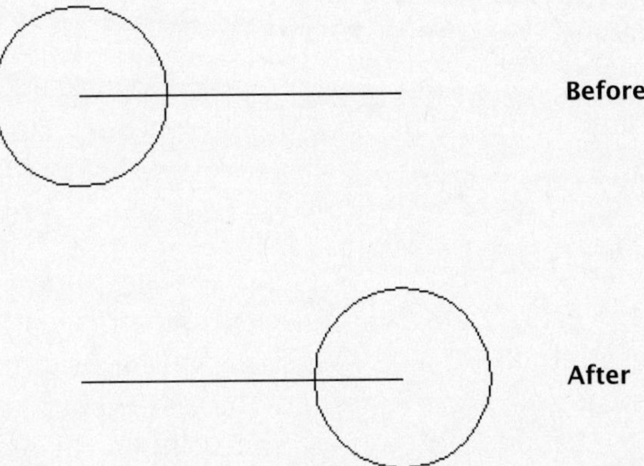

Mirroring Objects

The Mirror command is useful when the object to be drawn has one or more axes of symmetry. When *symmetry* exists you can draw one half or one quarter of the object and use the Mirror command to complete the drawing. The drawing in Figure 3-6 includes two axes of symmetry: the vertical and horizontal lines shown as dashed lines in the figure.

Figure 3-6
Mirror Example—Axes of Symmetry

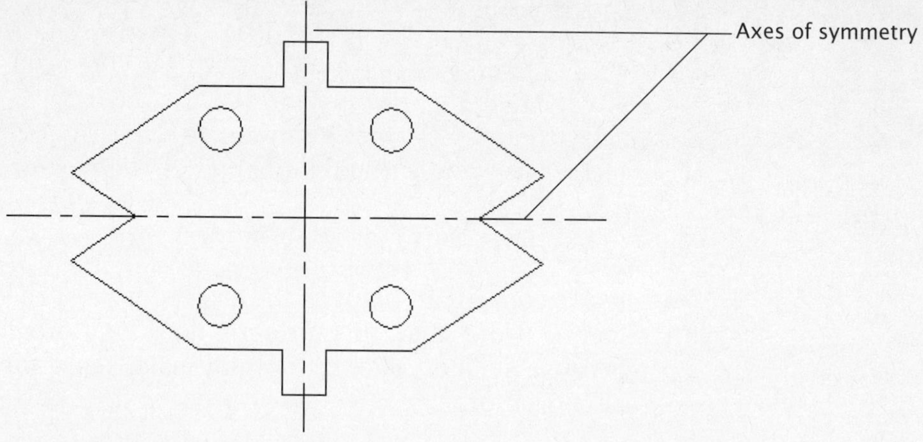

The Mirror command appears on the Construct pull-down menu. When you initiate this command, AutoCAD displays the prompt

```
Select objects:
```

After you select one or more objects and press ENTER, AutoCAD presents the prompt

```
First point on the mirror line:
```

Enter a point on the actual mirror line. If the mirror line is not a part of the drawing, select a point on an imaginary line that represents the axis of symmetry. Next AutoCAD displays the prompt

```
Second point:
```

Enter any other point on the mirror line. Finally AutoCAD shows the prompt

```
Delete old objects? <N>.
```

Now you can delete or retain the old image—that is, the object(s) you selected initially. If you press ENTER, the original objects are retained. If you type Y and press ENTER, the old objects are deleted, and the resulting image is a mirrored copy of the original. In most engineering drawings you will not delete the old objects.

Figure 3-7
Mirror Exercise—Horizontal Mirror Line

Try It

- Draw the circle and lines shown as the "Before" image in Figure 3-7.
- Copy the circle and lines to a location just to the right of their current location.
- Mirror the objects using a horizontal mirror line below the objects. The result should look like the "After" image.
- Mirror the objects in the "After" portion of Figure 3-7, using a vertical mirror line.

Your mirror lines need not all be vertical or horizontal. Figure 3-8 illustrates the result of using an inclined mirror line. The points on the original image and the corresponding points on the mirrored copy are equidistant from the mirror line. For example, the two points marked A represent a pair of corresponding points.

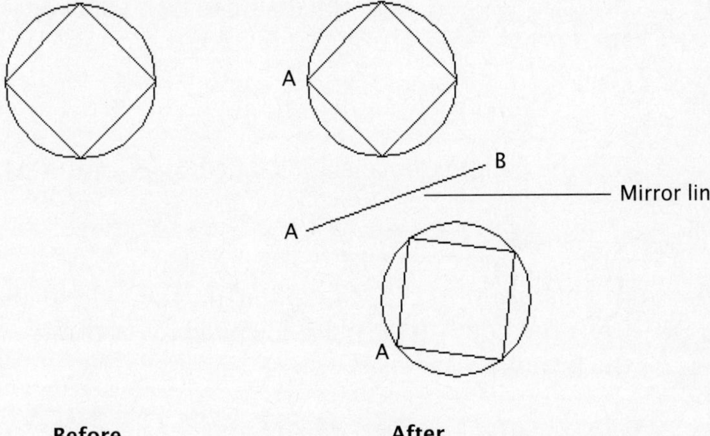

Figure 3-8
Mirror Exercise—Inclined Mirror Line

Try It

- Draw the circle and lines shown as the "Before" image in Figure 3-8.
- Copy the circle and lines to a location just to the right of their current location.
- Mirror the objects using an inclined mirror line, as shown in the figure. The result should look like the "After" image.
- Mirror the objects in the "After" portion of Figure 3-8, using a different inclined mirror line, and delete the old images.

Using the Offset Command

The Offset command is actually a special version of the Copy command. While the Copy command allows you to copy a group of objects, Offset allows you to copy only one object at a time. You use Offset to produce a copy of an object (usually a line, circle, or arc) that is *offset* from the original—that is, it is either parallel to or concentric with the original object. A copy of a line is exactly *parallel* to the original and the same length. A copy of a circle is a new circle with the same center as the original but with a larger or smaller diameter—that is, the two circles are *concentric*.

AutoCAD provides two methods for locating the new copy. You can specify its distance from the original, or you can specify a point through which the copy is to go.

Offsetting an Object by a Specified Distance Figure 3-9 includes three lines that have been offset by a specified distance. The Offset command was used to make copies of the sides of the triangle. Each line was copied to a location outside the triangle and at a given distance from the original line. As you can see, the new lines are exactly the same length as the originals.

You use the Construct pull-down menu to start the Offset command. AutoCAD displays the prompt

```
Offset distance or Through <Through>:
```

If this is the first time you have used the Offset command in the current drawing session, type the distance that you want between the objects, and then press (ENTER). AutoCAD responds with the prompt

```
Select object to offset:
```

Use the pickbox to select a single object. AutoCAD supplies the prompt

```
Side to offset?
```

At this prompt, pick any point on the side of the original on which you want the copy to be placed. The copy is drawn and AutoCAD redisplays the prompt

```
Select object to offset:
```

You can pick another object (including the offset copy you just completed), or you can end the command by pressing (ENTER).

If you had used the Offset command previously during the drawing session, AutoCAD would have remembered the previous offset distance. For example, if you had specified 0.25 as the offset distance, the first offset prompt would be

```
Offset distance or Through <0.25>:
```

You could have either accepted the value by pressing (ENTER) or entered a new distance.

Try It

- Draw a triangle similar to the one shown in Figure 3-9.
- Use the Offset command to copy the sides of the triangle 0.5 units outside the triangle. Your drawing should look like Figure 3-9.
- Offset the new lines, again to the outside of the old lines but with a different distance.
- Offset the sides of the triangle inward by a distance of 0.25.

Figure 3-9
Offset Lines Created with the Distance Option

You can offset circles in much the same way using the Distance option. The only difference is in the appearance of the result. A circle copied with Offset has a common center with the original but has a larger or smaller diameter. Figure 3-10 illustrates circles that have been copied using the Offset command.

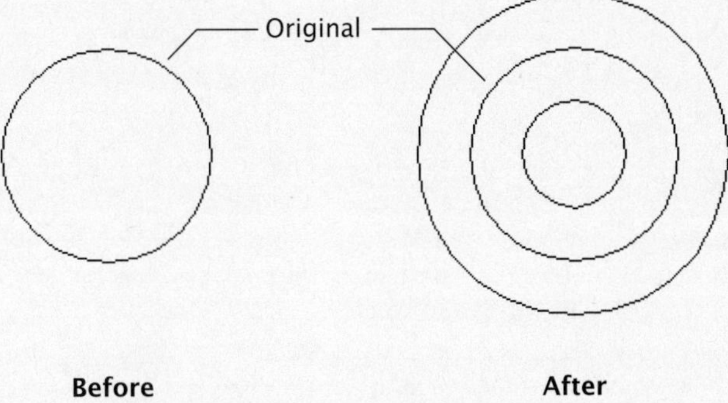

Figure 3-10
Offsetting Circles

Try It

- Draw a circle with a diameter of 3.0 units.
- Use the Offset command to make a copy of the circle outside the original.
- Make a copy, using the same distance, inside the original.

Offsetting an Object Through a Particular Point The Through option of the Offset command allows you to create a copy of the object that passes through a point of your choice. Using the Through option is a little different than using the Distance option, but the appearance of the result is the same for both options.

As you know, choosing Offset from the Construct pull-down menu yields this prompt:

```
Offset distance or Through <Through>:
```

Press (ENTER) to select the Through option. AutoCAD displays the prompt

```
Select object to offset:
```

After you select a single object to be offset, AutoCAD displays this prompt:

```
Through point:
```

Pick a point on the screen, and the object is copied through that point.

Try It

- Draw the line and circle as shown in the "Before" image of Figure 3-11. Place the center of the circle at the left end of the line.
- Use the Through option to offset the circle so that the copy passes through the midpoint of the line. Your drawing should look like the "After" image in Figure 3-11.
- Offset the line so that the copy is tangent to the new circle at the upper quadrant point.

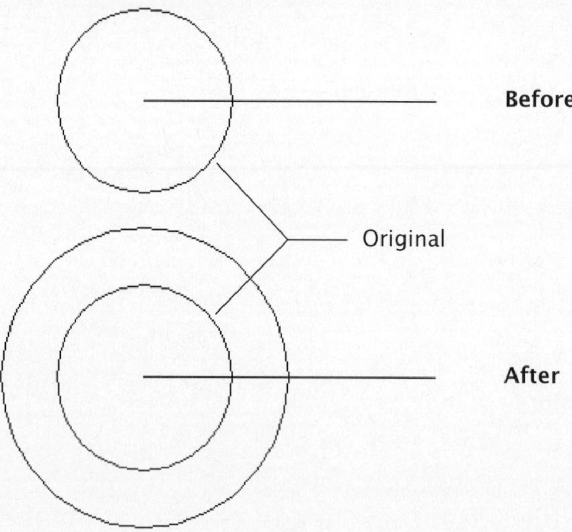

Figure 3-11
Offset Through Point

3-2 FINE-TUNING YOUR DRAWINGS

When you begin to create more complex drawings, you will need a few new editing techniques to help you. Two of these techniques are the Trim and Extend commands. You use Trim to trim away parts of objects that should not appear in the final drawing. In a similar way you use Extend to extend objects that are not complete. Using these commands is often easier than creating the correct image initially. You can also fine-tune your drawings by organizing them more carefully. This section explains how to use layers to separate different features of your drawing, as well as how to apply different linetypes and colors, and how to move to the various layers of your drawings.

Using the Trim Command

You use Trim to erase parts of objects that extend beyond known boundaries. To carry out the command, you must specify the boundary or boundaries and select the ends of the objects to be trimmed. Figure 3-12 illustrates a typical situation where Trim is useful. In the final drawing the horizontal lines stop at the inclined line on the right. The original set of horizontal lines was drawn by offsetting the top line. The task is to trim these lines back to the boundary. AutoCAD uses the term *cutting edge* to refer to the boundary. In Figure 3-12 only one cutting edge was used. However, the Trim command allows you to select as many cutting edges as you need for your editing project.

Figure 3-12
Trimming Lines with One Cutting Edge

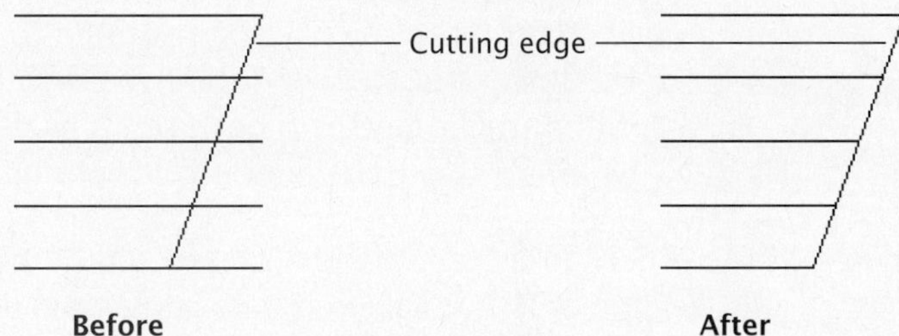

To start the Trim command, choose Trim from the Modify pull-down menu. AutoCAD responds with the following prompt:

```
Select cutting edge(s)...
Select objects:
```

The first line of this prompt tells you that the objects you select at this time will be used to trim other objects. Use any selection technique to pick the cutting edges. Press (ENTER) when you complete the selection.

Next AutoCAD displays the prompt

```
<Select objects to trim>/Undo:
```

Select objects one at a time using an aperture. The objects must extend beyond the cutting edge. The portion of the object that is trimmed depends on where you select the object. In Figure 3-12, for example, the right portions of the lines were trimmed because the lines were picked near the right ends. If the object to be trimmed does not intersect a cutting edge, AutoCAD displays the message

```
Entity does not intersect an edge.
```

and displays the prompt asking you to select objects. This prompt repeats until you press (ENTER) without selecting an object.

Try It

- Draw the lines shown in the "Before" image of Figure 3-12. Use Offset to draw the horizontal lines. The spacing is not important.
- Draw the inclined line to serve as a cutting edge. Trim the horizontal lines back to the inclined line. The result should resemble the "After" image.
- Draw a vertical line through the midpoint of the top line. Trim the left portions of the horizontal lines to the new vertical line.

The example in Figure 3-12 involves trimming several lines to a single cutting edge. Sometimes you will want to remove a segment of a line between two cutting edges. Figure 3-13 illustrates one such situation. The "Before" portion of the figure has two horizontal lines and two vertical cutting edges. The upper line is to be trimmed to the left cutting edge. The segment of the lower line between the two cutting edges is to be removed. The Trim command can perform both tasks easily.

Figure 3-13 illustrates two general rules about the Trim command:

- If the object to be trimmed is intersected by two or more cutting edges and the object is not selected between a pair of cutting edges, the object will be trimmed to the nearest cutting edge. (This applies to the upper horizontal line in the figure.)
- If the object is selected between cutting edges, the portion of the object between the cutting edges will be removed. (This applies to the lower horizontal line in the figure.)

Figure 3-13
Trimming Lines with Two Cutting Edges

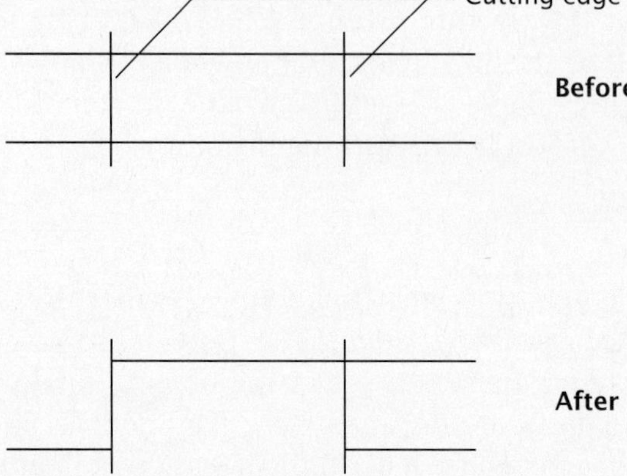

Try It

- Draw a pair of horizontal and vertical lines, as shown in Figure 3-13.
- Use the Trim command to trim the horizontal lines as shown in the "After" image at the bottom of the figure.

Trimming circles requires two cutting edges. The example in Figure 3-14 illustrates a common occurrence in engineering drawings. The object is closed on each end with semicircular arcs. The sides of the object are tangent to the arcs. In situations like this, you would draw the circles first. Then you would draw the lines tangent to the circles. You would finish the drawing by using the Trim command to remove the unwanted portions of the circle.

Figure 3-14
Trimming Circles

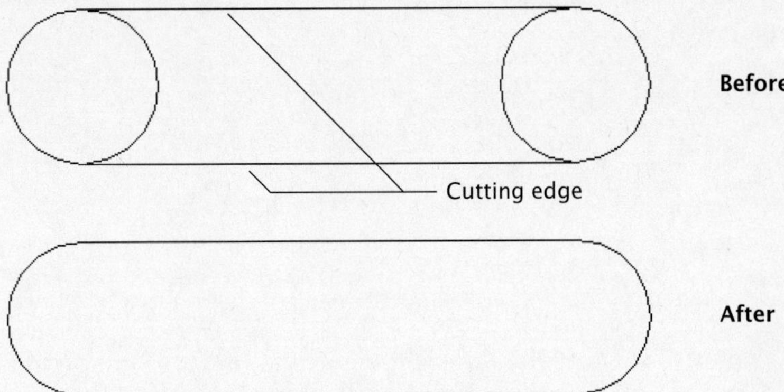

Try It

- Draw the lines and circles shown in the "Before" image of Figure 3-14. You may want to draw one circle and use the Copy command to produce the second arc.
- Complete the drawing by trimming the inside segments of the circles.

Using the Extend Command

The Extend command extends objects to selected boundaries. Figure 3-15 shows Extend being used to advantage. As you can see, the horizontal lines do not reach the inclined boundaries; you can use the Extend command to lengthen them so that they do.

To issue the Extend command, choose Extend from the Modify pull-down menu. AutoCAD displays the prompt

```
Select boundary edge(s)...
Select boundary:
```

The first line of this prompt tells you that the objects you select at this time will be used as the boundaries for the extension of other objects. Pick the objects you want to use as *boundary edges,* and then press ENTER. The next prompt is

```
<Select objects to extend>/Undo:
```

Select the objects you want extended, making certain to pick the end of the object nearest to the boundary to which the object will be extended. If there are two or more boundaries, the object will be extended to the boundary nearest the point you selected on the object. If the object to be extended will not intersect any boundary, AutoCAD displays the message

```
Entity does not intersect an edge.
```

and repeats the prompt asking you to select objects. This prompt repeats until you press ENTER without selecting an object.

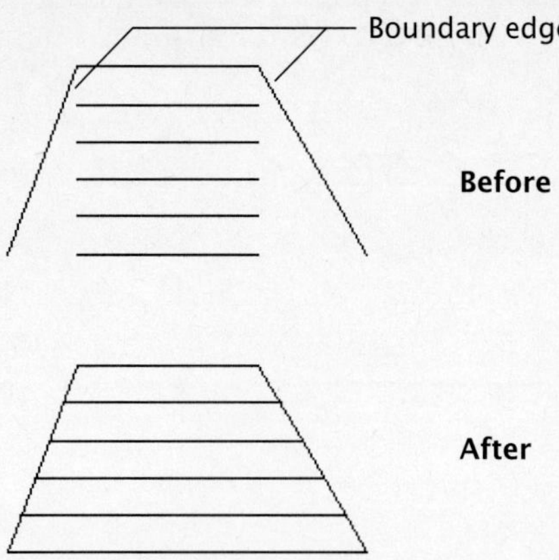

Figure 3-15
Extending Lines to Lines

Try It

- Draw the lines shown in the "Before" image in Figure 3-15, including the boundary edges.
- Use the Extend command to extend the horizontal lines both left and right to the boundary edges as shown. The result should look like the "After" image in Figure 3-15.

You can use circles as boundary edges with the Extend command. The circle may represent two boundary edges at once, as shown in Figure 3-16. If you select a circle as a boundary edge, the horizontal line can be extended to the left, and it meets the circle only once. However, the inclined line will, if fully extended, meet the circle twice.

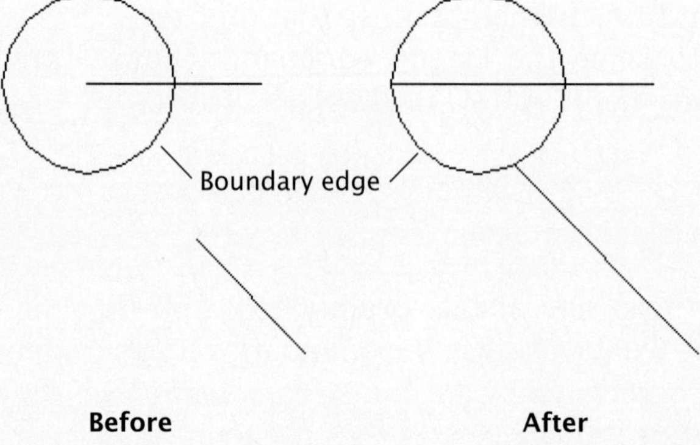

Figure 3-16
Extending Lines to Circles

Try It

- Draw the circle and the two lines shown in the "Before" image in Figure 3-16. Make certain that the inclined line will intersect the circle twice if extended.
- Use the Extend command to extend the lines as shown in the "After" image.
- Extend the inclined line so that it intersects the opposite side of the circle.
- Draw a third line that clearly does not intersect the circle. Use the Extend command to attempt to extend the new line to the circle, and observe the response.

Working with Layers

So far you have been drawing on a single layer, but with AutoCAD you can actually draw on many different layers. AutoCAD *layers* are similar to transparent overlays. Imagine a set of drawings used to build a house. The drawings show the foundations on one sheet, the electrical wiring on another, the plumbing on still another. In addition, the structural framing for the different floors and roof are drawn on their own sheets. With AutoCAD, instead of creating separate drawings, you can represent these various sheets as separate layers in a single drawing. Layers enable you to work with different components of your drawing separately, and also to view them together.

You can set up different layers, name them, and assign certain types of information to each. Then you can turn the layers on or off at will to reveal or conceal the information they contain. When you have finished the project, you can display the layers in any combination for printing.

You change the appearance of lines, called *linetypes*, as well as the color of lines on specified layers. For example, some drawings may include details that are not on the outside surface of the object but are hidden. In this situation you can use the Hidden linetype. Likewise, when a drawing includes many layers, it is helpful to assign a different color to each.

Although you can display many layers at a time, you can only draw on a single layer. The layer that you are working on is the *current layer*. So far you have been drawing on AutoCAD's default layer, which is called Layer 0. The name of the layer is displayed at the left end of the status line. The rectangle just to the left of the layer name shows the color assigned to layer 0. The default linetype assigned to layer 0 is the continuous linetype.

You can create layers, assign linetypes and colors, turn layers on or off, and more by using the Layer Control dialog box shown in Figure 3-17. To display this dialog box, choose Layer Control from the Settings pull-down menu. This dialog box displays all of the layers in a drawing and allows you to make several changes at once. As you can see in Figure 3-17, the current drawing includes two layers, CIRCLES and LINES, in addition to Layer 0. The first time you activate the dialog box, it lists only layer 0.

Figure 3-17
Layer Control Dialog Box

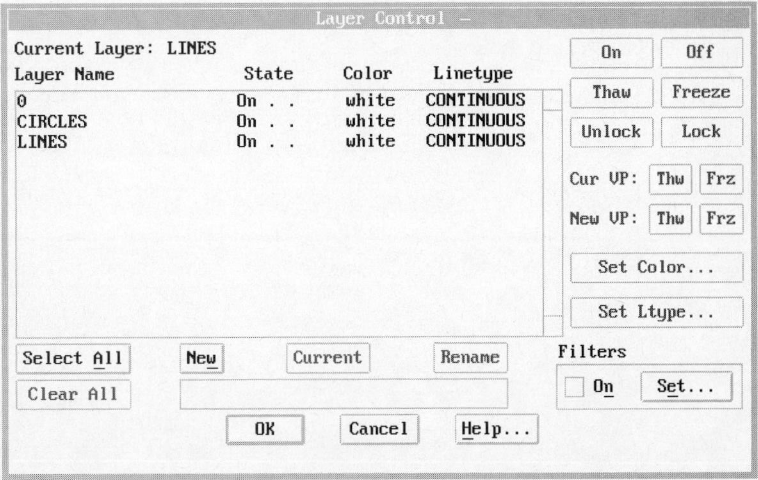

You must create new layers before you can change any of the features such as linetype or color. To add a layer, first type its name in the blank box just to the right of the Clear All button in the Layer Control dialog box. Then click on the New button, and the name of the layer is added to the list of layers.

Try It

- Activate the Layer Control dialog box.
- Create the two new layers CIRCLES and LINES.

Changing Linetypes So far all of your drawings have consisted of continuous (solid) lines. You usually use continuous lines to outline the visible details of the device. You can also use different linetypes to represent other information. Hidden lines and center lines are two of the most common conventional linetypes. Hidden lines consist of a series of short dashes separated by a short space. You use hidden lines to indicate that the feature of the device is an interior, or hidden, feature. Center lines are a series of long lines alternating with short lines. You can use them to mark the centers of circles.

You can assign AutoCAD's standard linetypes to layers or to specific objects in a drawing. First, however, you must load the linetypes. The linetypes are stored in the ACAD.LIN file.

Select LINETYP: from the SETTINGS screen menu, and the following prompt appears:

```
?/Create/Load/Set:
```

Respond to the prompt by typing ?, C, L, or S and then pressing ENTER. The results of the various responses are described in Table 3-1.

Table 3-1 Linetype Command Options

Response	Result
?	Displays the Select Linetype File dialog box shown in Figure 3-18. Press ENTER to display the standard linetypes on the text screen as shown in Figure 3-19.
C (Create)	Allows you to create a custom linetype, a feature that is beyond the scope of this text.
L (Load)	Loads the standard linetypes. If you type L and press ENTER, the prompt "Linetype(s) to load:" appears. Respond by typing * and pressing ENTER. The dialog box shown in Figure 3-18 appears, displaying the location of the ACAD.LIN file. Press ENTER to load the linetypes.
S (Set)	Sets the linetype for the layer.

Figure 3-18
Select Linetype File Dialog Box

```
Select Linetype File
Pattern: *.lin
Directory: C:\ACAD\SUPPORT
Directories:      Files:
\                 ACAD
..
<A:>
<B:>
<C:>
                                   Type it

                                   Default
File: ACAD
        OK     Cancel     Help...
```

Figure 3-19 shows a partial list of the standard linetypes.

Figure 3-19
Standard Linetypes

```
Linetypes defined in file C:\ACAD\SUPPORT\ACAD.lin:

      Name            Description
---------------- --------------------
BORDER
BORDER2
BORDERX2
CENTER
CENTER2

CENTERX2
DASHDOT
DASHDOT2
DASHDOTX2
DASHED

DASHED2
DASHEDX2
DIVIDE
DIVIDE2
DIVIDEX2
-- Press RETURN for more --
```

To change the linetype for a layer, first activate the Layer Control dialog box. Select the layer to be modified by clicking on its name; it will become highlighted. Next click on the Set Ltype button to display the Select Linetype dialog box shown in Figure 3-20. This dialog box lists the standard linetypes you saw a moment ago. Click on Next to see the remaining linetypes. To assign a linetype to the layer, click on the linetype name, and then click on OK.

Try It

- Display the list of linetypes.
- Load the standard linetypes.
- Activate the Layer Control dialog box.
- Set the CIRCLES layer linetype to Hidden. You must click on Next to display the Hidden linetype.
- Set the linetype on the LINES layer to Dashed.
- Make each layer the current layer, in turn, and draw lines and circles to test the results.

Figure 3-20
Select Linetype Dialog Box

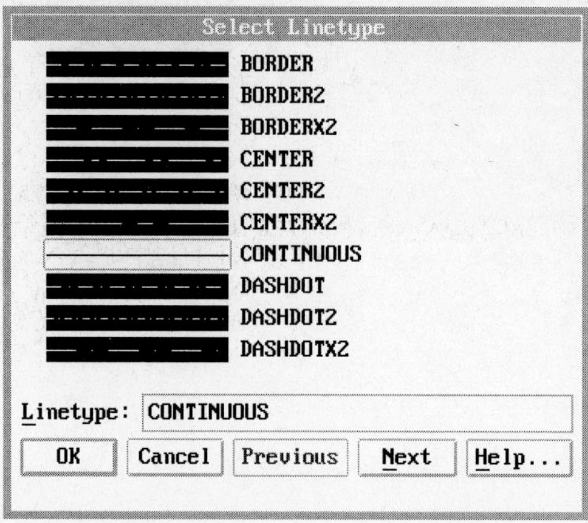

Using the Ltscale Command The Ltscale command lets you change the length of the spaces between the dashes or dots in the selected linetype. You can change this *line scale* by selecting Ltscale: from the SETTINGS screen menu. AutoCAD displays the prompt

```
New scale factor <Default value>:
```

If you have not changed the line scale, the default value is 1.0. You can change the line scale by typing a new value, at which point AutoCAD regenerates the drawing database and applies the new scale to all previously drawn objects. You cannot assign different line scales to different layers.

Figure 3-21
Comparing Line Scales

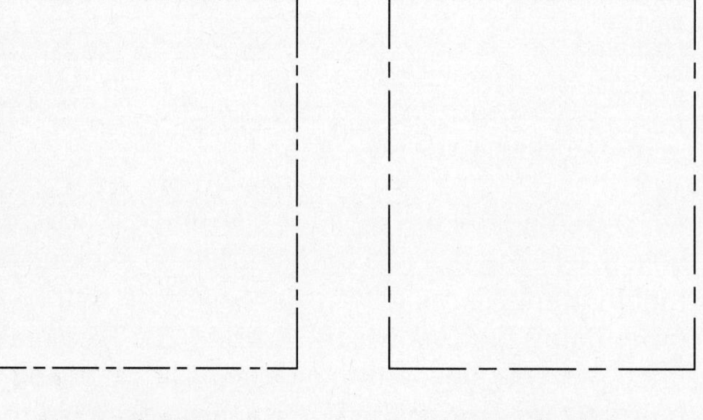

Line scale=0.5 **Line scale=1.0**

Figure 3-21 illustrates the effect of different line scales on the same objects. The rectangle on the left was drawn using the Center linetype with a line scale equal to 0.5. The rectangle on the right is drawn with a line scale equal to 1.0. As you can see, the smaller the line scale, the shorter the individual line segments that make up the linetype.

Try It

- Experiment with the Ltscale command, increasing the line scale to 2, 10, and 20—each time drawing an object or two to see what the new line scale looks like.
- Try decreasing the line scale to 0.5 and 0.1.

Choosing New Colors You can assign colors as well as linetypes to various layers. Clicking on the Set Color button in the Layer Control dialog box displays the Select Colors dialog box shown in Figure 3-22. This dialog box includes a full palette of the colors AutoCAD offers. (The actual colors are not shown, but the layout of the box is clear.) Normally you will use one of the nine standard colors displayed across the top of the dialog box. You select a color by clicking on the appropriate box. Colors are useful to help distinguish between different features and layers when more than one layer is on.

Figure 3-22
Select Color Dialog Box

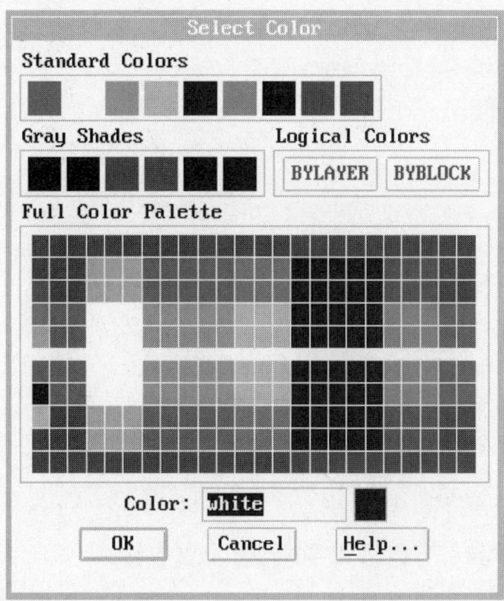

Try It

- Set the color of the CIRCLES layer to red.
- Set the color of the LINES layer to green.
- Make each layer the current layer in turn, and draw lines and circles to test the results.

Changing the Properties of an Object

You can use the Chprop command to change the properties of an object—including its color, layer, linetype, and thickness. The thickness property is associated with three-dimensional objects and will be discussed in Chapter 6. AutoCAD also provides the Change command for changing properties of objects and changing the location of the ends of lines and the size of circles and arcs. The Change command is discussed in Chapter 4.

Initiate the Chprop command by picking Change from the Modify pull-down menu and then choosing Properties. The following prompt appears:

```
Select objects:
```

Select the objects to be changed, and then press ENTER. The dialog box shown in Figure 3-23 appears. Select the property you want to change (Color, Layer, or Linetype) by clicking on the appropriate button. For each property you choose to change, a new dialog box appears. Select the new property, and click on OK to return to the Change Properties dialog box. When you complete the changes, click on OK. The dialog box disappears, and the objects are displayed with their new properties.

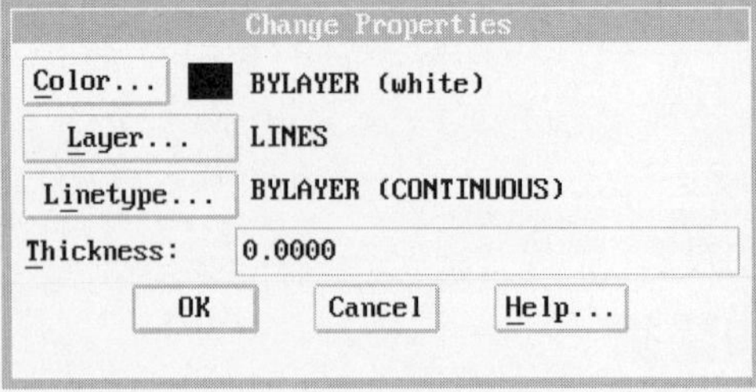

Figure 3-23
Change Properties Dialog Box

Try It

- Start the Chprop command.
- Pick a line on the LINES layer.
- Move the line to the CIRCLES layer.
- Change the color of a circle to Cyan.
- Change the linetype of a line to Dashed.

3-3 CORRECTING YOUR MISTAKES

Everyone makes mistakes when drawing. If you draw a single object in the wrong place, you can simply erase it and start over. However, if you erase a complex object by mistake, redrawing it could take a great deal of time. Fortunately, AutoCAD provides the UNDO and Redo commands for *undoing* mistakes and reversing the last undo operation. These commands work only in the current drawing session. If you leave an AutoCAD drawing and then return later to edit the drawing, these commands will not work.

Undoing Single Actions with the Undo Command

The Undo command selected from the Assist pull-down menu cancels the most recent command, and you can repeat this command to cancel many actions one at a time. You initiate the Undo command by picking Undo from the Assist pull-down menu, which is shown in Figure 3-24. This reverses your previous command.

You can initiate the Undo command to undo a single command by typing U and pressing ENTER. Many users find this procedure simpler than using the pull-down menu.

Help!
Cancel

Undo
Redo

Object Filters...
Object Snap ▷

Inquiry ▷

Calculator

Figure 3-24
Assist Pull-down Menu

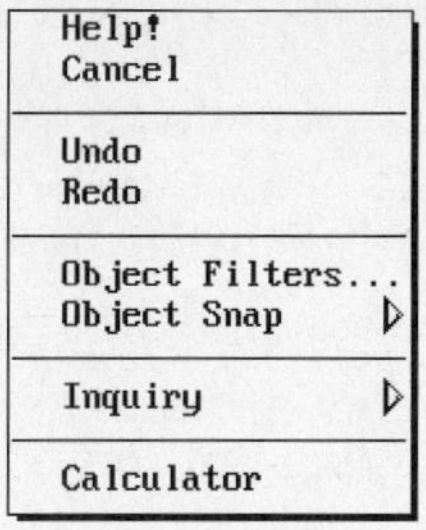

Try It

- Start a new drawing, and draw several lines and circles.
- Erase an object using the ERASE command.
- Move an object.
- Copy an object.
- Issue the Undo command, and observe the results. (Which command was reversed?)
- Issue the Undo command again, and observe the results.
- Issue the Undo command until the original set of objects is restored.

Undoing Multiple Actions with the Undo Command

You select the Undo command, from the screen menu, to cancel several commands at once. You can even mark groups of commands to be canceled. Undo cannot be initiated from a pull-down menu. To start the Undo command, select Edit, and click on next to display the rest of the Edit options. Select Undo from the screen menu. You will see the prompt

```
Auto/Back/Control/End/Group/Mark/<number>:
```

Respond by typing A, B, C, E, G, M, or a number and pressing ENTER. The results of certain responses are listed in Table 3-2. The Auto and Control options are beyond the scope of this text.

Table 3-2 Undo Responses and Results

Response	Result
<number>	Represents the number of commands that you want undone. The default value is 1. If you enter any other number and press ENTER, that number of commands will be undone.
M (Mark)	Places a mark in the sequence of commands. This option is useful if you want to experiment with some drawing steps before saving the results.
B (Back)	Undoes all of the commands back to the mark.
G (Group) E (End)	Entering G marks the beginning of a group of commands. Later entering E marks the end of the group. This group is treated as a single command when the Undo command is used.

Try It

- Draw a group of lines and circles.
- Edit them by using Copy, Erase, and Move.
- Use the Undo command to undo more than one editing or drawing step at once.
- Mark a place in the sequence, continue editing or drawing more objects, and then undo the sequence back to the mark.
- Experiment with the Group and End options.

Using the Redo Command

The Redo command re-executes the last command reversed by Undo. However, Redo restores only the last command. Initiate the command by choosing Redo from the Assist pull-down menu. Try this command as you experiment further with the Undo command.

3-4 CHANGING THE SCREEN DISPLAY

A number of AutoCAD commands allow you to control what is displayed on the screen. The most useful display commands, for the beginner, are Redraw, Zoom, and Pan.

Redrawing the Screen

The Redraw command removes the blips on the screen that accumulate as you draw and edit objects. Also, some editing commands cause part or all of an object to disappear. For example, if an object was entirely or partially behind another object that was erased, it will seem to have disappeared. Redraw will restore the image.

To initiate the Redraw command type `REDRAW` in the command area, and then press ENTER. The screen is redrawn or refreshed. It is good practice to use Redraw periodically.

Zooming In to Get a Close-up View

The Zoom command allows you to *zoom* in on, or enlarge, part of a drawing. Some drawings have so much detail that it is difficult, if not impossible, to select objects and points for editing. If so, you can zoom in on a section of the drawing to magnify it. The Zoom command does not change the actual size of objects; rather it changes your view of them. (To change the size of objects in a drawing, you use the Scale command, which is discussed in Chapter 4.)

Choosing Zoom from the View pull-down menu does not present the entire set of options that you can use with the command. To see all the options, type `ZOOM` in the command area, and then press ENTER. AutoCAD displays the main Zoom prompt:

```
All/Center/Dynamic/Extents/Left/Previous/Vmax/Window/
<Scale(X/XP)>:
```

Respond to this prompt by typing either A, C, D, E, L, P, V, or W. Each response and result is described in Table 3-3.

Table 3-3 Zoom Responses and Results

Response	Result
A (All)	Displays the area of the drawing defined by the limits or extents, whichever is greater. *Extents* is the area actually occupied by any part of a drawing.
C (Center)	Displays a view based on a point you select as the center of the screen after the Zoom is executed. You are prompted for a magnification factor or a height. If you enter a numerical value, it is interpreted as the height in the drawing units being used. A value followed by an X (for example, 5X) is interpreted as a magnification factor.
D (Dynamic)	This option is too complex to be useful at this time.
E (Extents)	Displays the entire drawing, forcing it to the left area of the screen. This option is useful when looking for objects that disappeared from view during an editing command such as Copy or Move.
L (Left)	Displays a view based on a point you pick as the lower-left corner of the new display.
P (Previous)	Restores the previous display created by the Zoom command in the current editing session. AutoCAD remembers the Zoom sequences so you can back up through the displays. If you back up through all of the zooms, AutoCAD displays the message "No previous view saved."
V (Vmax)	Creates the largest view that does not require a regeneration.
W (Window)	Enlarges a rectangular area to the size of the screen area. You are prompted to enter a first Corner and the other Corner.
Scale(X/XP)	This is the default option. Enlarges or reduces the drawing display. If you enter a numerical value followed by an X (for example, 5X), the factor applies to the current display. A factor without the X applies to the area defined by the limits of the drawing. The XP suffix applies to paper space units and is beyond the scope of this module.

The Zoom command is transparent, which means that you can use it while another command is in progress. Typing an apostrophe before the Zoom command temporarily suspends the current command while you complete the zoom operation.

The All option is one of the three most useful Zoom options. When you work on a complicated drawing, parts of the drawing may disappear from view. You can use the All option to bring the entire drawing back into view. Occasionally you "lose" an object by moving or copying it to some remote location off the screen. You can use the All option to locate the "lost" object and erase it if necessary. After the main Zoom prompt

```
All/Center/Dynamic/Extents/Left/Previous/Vmax/Window/
<Scale(X/XP)>:
```

appears, type A and press ENTER. The entire drawing comes into view.

Try It

- Make a drawing consisting of two circles. Move one of the circles, using a second point that moves the circle out of view. The circle is "lost."
- Use the All option of the Zoom command to bring the errant circle into view. Erase that circle and use All again.

The Window option is another useful Zoom option. In a particularly crowded drawing it may be impossible to pick out a detail that you need for editing. For example, you may be trying to see the intersection of two objects to use with the INT Osnap mode. You can enlarge the detail around the intersection using the Window option.

You initiate the Window option by typing `W` and pressing ENTER at the main Zoom prompt. At the

```
First corner:
```

prompt, pick the first corner of a window that contains the detail you want to enlarge. At the

```
Other corner:
```

prompt, pick a point on the opposite (diagonal) corner. Now the section of the drawing in the window is enlarged. The center of the window is the center of the screen. Unless you choose a rectangle that is in proportion to the screen dimensions, objects outside the window are displayed.

Figure 3-25
Using the Zoom Window Option (Before)

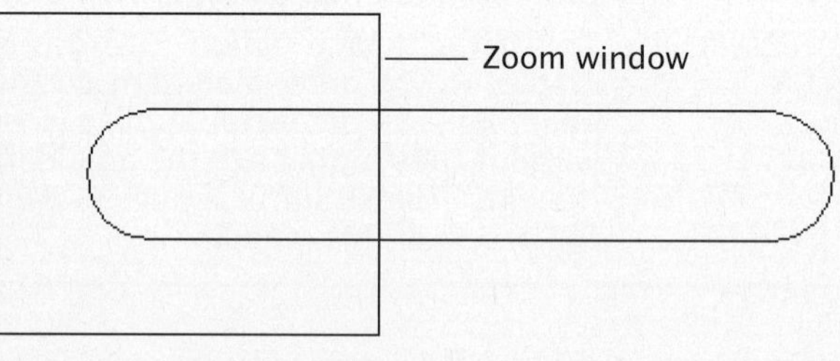

Before

Figures 3-25 and 3-26 illustrate the Window option. Figure 3-25 shows the entire drawing area and a rectangle representing the zoom window. The result of the zoom is shown in Figure 3-26.

Figure 3-26
Using the Zoom Window Option (After)

After

Try It

- Draw several objects on the screen.
- Use the Window option to enlarge a portion of the drawing. Use the Window option several times to enlarge part of each previous enlargement.
- Recover the original display by using the All option.

Previous is another handy Zoom option. To initiate this option, type P and press ENTER at the main Zoom prompt. AutoCAD recovers the preceding display. If you continue to use the Previous option, you eventually return to the initial display from the current drawing session. If you use the option again, AutoCAD displays the message

```
No previous view saved.
```

Try It

- Use the Previous option to recover the previously stored display.
- Continue to use the Previous option until there are no previous views saved.

Panning to See Objects Off the Screen

At times, objects you have drawn will move out of the screen area, perhaps as the result of a zoom operation. To see the portion of the drawing that is off the screen, you can use the All option of the Zoom command, but this may reduce the image too much. Using Pan lets you *pan* the drawing, bringing a different image into view without changing the magnification of the display. The Pan command does not change any of the coordinates of the drawing; rather it moves the drawing so that a different portion is visible. Figures 3-27 and 3-28 illustrate the use of the Pan command.

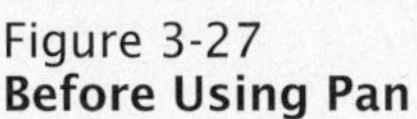

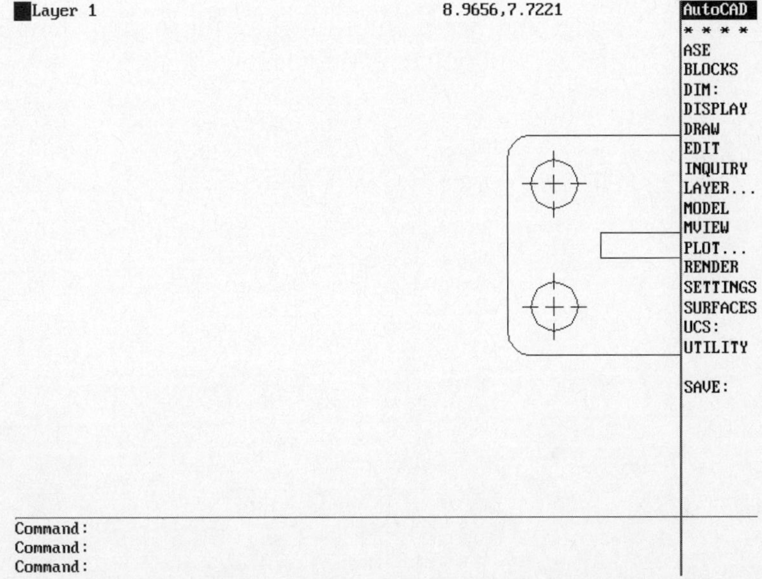

Figure 3-27
Before Using Pan

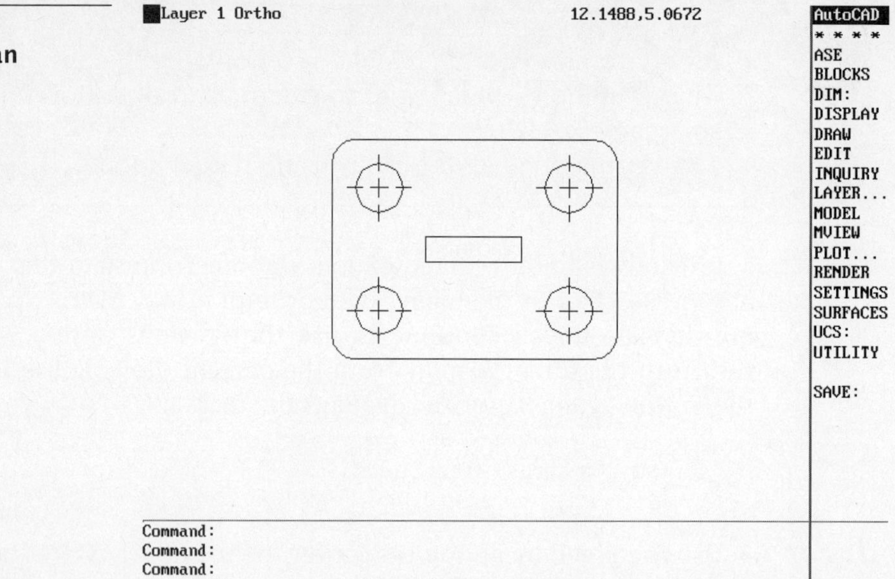

Figure 3-28
After Using Pan

In Figure 3-27 part of the plate is off the right side of the screen. The entire plate must be visible to make a copy. The image is moved to the left with the Pan command, as shown in Figure 3-28.

To issue the Pan command, choose Pan from the View pull-down menu. You will see the prompt

```
Displacement:
```

The displacement is the distance the drawing is to be moved. You can enter a displacement directly by entering a pair of coordinate values; however, it is generally easier to select a point with the mouse. If you do, you see the prompt

```
Second point:
```

Select another point with the mouse, and the distance between the first and second points is the displacement.

Try It

- Draw several shapes (or use the shapes that are already on screen).
- Use the Zoom command to enlarge part of the drawing.
- Practice using the Pan command with the two options for entering the displacement.
- After you have panned around the drawing a few times, restore the original image by using the All or Previous option of the Zoom command.

Application 1: OPTICAL DISK PICKUP SYSTEM

Optical Engineering

A *laser disk* is similar to a conventional recording disk. The grooves form a spiral curve. The information on a conventional disk is stored as physical deformations in the shape of the groove. The information is played back by running a pickup needle through the groove. Eventually the deformations wear out and the recording deteriorates. The information on laser disks is also stored as deformations, but the deformations are formed by high-powered lasers. The data on the disk is in the form of binary code—a series of 0s and 1s. The information is read by a low-powered laser beam from a laser diode. The laser diode is focused with a lens, and the reflected light is, in turn, focused on a detector. Finally the data is sent to an electronic device, called an *optical disk pickup system*, for conversion to sound or graphic images.

1. Identify the Object and Its Function

The object is the schematic of an optical disk pickup system typically used for audio and video optical disks. The system is designed to read the data recorded on a special optical disk.

2. Research Models and Determine Dimensions

There are several optical disk pickup systems on the market today. You will find basic information about these systems in textbooks on optical systems. The system shown in Figure 3-29 represents a typical design. Since you will be drawing a schematic, or diagram, of the system, dimensions are not necessary. Draw the size of the individual objects so that the elements are proportional to one another.

3. Make a Hand-Drawn Sketch

Use Figure 3-29 as the rough sketch. Plan the location of the components so that they line up properly. You will probably do best if you draw the lenses first.

4. Make Appropriate Screen Adjustments

Use New to start the drawing. Save the drawing as OPTICAL.

5. Draw, Print or Plot, and Save the Drawing File

Draw the schematic as shown. The lenses are arcs. You draw an arc by first drawing a circle and intersecting it with a line. Then you trim away the unwanted part of the circle. The other face of the lens is a mirror image of the first face. After you have drawn one lens, the remaining drawing is quite straightforward. Do not attempt to add the text.

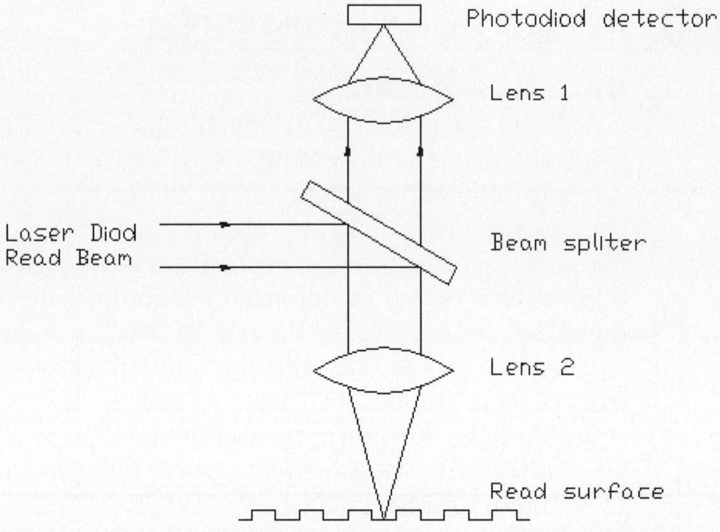

Figure 3-29
Optical Disk Pickup Schematic

What If

What if the drawing is too long vertically? You can shorten the drawing by shortening the light rays between lens 1 and the reflecting mirror. Using a horizontal line as a cutting edge, trim the lines between the mirror and the lens. Finally, move the lens and the photodiode detector down. Use the top surface of the beam splitter as a boundary edge, and extend the vertical lines to intersect the mirror. You can use the same technique to shorten the lines between lens 2 and the beam splitter.

SUMMARY

In this chapter you've added several new editing tools to your repertoire. You can copy, move, and mirror objects. The Offset command is especially convenient if you need parallel or concentric copies of objects. You have learned how to extend and trim objects. Layers are a powerful tool you can use to organize a drawing. Linetypes and colors add a professional quality to the result. The Chprop command is useful when you need to change the properties of selected objects. You can correct mistakes by using the Undo and Redo commands. Finally, the Redraw command permits you to refresh your screen, and the Zoom and Pan commands help you when you need to see details close up.

Key Words

base point
boundary edge
concentric
current layer
cutting edge
extents
laser disk
layer
line scale
linetype
offset
optical disk pickup system
pan
parallel
symmetry
undo
zoom

Exercises

Reproduce the drawings shown in the following exercises. Do not try to add text or dimensions. Try to add simple arrowheads on the direction lines in the schematics.

Exercise 3-1
Reflecting Telescope Schematic

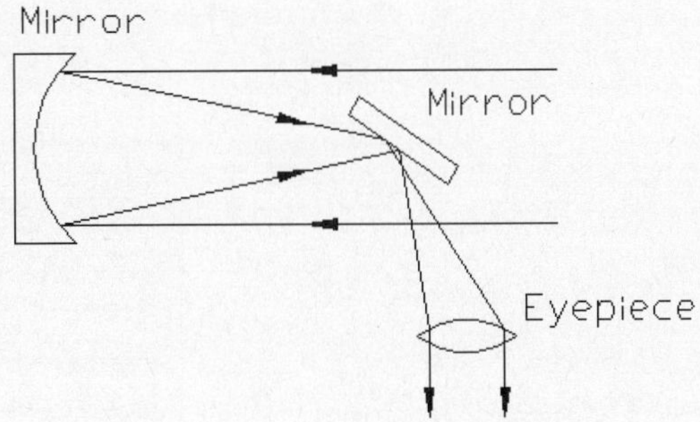

Exercise 3-2
Tool

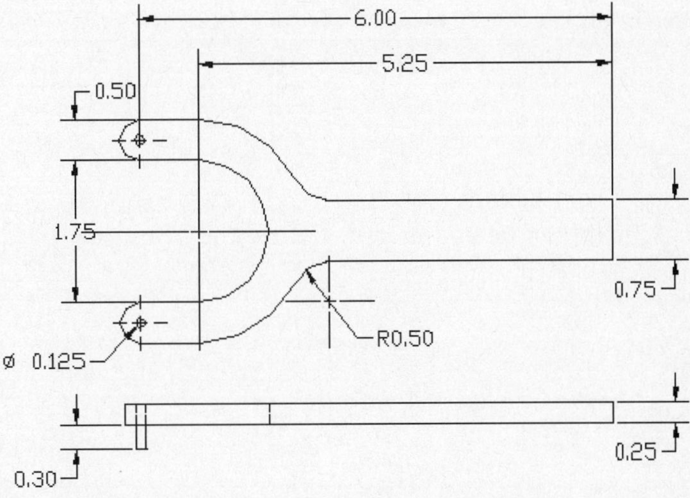

Exercise 3-3
Bracket

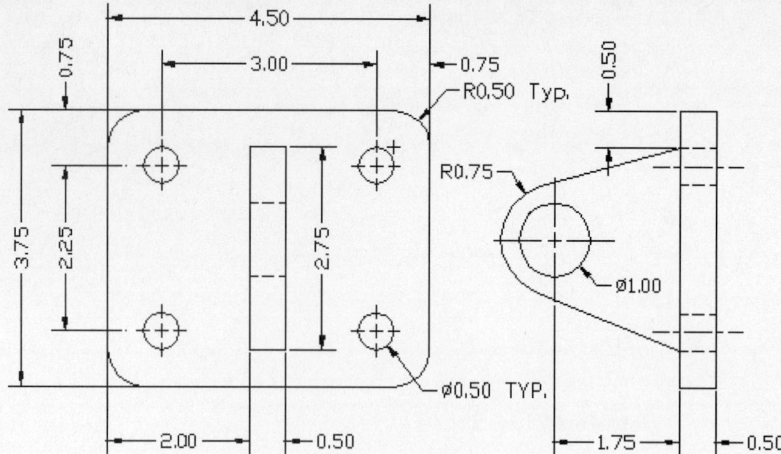

Exercise 3-4
Stair Detail

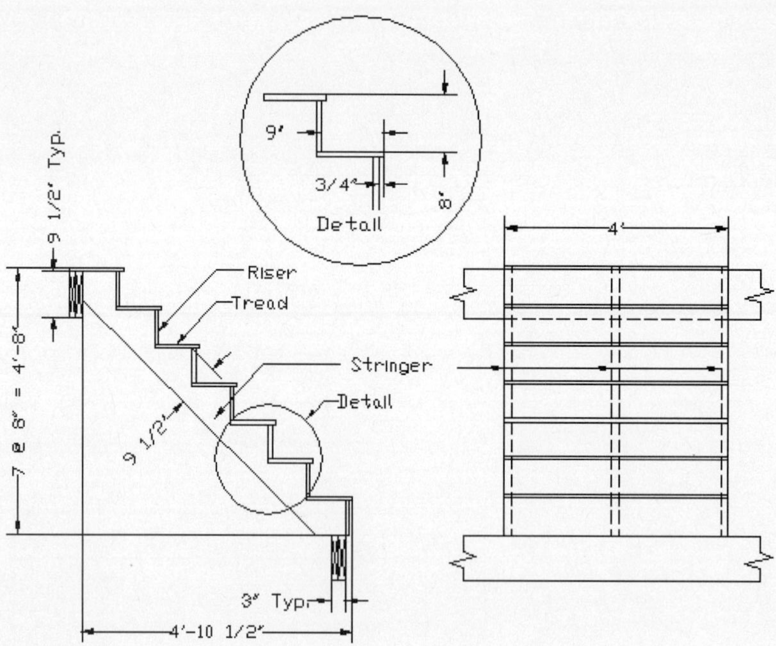

The thickness of the treads and risers is 3/4". The thickness of the support beams is 2.5". Offset and trim may be used to advantage in this problem.

Exercise 3-5
Printing Press Schematic Diagram

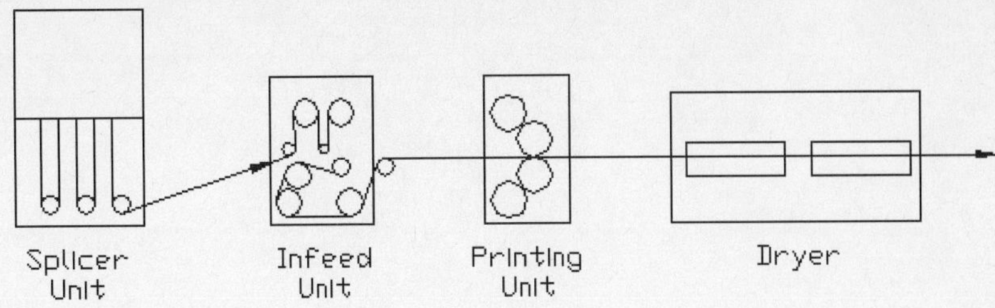

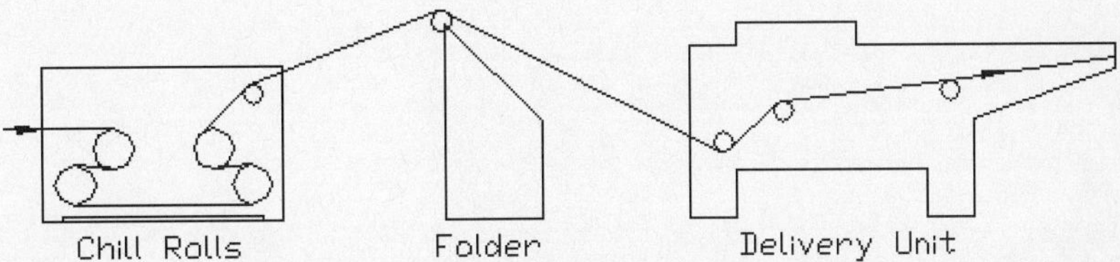

Adjust the limits to accommodate the overall length of the diagram. The dimensions of the dryer are approximately 15 feet by 7 feet. Draw the elements approximately to scale, using these dimensions as a guide.

Use Copy and Mirror while drawing some of the elements. The lines representing the paper path are tangent to the rollers.

Exercise 3-6
Foundation Plan

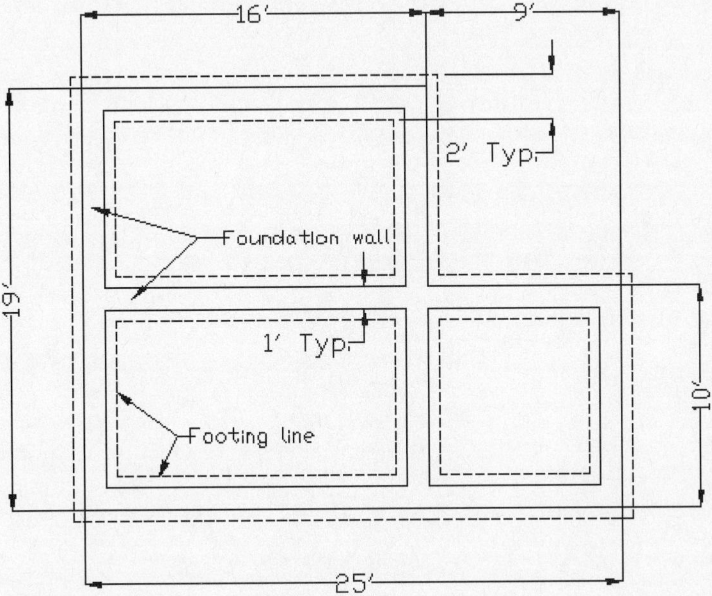

Select Engineering units. Set Upper Limits to 48',36'. Set Ltscale to 18. Enter data with the foot (') symbol. Save this drawing because you will use it for an exercise in Chapter 5.

4 Using Additional Drawing and Editing Tools

Microprocessors

Microprocessors are miniature computers that perform a wide range of functions. They are programmed to control anything from children's toys to automobile systems to remote sensing devices. The microprocessor is made from a combination of solid-state devices, the transistor being the oldest and most common. The microprocessor, fabricated as an integrated circuit, is encased in plastic for durability. Connecting pins are included in the assembly. The computer that you are using to run AutoCAD could not exist without microprocessors. CAD systems are used to design the integrated circuits employed in every modern electronic device, including computers. At the end of this chapter you will draw an electronic circuit designed to measure the operating characteristics of an element used in a microprocessor.

INTRODUCTION

In this chapter you learn how to set up a prototype drawing, how to draw arcs and polygons, and how to add text to your drawings. In addition, you learn how to use the Fillet and Chamfer commands to modify the corners of objects. You also learn how to manipulate objects with the Rotate, Scale, and Stretch commands. Finally, you learn how to use the Change command to change various properties of existing objects.

4-1 SETTING UP A PROTOTYPE DRAWING

As you made drawings in earlier chapters, you had to take the time to modify various settings to fit the needs of the particular drawing. It is more efficient to set up *prototype drawings* that contain the desired settings. These prototypes are simply blank drawings that you use to start a new drawing. They can include settings such as units, limits, and layers, with preset linetypes and colors. They can also include standard borders and title blocks. A *border* is the rectangular boundary around the entire drawing. The *title block*, usually found in the lower-right corner of the drawing, is where you add the company name and other identifying information.

To set up any prototype drawing, begin a new drawing as usual. Adjust the limits and units settings, set up layers as needed, add the border, and save the drawing. The name you use when you save the drawing is the name of the prototype drawing. Now the drawing is available to be used as a prototype.

When you start a new drawing, AutoCAD displays the Create New Drawing dialog box shown in Figure 4-1. Double-click in the upper-right box and type the name of the drawing to be used as a prototype. If necessary, click on the No Prototype box to remove the X, and then enter the new drawing name in the lower-right box; this prevents you from overwriting the prototype with the new drawing. Finally, click on OK. AutoCAD uses the settings from the prototype drawing in the new drawing you are about to create.

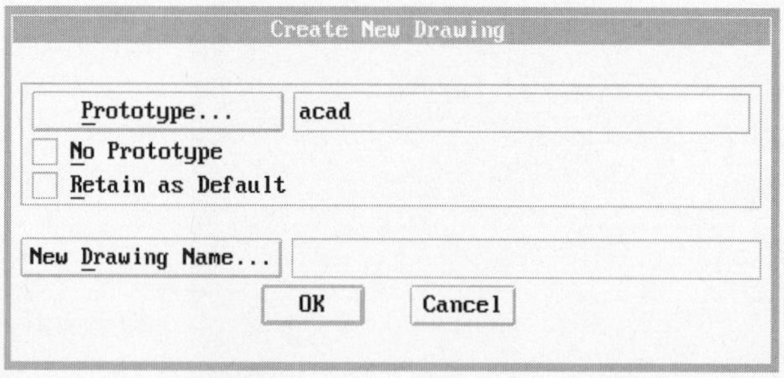

Figure 4-1
Create New Drawing Dialog Box

Create New Drawing
Prototype... acad
No Prototype
Retain as Default
New Drawing Name...
OK Cancel

Try It

- Create a prototype drawing called ENGIN.
- Set the units to Engineering with two decimal places. Set the limits as follows: Lower -1',-1'; Upper 35',26'. Set Snap and Grid to 6".
- Make layers with the following linetypes and colors:

Layer	Linetype	Color
Border, CONT	Continuous	Black
CEN	Center	Green
HIDE	Hidden	Blue
TEXT	Continuous	Red

- Create a second prototype drawing called DECIMAL using decimal units with 3 decimal places and the default limits. Use the remaining settings as used in the ENGIN prototype.

4-2 DRAWING WITH SOME NEW TOOLS

Arcs and polygons are two objects that you can draw without editing another object. You use arcs to form images that include only part of a circle. The AutoCAD polygon is any closed object with equal sides and equal interior angles. These polygons are used to represent bolt heads and wrenches, among other things.

Drawing Arcs

An *arc* is a portion of a circle. If you select Arc from the Draw pull-down menu, AutoCAD displays the Arc pull-down menu shown in Figure 4-2.

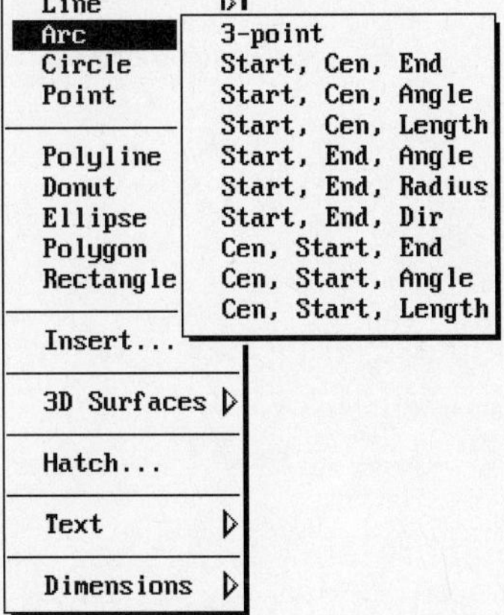

Figure 4-2
Draw and Arc Pull-down Menus

Most of the options in this menu include the following words or abbreviations:

Start	The start point of the arc.
End	The endpoint of the arc.

Cen	The center of the arc.
Length	The length of the chord between the start and endpoints.
Angle	The included angle defined by the start point, the endpoint, and the center of the arc.
Radius	The radius of the arc.
Dir	The direction of the tangent at the start point.

If you select any of the options for drawing arcs, you are prompted for the data in order. For example, if you choose Start, Cen, End, AutoCAD first asks for a start point, then a center point, and finally an end point. You can enter coordinates from the keyboard or pick points with the mouse in response to the prompts. The three most common options are 3-point; Start, Cen, Angle; and Start, End, Radius.

When using the 3-point option, you simply select three points on the arc. Start the 3-point option by picking it from the Arc pull-down menu. The first prompt is

```
Center/<Start point>:
```

Pick any point as the start point for the arc. The next prompt is

```
Center/End/<Second point>:
```

Again, pick any point as the second point on the arc. A rubber band forms after you pick the second point. You can see how the arc is being formed as you move the crosshairs around the screen. The prompt

```
End point:
```

appears. Now pick the endpoint, and the arc will be completed. Figure 4-3 illustrates a three-point arc.

Figure 4-3
Arc: 3-point Option

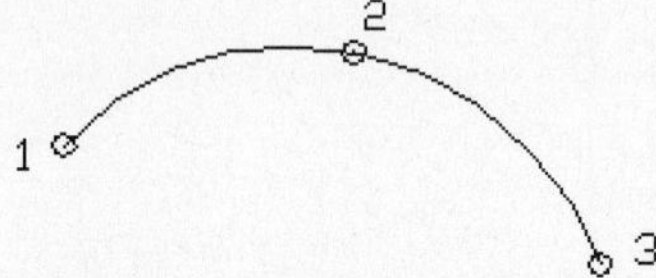

Try It

- Draw a 3-point arc similar to the one shown in Figure 4-3.
- Draw another arc that opens upward.

You can also draw an arc by specifying the start point, the center point, and the included angle. Two such arcs are shown in Figure 4-4. The Arc command does not add the angular dimensions shown in the figure. The included angle is the central angle of the arc (the angle between lines drawn from the center to the endpoints of the arc). You start this option by selecting Start, Cen, Angle from the Arc menu.

The first prompt is

```
Center/<Start point>:
```

Pick any start point. AutoCAD remembers the order of the points (Start and Center) for this option, therefore the next prompt is

```
Center:
```

Pick any point for the center of the arc. The next prompt is

```
Angle/Length of chord/<End point>:
Included angle:
```

This seems a double prompt. Again, AutoCAD remembers that you are using the Start, Cen, Angle option and chooses Angle response automatically and prompts you for the angle. If you move the crosshairs, an arc is formed. You can pick a point with the mouse to establish an angle, but it is more common to enter a positive or negative angle from the keyboard.

Figure 4-4
Arc: Start, Cen, Angle Option

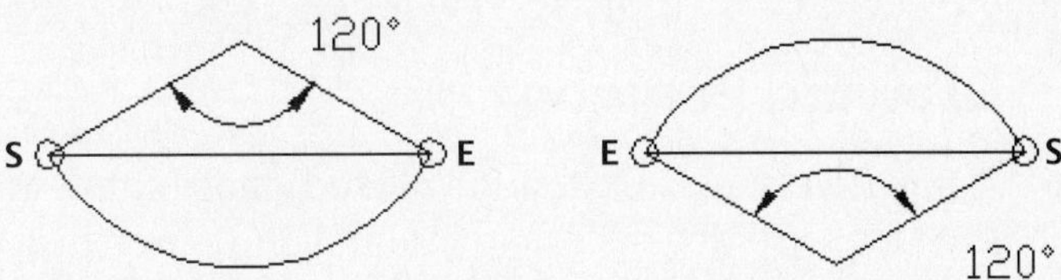

Figure 4-4 also illustrates the effects of choosing a different start point (S) and endpoint (E). The angle is the same for each arc (+120 degrees). As you can see, the arc is drawn so that it goes from the start point to the endpoint in a counterclockwise direction.

Try It

- Draw the two arcs shown in Figure 4-4.
- Draw two more arcs using the same start and endpoints but with a negative (-120-degree) angle.
- Draw another set of arcs using the same points but with different angles.

You can also draw arcs using the Start, End, Radius option, which is illustrated in Figure 4-5. Select Start, End, Radius from the Arc pull-down menu and the prompt

```
Center/<Start point>:
```

appears. Pick a start point for the arc. At the next prompt

```
End point:
```

pick the endpoint. The next prompt is

```
Angle/Direction/Radius/<Center point>:
Radius:
```

You can enter the radius by moving the mouse until you are satisfied with the arc, but it is more common to type the value of the radius from the keyboard.

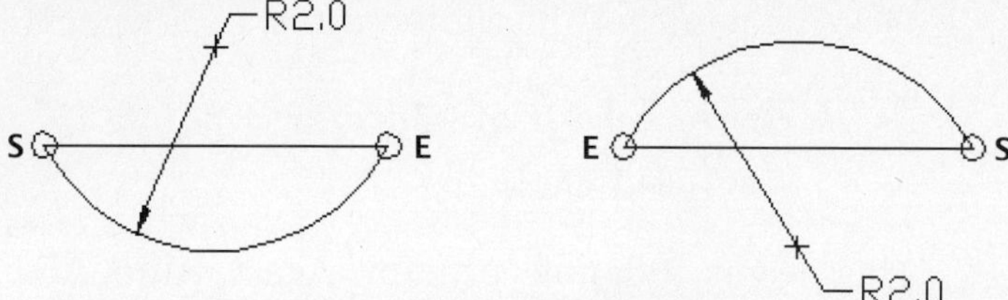

Figure 4-5
Arc: Start, End, Radius Option

Try It

- Draw the two arcs shown in Figure 4-5.
- Draw arcs with the same start point and endpoint, but use values for the radius that are larger and smaller than 2.

Drawing Polygons

A *polygon* is any multisided closed figure made up of lines. The lengths of the sides are not necessarily equal. Polygons drawn with the Polygon command, however, have equal sides and equal interior angles.

To draw a polygon, choose the Polygon command from the Draw pull-down menu. The first prompt is

```
Number of sides:
```

You can draw polygons with any number of sides between 3 and 1024. After you specify the number of sides, AutoCAD displays the prompt

```
Edge/<Center>:
```

This prompt allows you to specify the length and position of an edge, or to specify the center and radius of either a *circumscribing* or an *inscribing* circle. Figure 4-6 illustrates polygons drawn using these three options.

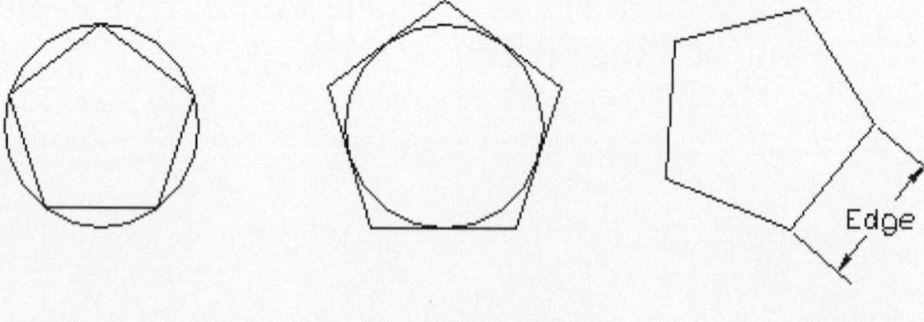

Inscribed Option **Circumscribed Option** **Edge Option**

Figure 4-6
Polygon Options

To choose the Center option, you pick a point on the screen. This point is the center of either an inscribing or circumscribing circle. AutoCAD displays the prompt

```
Inscribed in circle/Circumscribed about circle (I/C):
```

Now choose I or C to create either an inscribed or circumscribed polygon. Finally, AutoCAD presents the prompt

```
Radius of circle:
```

You supply a radius to complete the inscribed or circumscribed polygon.

If you select the Edge option by typing E and pressing ENTER at the

```
Edge/<Center of polygon>:
```

prompt, you are prompted in turn for the

```
First endpoint on edge:
```

and the

```
Second endpoint on edge:
```

By picking two points, you determine the size, location, and orientation of the polygon.

Try It

- Start a new drawing called POLYGON, using the DECIMAL drawing you created earlier as a prototype.
- Draw two circles each with a 1.0-unit radius.
- Draw an inscribed polygon using the left circle and a circumscribed polygon using the right circle.
- Draw a polygon with the Edge option, using the edge of one of the previous polygons as the edge of the new polygon.

4-3 ADDING TEXT TO DRAWINGS

Text is an essential part of all engineering drawings. For example, you use text to describe the materials to be used and to add title blocks that indicate who prepared the drawing.

Adding text to a drawing involves two steps. First you use the Dtext command to insert the text, placing it in the correct location on the drawing, aligning it, and adjusting its size. Second you use the Style command to design the text style, selecting the appearance of the characters, choosing the height to width ratio, and picking the slope and orientation of the characters.

Adding Text with the Dtext Command

You can use the Dtext (dynamic text) command to enter text into your drawings. When you use Dtext, AutoCAD displays a box equal to the size of the characters and displays the text on the screen as you are typing so you can judge the length of the lines. You can also continue the text on multiple lines.

To start the Dtext command, select Text from the Draw pull-down menu, and then choose Dynamic. The main Dtext prompt appears:

```
Justify/Style/<Start point>:
```

If you choose the Start point option, the text will be left justified. Choose the Style option to change from one style to another. You can initiate the Justify option by typing `J` at this prompt and pressing (ENTER); another prompt appears offering you 14 more options for justifying text.

The Start point and Justify options of the Dtext command are discussed in detail in this section.

Using the Start Point Option The Start point option results in left-justified text, as illustrated in Figure 4-7. The plus signs (+) in this and subsequent figures indicate the justification points of the lines of text. They do not appear when you enter text. They are shown to identify where the text lines up with the points you select when you start a line of text.

To initiate the Start point option, you select a start point at the main Dtext prompt, using any selection technique. The start point is indicated by the + in the figure. Then the following prompt appears:

```
Height <0.2000>:
```

The number is the default height of the characters and is equal to the value that was used last with the Dtext command. Type a new value and press (ENTER), or press (ENTER) to accept the default value. The next prompt is

```
Rotation Angle <0>:
```

The *rotation angle* is the angle the text line makes with the horizontal. Enter a new value, or press (ENTER) to accept the default value. After you set the angle, a square the size of the characters appears at the start point. At the final prompt

```
Text:
```

type the text. You can enter multiple lines of text by pressing (ENTER) at the end of each line. Press (ENTER) twice to end the Dtext command.

Figure 4-7
Dtext Using the Start Point Option

Try It

- Use the Start point option to enter the text shown in Figure 4-7.
- Enter the same text again in another location, changing the height to 0.5.
- Enter the same text a third time using a rotation angle of 45.

You can use the Align option to *align* text between two points in the drawing. These points set the slope of the text line, and the text is forced to fit between the points. The Align option does not prompt you for a height. Instead the height is adjusted depending on the number of characters in the line of text. Figure 4-8 illustrates the Align option, showing the effects of choosing different distances between the two aligning points. The Align, Fit, Center, Middle, and Right options of this Justify option prompt are discussed in this section. The other options are beyond the scope of this text.

To initiate the Align option, type J and press ENTER at the

```
Justify/Style/<Start point>:
```

prompt. At the next prompt,

```
Align/Fit/Center/Middle/Right/TL/TC/TR/ML/MC/MR/BL/BC/BR:
```

type A and press ENTER. The next prompt is

```
First text line point:
```

Pick a point on the screen and the prompt

```
Second text line point:
```

appears. Pick a second point to fix the alignment. AutoCAD displays the small square showing the alignment of the characters. At the prompt

```
Text:
```

you can type the text. After you enter the text, the size of the characters is adjusted to fill the distance between the two points. At the "Text:" prompt, if you enter some text, press ENTER, and then continue typing text on a second line, the characters on the two lines will have different sizes.

Aligned Text

Aligned Text

Figure 4-8
Dtext Using the Align Option

Try It

- Use the Align option to enter the two lines of text shown in Figure 4-8, using two different pairs of align points.
- Enter a longer line of text, continuing it on a second line. Note the appearance of the characters.

The Fit option is illustrated in Figure 4-9. It is similar to Align with one major difference: The height of the characters is fixed. The width of the characters is adjusted to fit the line of text between the two text points.

To initiate the Fit option, type `J` and press ENTER at the

```
Justify/Style/<Start point>:
```

prompt. At the prompt

```
Align/Fit/Center/Middle/Right/TL/TC/TR/ML/MC/MR/BL/BC/BR:
```

type `F` and press ENTER. The next prompt is

```
First text line point:
```

Pick a point on the screen, and the prompt

```
Second text line point:
```

appears. Pick a second point to fix the alignment. At the prompt

```
Height <0.2000>:
```

enter a new height or accept the default value. The small square appears. At the prompt

```
Text:
```

type the text, pressing ENTER twice when you're done. Now the characters are adjusted to fill the distance between the two points.

Figure 4-9
Dtext Using the Fit Option

Try It

- Use the Fit option to enter the two lines of text shown in Figure 4-9, using two different pairs of fit points.
- Enter a longer line of text, continuing it on a second line. Note the appearance of the characters.

The Center and Middle options are very similar. Each prompts you for a point and centers the text horizontally about that point (if the rotation angle is 0). The Center option centers the text above an imaginary line through the point. The Middle option centers the characters vertically about the point. These options are illustrated in Figure 4-10.

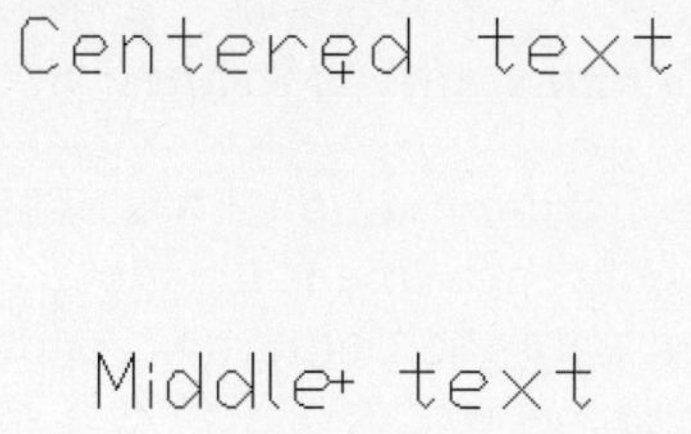

Figure 4-10
Dtext Using the Middle and Center Options

Centered text

Middle text

To initiate the Center option, type J and press ENTER at the

```
Justify/Style/<Start point>:
```

prompt. At the prompt

```
Align/Fit/Center/Middle/Right/TL/TC/TR/ML/MC/MR/BL/BC/BR:
```

type C and press ENTER. The next prompt is

```
Center point:
```

Pick a center point with the mouse or enter the coordinates from the keyboard. At the prompt

```
Height <0.2000>:
```

enter the height. At the prompt

```
Rotation angle <0>:
```

enter the rotation angle. The small square appears to show the size of the characters, and the prompt

```
Text:
```

appears. Enter the text as before. The text temporarily appears to the right of the center point. After you press ENTER twice, the text shifts to the left and centers itself around the center point.

To initiate the Middle option, type J and press ENTER at the

```
Justify/Style/<Start point>:
```

prompt. At the prompt

```
Align/Fit/Center/Middle/Right/TL/TC/TR/ML/MC/MR/BL/BC/BR:
```

type M and press ENTER. The next prompt is

```
Middle point:
```

Pick a point to serve as the middle point for your text. Then enter a height and a rotation angle, and enter your text, as you did with the Center option, pressing ENTER twice when you're done. The plus (+) marks in Figure 4-10 show how the text is positioned vertically about the center and middle points.

Try It

- Use the Center and Middle options to enter the text shown in Figure 4-10.
- Repeat the options, entering multiple lines of text without restarting the command. Observe how each line is arranged about the selected point.
- Enter some more text with the Center and Middle options, using a rotation angle other than zero.

The Right option illustrated in Figure 4-11 allows you to right justify lines of text. You select a point that establishes the right edge of the text. As you type the text, it temporarily appears to the right of the selected point. When you press ENTER twice, the text shifts to the left and becomes right justified.

To initiate the Right option, type J and press ENTER at the

```
Justify/Style/<Start point>:
```

prompt. At the prompt

```
Align/Fit/Center/Middle/Right/TL/TC/TR/ML/MC/MR/BL/BC/BR:
```

type R and press ENTER. At the prompt

```
Endpoint:
```

pick a point to serve as the right end of the lines of text. The prompt

```
Height <0.2000>:
```

appears. After you enter the height, AutoCAD displays the prompt

```
Rotation angle <0>:
```

Enter the rotation angle and the prompt

```
Text:
```

appears. Enter the text, pressing ENTER twice to complete the command.

Try It

- Enter the text shown in Figure 4-11.
- Enter more text using a different value for the height, and observe the difference in the actual size of the characters.
- Enter text using a different rotation angle.

Figure 4-11
Dtext Using the Right Option

This text used
the Right
Option. Its height
is 0.30 and its
angle is 0.

Creating New Text Styles

So far you have been using the STANDARD text style that AutoCAD supplies. You can, however, create as many new styles as you need for a given drawing. To define a new text style, you must name the style; choose a font; set the height, the width factor, and an obliquing angle; and, finally, decide whether you want the characters to be backward, upside-down, or arranged in a vertical line. An advantage of creating new styles is that, if you redefine any part of a previously defined style, all of the text entered in that style is changed automatically.

To begin creating a new text style, choose the Style: command from the SETTINGS screen menu. AutoCAD displays the prompt

```
Text style name (or ?)<STANDARD>:
```

The name in angle brackets is the current style. It will be the STANDARD style, unless you have been using another style. Enter a name for the new style, and the Select Font File dialog box shown in Figure 4-12 appears. To see the names of the available fonts, scroll through the Files box. When you find the font that fits your needs, click on its name and then click on OK. The message "New Style" appears in the command area, and the dialog box disappears.

Figure 4-12
Select Font File Dialog Box

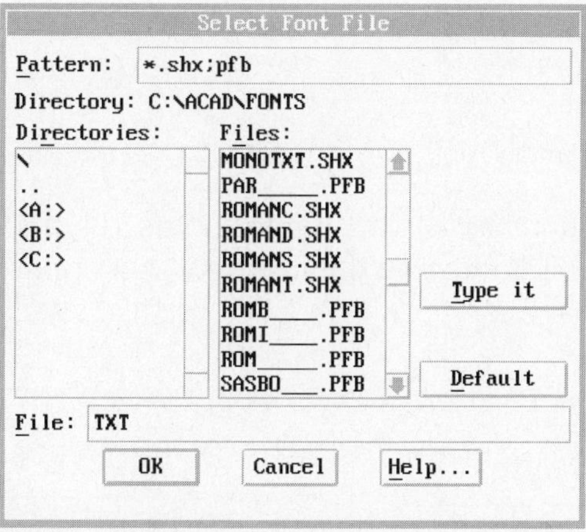

The next prompt is

```
Height <0.0000>:
```

Enter a height or accept the default value. If you enter 0, you are prompted for the height when you enter text. If you enter any other value, the height is fixed. It is better practice to enter 0 so you can adjust the height when you enter text.

At the next prompt

```
Width factor <1.000>:
```

enter a value or accept the default value. This factor controls the ratio of the width to the height of the letters. The normal value is 1, but you can use other values for special effects. For most engineering applications, a width factor of 1 is standard. The next prompt is

```
Obliquing angle <0>:
```

You can either enter an angle or press ENTER to accept the default value. A positive value slants the letters to the right while a negative value slants the letters to the left. For engineering drawings, it is standard to accept the default value, which results in upright letters.

At the prompt

```
Backwards? <N>:
```

enter Y if you want the text to read backward. Otherwise, accept the default value of N. The next prompt is

```
Upside-down? <N>:
```

Enter Y if you want the text to appear upside-down. Otherwise, accept the default value of N. At the next prompt

```
Vertical? <N>:
```

enter Y if you want the text to read vertically. Otherwise, accept the default value of N. If you need to enter a label along the edge of a drawing, vertical text is useful.

When you have responded to these prompts, the message

```
style is now the current text style
```

appears, where *style* is the name you used at the first prompt.

Figures 4-13 and 4-14 illustrate a variety of styles. The NEW style has no unusual characteristics. NEW1 is a vertical style, and NEW2 is backward.

Figure 4-13
Comparing New Text Styles

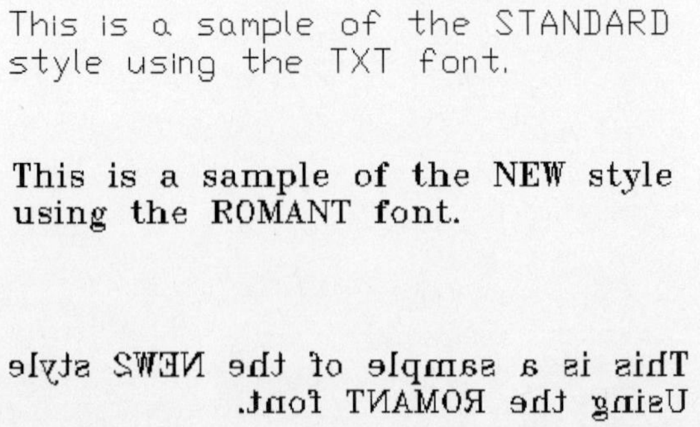

This is a sample of the STANDARD
style using the TXT font.

This is a sample of the NEW style
using the ROMANT font.

This is a sample of the NEW2 style
Using the ROMANT font.

Figure 4-14
Additional Text Styles

This text used the
NEW1 style. The
font is ROMANDt.

This text uses the
ROMANDT font. The
obliquing angle is
10°.

This text uses the
TXT font. The
obliquing angle is
20°.

Changing Text Styles After you have created one or more text styles, you can use these styles instead of the STANDARD style that AutoCAD provides. To change to a new style initiate the Dtext command. At the prompt

```
Justify/Style/<Start point>:
```

enter S and press ENTER. The prompt

```
Style name (or?)<STANDARD>:
```

appears. Type the name of the new style and press ENTER. The prompt

```
Justify/Style/<Start point>:
```

reappears. Continue to enter text using the new style. If you do not remember the style names that you created, type ? and press ENTER to display the list of style names. The default style name will be the last style that you used. Therefore you will see STANDARD initially.

Try It

- Create the three styles NEW, NEW1, and NEW2 using the ROMANT font.
- Change to the NEW style, and enter the middle lines of text in Figure 4-13.
- Change to the NEW2 style, and enter the lower lines of text in Figure 4-13.
- Change back to the NEW style, and enter the message "This text is inclined and is the NEW style." Enter the text at a 20-degree angle.
- Change to the NEW1 style, and enter the vertical text in Figure 4-14.
- Use the STYLE command to redefine the NEW style.
- Change the font to ROMANS with an obliquing angle of -10 degrees.
- After you see the result, change the font back to ROMANT.

Creating Special Characters with Control Codes

A number of special characters are common in engineering drawings, including the degree symbol (°), the tolerance symbol (±), the percent symbol (%), and the diameter (ø) symbol. To create these symbols and underscore or overscore text, you use the special *control codes* shown in Table 4-1.

Table 4-1 Special Control Codes

Symbol	Control Code Sample Entry	Effect
‾ (overscore)	%%OOverscore%%O	Overscore
_ (underscore)	%%UUnderscore%%U	Underscore
° (degree)	230%%D	230°
± (tolerance)	4.5%%P0.01	4.5±0.01
ø (diameter)	%%C 2.5	ø 2.5
% (percent)	50 %%%	50 %

Try It

- Use the Dtext command to enter the text shown in the right portion of Figure 4-14, using the control code for the degree symbol.
- Enter the text shown in Table 4-1. Notice that the codes appear initially but disappear after the line is complete, leaving only the final result.

4-4 MANIPULATING OBJECTS

Often you will need to manipulate objects after you initially draw them. Corners of objects, which are usually drawn with sharp intersections, can be modified by using the Fillet and Chamfer commands. You can draw one or more objects with one orientation and then easily change their orientation by using the Rotate command. In addition, you can copy an object to a new location and change its size with the Scale command, which alters the size but not the shape of an object. If you need to change the shape of an object in a single dimension, you use the Stretch command. Finally, you can use the expanded version of the Chprop command, Change, to relocate the endpoints of lines, edit text, and change the sizes of circles.

Using the Fillet Command

The Fillet command is designed to alter the intersection of lines or arcs. The command fillets, or rounds off, the corners with an arc tangent to the two objects. The original objects are trimmed back to the arc. Figure 4-15 illustrates the results of using the Fillet command on a pair of lines and on a line and an arc. The dashed lines represent the portion of the objects removed by the command. The fillet arc is labeled in the figure. As you can see, the Fillet command works even if the two objects do not actually intersect. The only requirement is that they would intersect if extended.

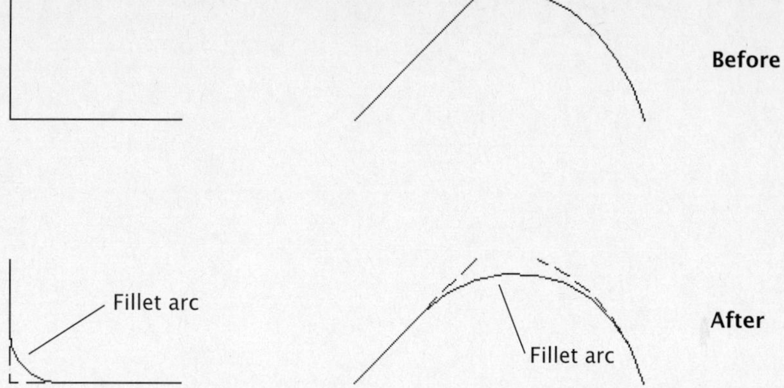

Figure 4-15
Fillet Examples

The Fillet command requires that you enter the radius of the arc before you select the objects. After the radius is set, you start the command again and select the objects.

Start the Fillet command by selecting Fillet from the Construct pull-down menu. At the prompt

```
Polyline/Radius/<Select first object>:
```

type R and press (ENTER) to signal that the radius is to be entered or changed. At the next prompt

```
Enter fillet radius <0.0000>:
```

enter the radius. The default value is 0.0000 unless you have set another value during the drawing session.

Restart the Fillet command to fillet two objects. At the prompt

```
Polyline/Radius/<Select first object>:
```

pick a line. At the prompt

```
Select second object:
```

pick another line. AutoCAD will draw the fillet and end the command.

If the fillet radius is too large for the length of the lines, AutoCAD responds with the message "Radius is too large." If necessary, try again with a smaller radius.

The Fillet command works equally well on outside corners. In technical terms, the fillets on outside corners are called *rounds,* and those on inside corners are called fillets. The arcs in the four inside corners of the lower-left object in Figure 4-16 are fillets. The arcs in the two outside corners are rounds.

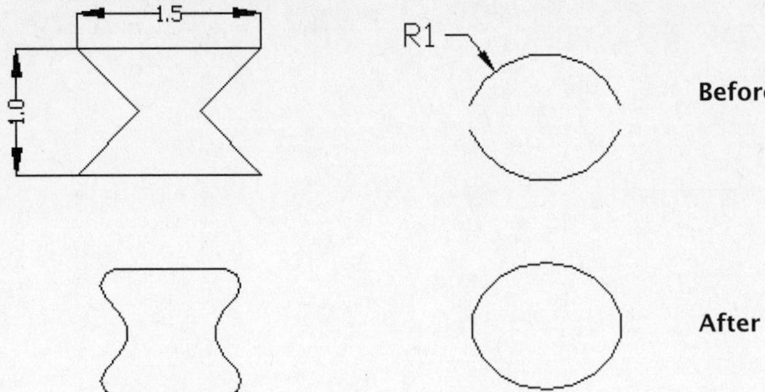

Figure 4-16
Fillet Exercise

Try It

- Draw the objects shown in the "Before" section of Figure 4-16.
- Add fillets to the left object, using a radius of 0.125 for the four inside corners and 0.25 for the two outside corners.
- Use Undo to restore the objects, and use a radius of 0.25 for all the corners.
- Use Undo again to restore the object and use a radius of 0.20 to fillet all of the corners.
- Use a radius of 0.40 to fillet the two arcs as shown in Figure 4-16.

Using the Chamfer Command

The Chamfer command modifies the intersection of two lines (but not arcs) by *chamfering*, or cutting off the corner, of the intersection with a straight line. Chamfer requires two distances to determine how far back from the intersection to make the cut: The first distance is measured along the first line, and the second distance is measured along the second line.

The result of chamfering lines is illustrated in Figure 4-17. The figures on the left use different chamfering distances. The lines on the right are chamfered with equal distances. Note that the lines do not need to intersect to be chamfered; AutoCAD finds the apparent intersection point and completes the chamfer. To complete a chamfer process, you initiate the Chamfer command twice: once to set the chamfer distances and then again to chamfer the lines.

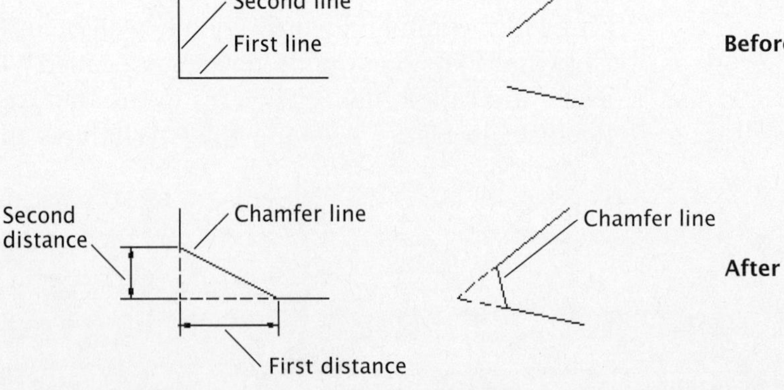

Figure 4-17
Chamfer Examples

To start the Chamfer command, select Chamfer from the Construct pull-down menu. At the prompt

```
Polyline/Distances/<Select first line>:
```

type D and press ENTER to signal that you want to enter or change the distances.

At the prompt

```
Enter first chamfer distance <0.0000>:
```

enter the first chamfer distance. The default value is 0.0000 if you are using the command for the first time in the drawing session. At the prompt

```
Enter second chamfer distance <>:
```

enter the second distance. The default value for the second distance is the first distance.

Once you have set the distances, press ENTER to restart the Chamfer command. At the prompt

```
Polyline/Distances/<Select first line>:
```

pick a line using the aperture. At the prompt

```
Select second line:
```

pick another line. AutoCAD completes the chamfer and terminates the command. Since the chamfer operation trims the extra parts of the lines, the command does not work if a chamfer distance is too large. The command cannot eliminate an entire line.

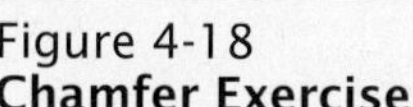

Figure 4-18
Chamfer Exercise

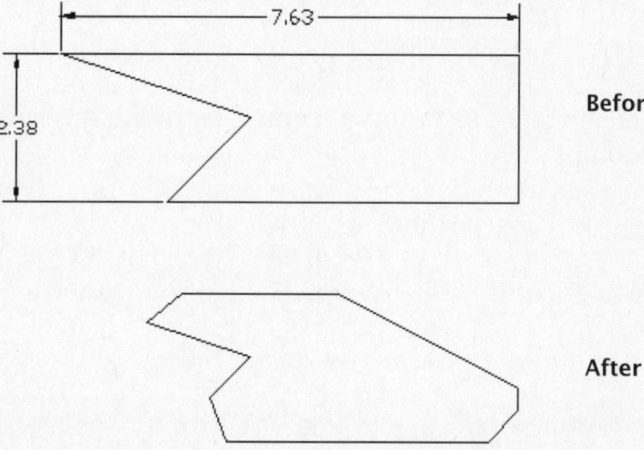

Try It 

- Make a drawing similar to the "Before" object in Figure 4-18. Use the given dimensions as a guide.
- Chamfer the corner at point A using distances of 1.5 and 2. Chamfer the corner at point B using distances of 1.5 and 3.
- Chamfer the corner at point C using equal distances of 1.
- Chamfer the corner at point D using equal distances of 0.5.

Rotating Objects

The Rotate command rotates objects about a specified point. Rotating an object involves three steps: First you select the object or objects to be rotated. Second you select the proper point for the center of rotation. Third you determine the amount of rotation.

The drawing in Figure 4-19 shows an object in an incorrect position and the same object rotated so that it is in the correct position. In this example, the object is rotated 90 degrees clockwise, with point A as the center of rotation.

Figure 4-19
Rotate Example Using Rotation Angle Option

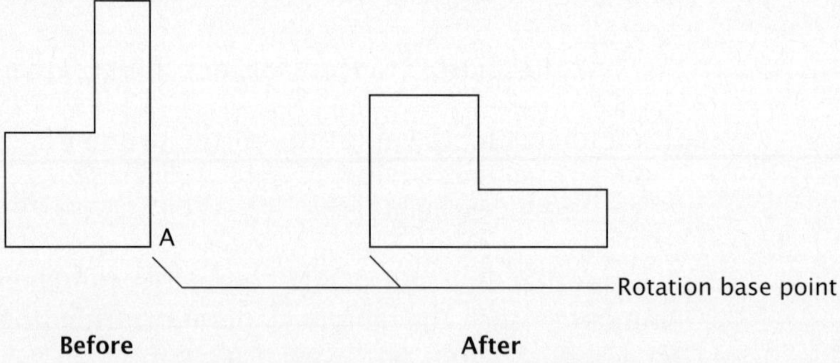

Start the Rotate command by selecting Rotate from the Modify pull-down menu. At the prompt

```
Select objects:
```

select the objects to be rotated by using any selection techniques. At the prompt

```
Base point:
```

pick an appropriate point. The next prompt

```
<Rotation angle>/Reference:
```

gives you two ways to enter the rotation. Entering an angle and pressing ENTER automatically selects the Rotation angle option and completes the command. A positive angle causes a counterclockwise rotation, and a negative angle causes a clockwise rotation.

Try It

- Draw an object similar to the "Before" image in Figure 4-19.
- Rotate the object 90 degrees clockwise about point A, as shown in the figure.
- Rotate the object 90 degrees counterclockwise about the lower-right corner of the object in its "After" position.
- Continue to rotate the object until you return it to its original orientation.

On occasion you may need to rotate an object without knowing the precise angle of rotation. If this is the case, type R and press ENTER at the prompt

```
<Rotation angle>/Reference:
```

In the exercise shown in Figure 4-20, for example, the problem is to rotate the arc so the two endpoints are on the horizontal line. In this case you do not know the angle of rotation (labeled "Reference angle") in the figure. If you know the current orientation of some line, real or imaginary, and you know the new orientation, you enter the two angles at the prompts

```
Reference angle <0>:
```

and

```
New angle:
```

AutoCAD uses the difference between the angles to compute the rotation angle.

Alternatively, you can respond to the prompt

```
Reference angle <0>:
```

by picking a point, usually the base point, as the first point in the reference direction. AutoCAD then prompts you for a

```
Second point:
```

Pick a second point along a line in the reference direction. AutoCAD uses the second point with the first point to establish the reference direction (see Figure 4-20). Now you must establish the new orientation the reference direction is to take. At the prompt

```
New angle:
```

pick another point along a real or imaginary line through the base point to establish the new direction (see Figure 4-20). AutoCAD calculates the angle between the two directions and uses the result as the rotation angle.

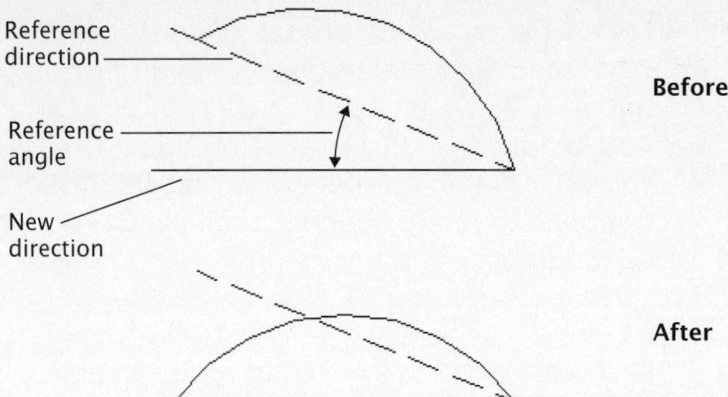

Figure 4-20
Rotate Exercise Using the Reference Option

Try It

- Draw an arc similar to the one shown in the "Before" image of Figure 4-20.
- Draw a horizontal line through lower end of the arc.
- Using the Reference angle option, rotate the arc so that both endpoints are on the horizontal line.
- Rotate the arc and the horizontal line so that a line making an angle of 45 degrees with the +X axis makes an angle of 45 degrees with the +Y axis.

Scaling Objects

You use the Scale command to increase or decrease the size of objects in a drawing without changing their original relative proportions. You must specify a scale factor to enlarge or reduce the size of an object, and you establish a base point to show which point on the object remains stationary while all of the other points move.

There are three ways to define the scale factor. The first, and most common, way is to enter the scale factor from the keyboard, assuming you know the exact factor. The second method is to scale an object visually by moving the cursor, observing the image, and picking a satisfactory new size. This method is not very precise and is generally not used. The third method is to reference a length in the original image to a known new length and let AutoCAD compute the scale factor for you.

When you choose the Scale command from the Modify pull-down menu, you are prompted to select the objects to be scaled. After you complete the selection process, the prompt

```
Base point:
```

appears. This point is the only point on the objects that does not move. The next prompt

```
<Scale factor>/Reference:
```

is asking for a numerical scale factor. If you know the scale factor, enter it by typing the value and pressing ENTER.

Try It

- Draw two circles of different sizes. Use the Scale command to increase the diameter of the smaller circle so that the two circles are the same size. Keep the left end of the horizontal diameter stationary.
- Use Undo to restore the circle to its original size. Scale the other circle to 1/2 its size, keeping the center of the circle stationary.

If you do not know the exact scale factor, you can select the Reference option by typing R and pressing ENTER at the

```
<Scale factor>/Reference:
```

prompt. The next prompts ask you for the lengths to be used in calculating the scale factor. Your response to the first of these prompts

```
Reference length <1>:
```

is used in the denominator of the scale factor. You can accept the default value of 1 or pick two points on the screen. The distance between the points is the *reference length.* Your response to the second prompt

```
New length:
```

may be a numerical value or, again, two points on the screen. This data is used in the numerator to calculate the scale factor.

Try It

- Draw two squares of different sizes. Use the Scale command with the Reference option the make the squares the same size.
- Use the Reference option to change the size of either square by a factor of 4/3.

Stretching Objects

You use the Stretch command to *stretch* an object, which means to increase or decrease the dimension of an object in one direction only. For example, you can use the command to change a square into a rectangle by stretching the square either horizontally or vertically. In the drawings shown in Figure 4-21, the objects on the left were stretched: the two dimensions of both objects were increased by different factors. In such cases you cannot use the Scale command; instead, you need to use the Stretch command.

Figure 4-21
Stretch Example

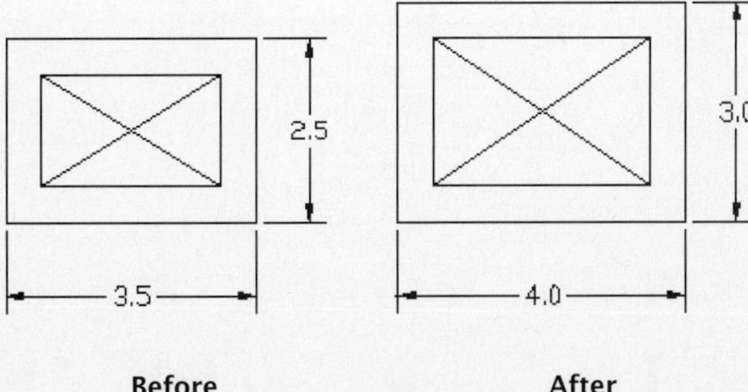

The Stretch command enables you to move parts of an object that are connected to the remainder of the object. The connecting lines are stretched. In Figure 4-21, the right wall was moved, and the horizontal and diagonal lines connecting the right wall to the left wall were stretched correspondingly. When you use Stretch, you use a crossing window to select the objects to be moved. The crossing window that is used with Stretch is identical to the crossing C window discussed in Chapter 2. These objects must be entirely within the window. The objects cutting the boundary of the crossing window are the ones being stretched. While the name of the command is Stretch, the command can be used to shorten as well as lengthen the connecting lines.

To start the Stretch command, pick Stretch from the Modify pull-down menu. At the prompt

```
Select objects to stretch by window...
Select objects:
```

type C and press ENTER to use a crossing window. Pick points for the crossing window so that the window includes the object(s) to be moved and crosses the objects to be stretched. At the prompt

```
Base point:
```

pick a point on the object to be moved. At the prompt

```
New point:
```

pick the new location for the base point. The object(s) will be stretched as indicated, and the command will end.

Try It

- Draw the rectangle and diagonal lines shown on the left in Figure 4-21. Use the dimensions shown for the outside rectangle. The dimensions of the inside rectangle are not important.
- Use the Stretch command to increase the horizontal dimension from 3.50 to 4.00. Keep the lower-left corner of the rectangle stationary.
- Use the Stretch command again to increase the vertical dimension from 2.50 to 3.00.
- Use the Stretch command to restore the horizontal dimension to its original length.

Using the Change Command

In Chapter 3 you used the Chprop command to change selected properties of objects in a drawing. The Chprop command is a shortened version of the Change command, which allows you to make many different changes, depending on the object you select. The possible changes are listed in Table 4-2.

Table 4-2 Uses of the Change Command

Object Type	Changes
Lines	Changes the endpoints of selected lines. The lines will end at a common change point of your choice unless ORTHO is turned on.
Circles	Leaves the center of the circle unchanged while changing the radius so the circle goes through the change point.
Text	Edits the line of text to allow changes in the location, height, style, and rotation. The entire text string may be re-entered.
Block	Changes the insertion point and rotation of blocks.
Attributes	Enables you to edit attribute definitions much as you edit text.

You will experiment with the first three of these options in this chapter. Blocks are presented in Chapter 5. Attributes are a special feature of blocks and will not be covered.

Figure 4-22 illustrates how you can use the Change command to change lines and circles. The two lines in the upper illustration did not originally meet. The Change command was used to move the left endpoints of the lines to a common point, the change point. Since the other ends of the lines were not moved, the line lengths were also changed. In the lower illustration the Change command was used to change the radius of the circle shown on the left. The circle on the right now goes through the designated change point.

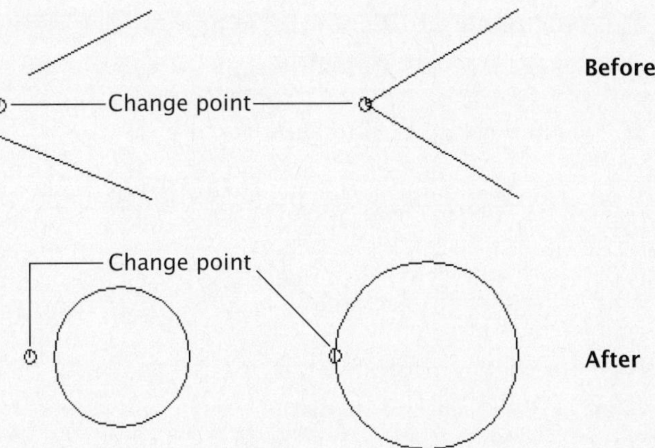

Figure 4-22
Change Example with Lines and Circles

To start the Change command, pick Change from the Modify pull-down menu and then choose Points. At the prompt

```
Select objects:
```

pick a point on the end of the line to be moved. Pick another line if you are changing more than one line at a time. If you are changing a circle, pick the circle. Press ENTER to end the selection process. At the prompt

```
Properties/<Change point>:
```

pick the point where you want the endpoints of the line or the circumference of the circle relocated. If you select the Properties option by typing P and pressing ENTER, AutoCAD displays a list of properties to be changed.

Try It

- Draw the lines and circle shown as the "Before" images on the left in Figure 4-22. The exact size and location are not important.
- Use the Change command to move the left ends of the lines so they go through a common point. Use Undo to restore the lines. Use the Change command to move the other ends of the lines to a common point near the center of the drawing.
- Use the Change command to increase the radius of the circle. Change the size of the circle again, so that it goes through the end of one of the lines.

You can also use the Change command to edit text. At the prompt

```
Select objects:
```

pick a point on the line of text to be edited and press ENTER. At the prompt

```
Properties/<Change point>:
```

pick the same point. The following message and prompt appears:

```
Text style <current style name>
New style or RETURN for no change:
```

Type the name of the new style and press ENTER, or press ENTER to keep the current style. At the prompt

```
New height <current height>:
```

type the new height, or press ENTER to keep the current height. At the prompt

```
New rotation angle <current rotation>:
```

type the new rotation angle, or press ENTER to keep the current rotation angle. Finally, at the prompt

```
New text <current text line>:
```

type the new text line from the beginning and press ENTER. If you are not changing any of the text, press ENTER to terminate the command.

Standard Style, height = 0.3

New style, height = 0.25

Figure 4-23
Editing Text with Change

Try It

- Make a drawing with one line of text similar to the "Before" image in Figure 4-23. Use the STANDARD style with a height equal to 0.3.
- Copy the text to a location just below the original. Create a new style using the ROMAND font.
- Use the Change command to change the lower line of text as shown in the figure.
- Experiment with the Change command to move the start point, change the height, and change the rotation angle of a line of the text.

Application 1: DIGITAL ELECTRONICS CIRCUIT

Electrical and Electronics Engineering

Digital electronic circuits are designed to perform a wide variety of tasks in the computer and communications industries. Before any electronic instrument goes into production, performance tests are conducted to certify that the instrument meets or exceeds its advertised specifications. The same sort of testing begins at the most basic level, the individual elements in the instrument. This application is the design of a circuit to test the transfer characteristic of a solid-state device, known as the 7400 TTL NAND gate.

The five-step process can now be used to prepare the circuit diagram.

1. Identify the Object and Its Function

The circuit is to be designed so that one voltage on the input side of the NAND gate can be varied while the other voltage on the input side remains constant. The circuit is to provide a way of measuring the voltage on the output side of the gate. The data, the variable input voltages and the corresponding output voltages will be read, recorded, and plotted.

2. Research Models and Determine Dimensions

There may be several ways of arranging the circuit so that it satisfies the needs of the experiment. You need to do a little research in a standard electronics textbook to become familiar with the NAND gate. In addition, you choose the device to control the voltages on the input side of the gate as well as measuring the output voltage. You will probably be able to use a standard variable resistance in combination with a fixed resistance voltage source to vary the input resistance. You can use an oscilloscope to measure the fixed input voltage as well as the variable output resistance.

3. Draw a Rough Hand Sketch

Use Figure 4-24 as the basis for your rough sketch. The circuit diagram includes a resistor, a ground symbol, and a repeated node symbol. It is important to plan the size of the symbols and the lengths of the connecting elements so that the finished drawing looks professional. You can add the text after drawing the circuit diagram. Make sure that the height and style of the text are in proportion to the rest of the drawing.

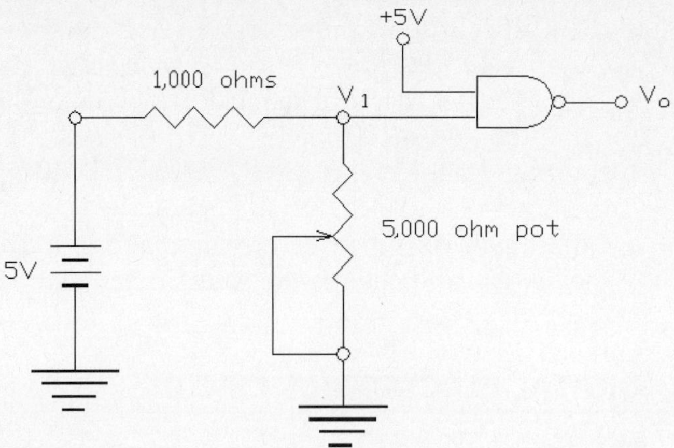

Figure 4-24
Circuit Diagram for Testing a NAND Gate

4. Make Proper Screen Adjustments

Set up a prototype drawing called CIRCUITS. Make a layer for the text and name it TEXT. Make another layer, called ELEM, on which to draw the basic elements before you copy them to the proper locations in the circuit diagram. You will turn off this layer when you have completed the diagram. For the different layers, set colors that are comfortable for you to look at. Save the prototype drawing after you draw the elements but before you draw any part of the diagram. Start a new drawing, called CIRC1, using the CIRCUITS prototype.

5. Draw, Print, and Save the File

Draw the actual circuit on layer 0 and add the text to the TEXT layer. When you have completed the drawing, compare it to Figure 4-24 and save the file.

What If

What if you discovered that you drew the circuit diagram on the ELEM layer? How would you correct the error?

What if the elements in the diagram were too close together to accommodate the text clearly? How would you move the elements apart without redrawing them or using the Move command?

SUMMARY

In this chapter you learned how to set up prototype drawings to include layers, units, limits, colors, and other settings. You have added to your collection of drawing and editing tools so you can now draw arcs and polygons, design text, and add text to your drawings. You can use five new editing commands—Fillet, Chamfer, Rotate, Scale, and Stretch—to draw increasingly complex objects. Finally you can use the Change command to relocate the endpoints of lines, resize circles, and edit text.

Key Words

align
arc
border
chamfer
circumscribe
control code
fillet
inscribe
polygon
prototype drawing
reference length
rotation angle
scale
stretch
title block

Exercises

Reproduce the following drawings using the given dimensions when they are provided. Do not add dimensions, but reproduce the text whenever possible. Use a prototype drawing when appropriate.

Exercise 4-1
Custom Switch Plate

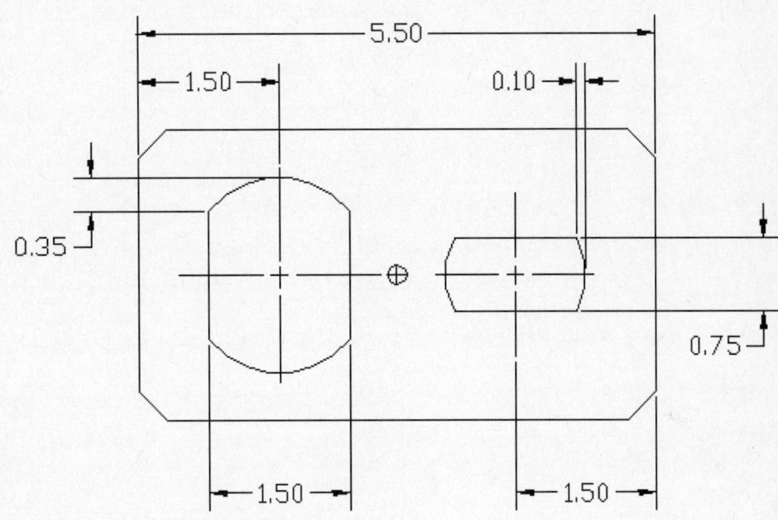

Center Hole diameter = 0.2
Chamfer Distance = 0.25

Exercise 4-2A
Fixture

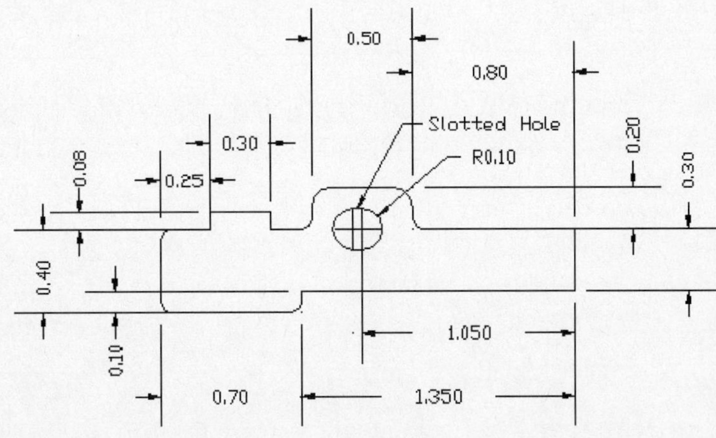

Exercise 4-2B
Slotted Hole Detail

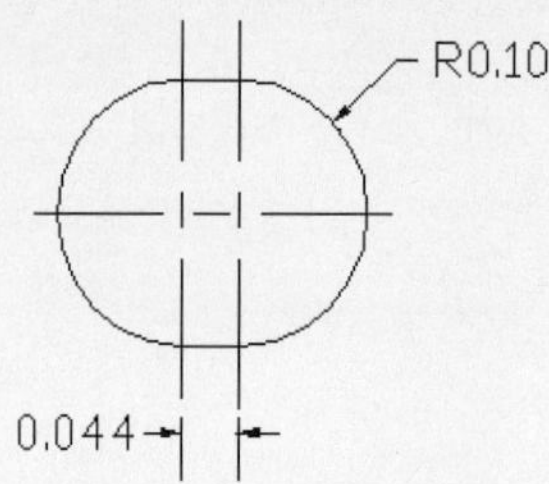

Exercise 4-3
Wrench

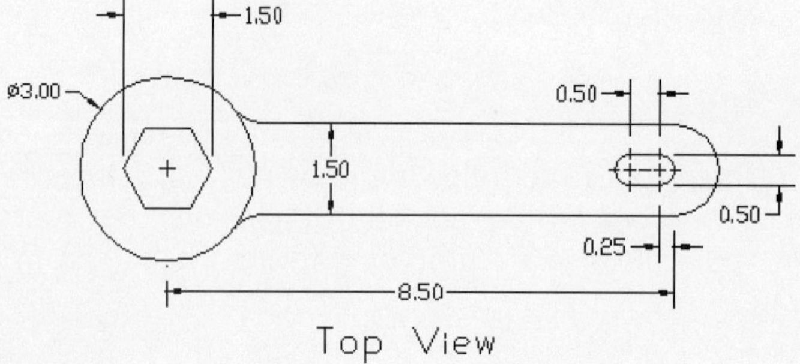

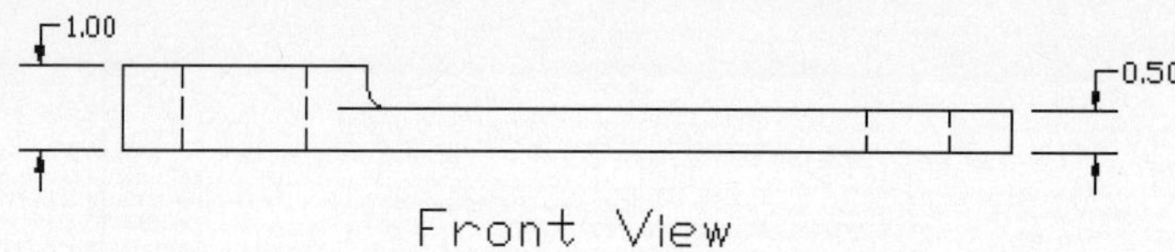

Draw the two views of the wrench as shown in Exercise 4-3. Save the drawing. Increase the length of the handle by 1/2 inch without changing any of the other dimensions.

Exercise 4-4
Circuit Diagram

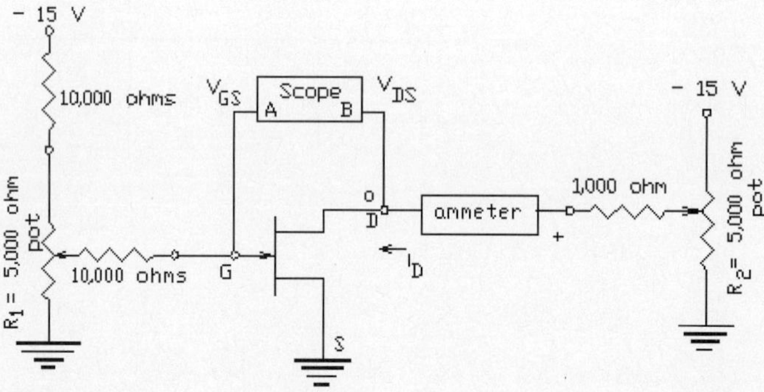

Use the CIRCUIT prototype, and add the new element symbols to the ELEM layer as shown in Exercise 4-4.

Exercise 4-5
Border and Title Block

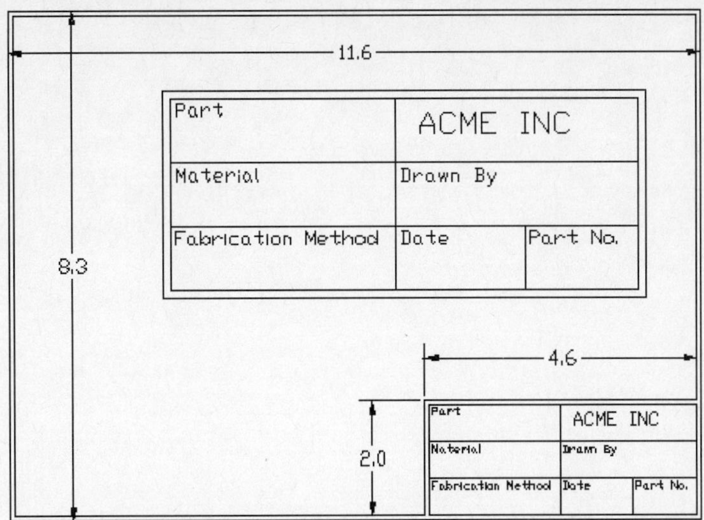

Add the Border and Title Block to each of your prototype drawings as shown in Exercise 4-5. Put your name in the Drawn By area.

Exercise 4-6
Gasket

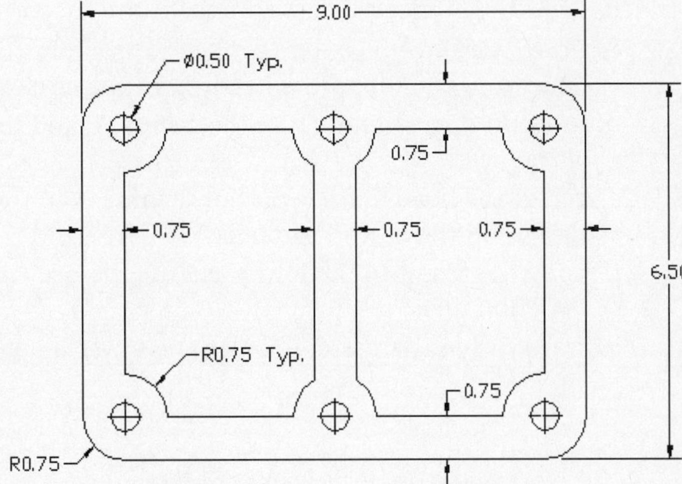

Draw the gasket as shown in Exercise 4-6. Save the drawing. Change the length from 9 to 11.5 and the height from 6.5 to 8. The new gasket is symmetrical about the center holes.

Exercise 4-7
Standard Bolt with Square Head and Nut

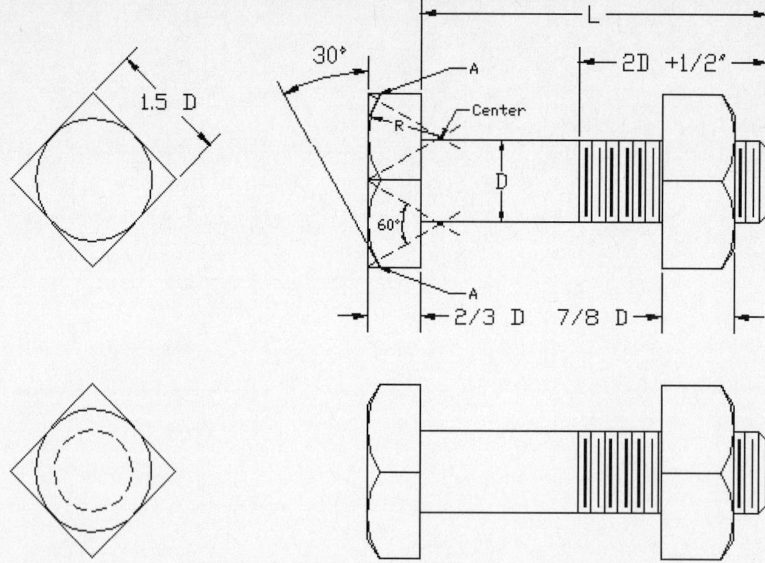

a. Draw the square as a polygon and the outline of the bolt head thickness, using the dimensions of a 1-inch-diameter bolt.
b. Draw the 60-degree dashed lines from the corners of bolt head.
c. Draw circles with centers at the intersections of the dashed lines and tangent to the top of the head. Trim the circles as shown.
d. Draw 30-degree lines from the points A, and lines to finish the outline of the head.
e. Mirror the head to form part of the nut. Add the rest of the nut, the bolt shaft, and the thread symbols.
f. Copy the result to the lower position before erasing the dashed construction lines.
g. Erase the construction lines on the lower image.

5 Adding More Tools to Your Drawing Kit

Composite Materials

Composites combine different materials in a matrix to take advantage of the strengths of the separate materials. An early example of composite materials is reinforced brick made from straw and mud. The tensile strength of the straw kept the bricks from cracking. Modern reinforced concrete is a direct descendent of reinforced bricks. Steel reinforcing bars replaced the straw, and concrete replaced the mud. Even more interesting are composites that use carbon and glass fibers in an epoxy matrix. These composites are strong and lightweight. The combination of strength, light weight, and heat resistance is especially suited to applications in aircraft and space vehicles. With their high strength-to-weight ratio, such composites are ideal for use in high-performance sports equipment. At the end of this chapter, you will draw a modern bicycle wheel made of carbon, Kelvar, and glass fibers molded over a foam core.

INTRODUCTION

This chapter introduces a whole spectrum of new drawing and editing tools. You learn how to draw two new objects: ellipses and points. You discover how to add crosshatching to clarify the interior details of parts. You also learn how to use the Measure and Divide commands to draw points at evenly spaced distances along lines, circles, and arcs. Then you use the Array command to make copies of objects in rectangular or circular patterns. You learn how to combine a collection of objects into one "super" object called a block. You can insert blocks into other drawings and edit them with the aid of the Explode command. You learn how to add dimensions to the objects in your drawings. Finally, you learn how to plot your drawing.

5-1 DRAWING WITH SOME NEW TOOLS

This section explains how to draw ellipses and points and how to add hatch patterns within objects. The Ellipse command allows you to draw this special closed curve. The Point command enables you to add visible points to your drawings. The commands PDMODE and PDSIZE control the appearance and size of the point symbol. With the Hatch command you can draw hatch patterns within the boundaries of objects.

Drawing Ellipses

An *ellipse* is one of the curves generated by passing a plane through a solid cone. In engineering drawings, a circle appears as an ellipse when the plane containing the circle is not normal to your point of view.

The ellipse is used in engineering drawings to show the view of a circle that you see if you look at the circle from an arbitrary direction. In Figure 5-1 an ellipse represents one view of a circle. The circle goes through the plate on the left. If you view the plate along line C–B, you see the normal or orthographic view of the circle. Viewed from this direction the image of the circle is not distorted. If you look at the circle along line A–B, however, the image of the circle is an ellipse.

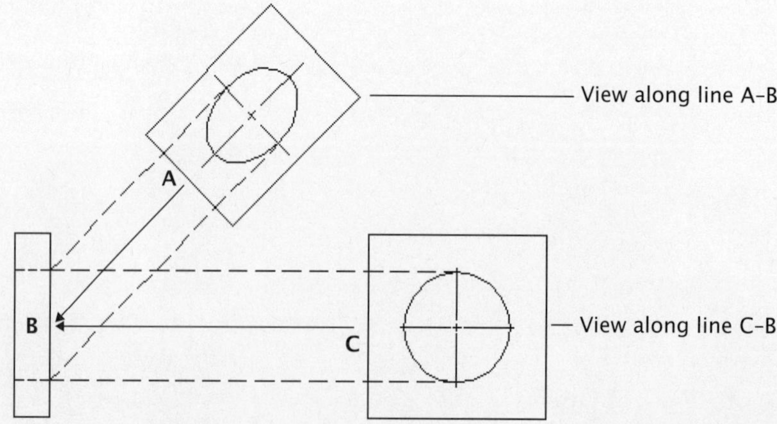

Figure 5-1
Representing a Circle with an Ellipse

The ellipse is defined by two axes. The long or *major axis* is the diameter of the circle that the ellipse represents. The short or *minor axis* is the distorted length of the diameter of the circle. The ellipse is drawn by connecting the ends of two axes with a curve.

You start the Ellipse command by selecting Ellipse from the Draw pull-down menu. AutoCAD then presents two options, as shown in Figure 5-2. You can select Center, Axis, Axis to pick the center point and points on one end of each axis. Alternatively you can select Axis, Eccentricity to pick points on both ends of one of the axes and then pick a point on one end of the other axis.

Figure 5-2
Ellipse Pull-down Menu

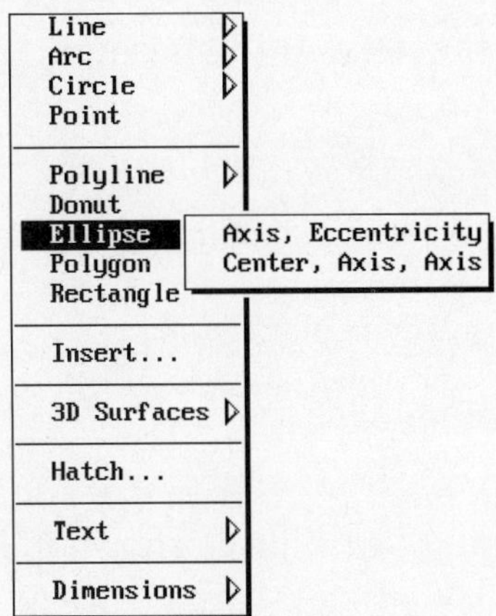

If you select Center, Axis, Axis, AutoCAD displays the prompt

```
<Axis endpoint 1>/Center:
Center of ellipse:
```

Pick the center point. At the next prompt

```
Axis endpoint:
```

pick the end of one of the axes. Finally, at the prompt

```
<Other axis distance>/Rotation:
```

pick the end of the other axis.

Figure 5-3
Ellipse Options

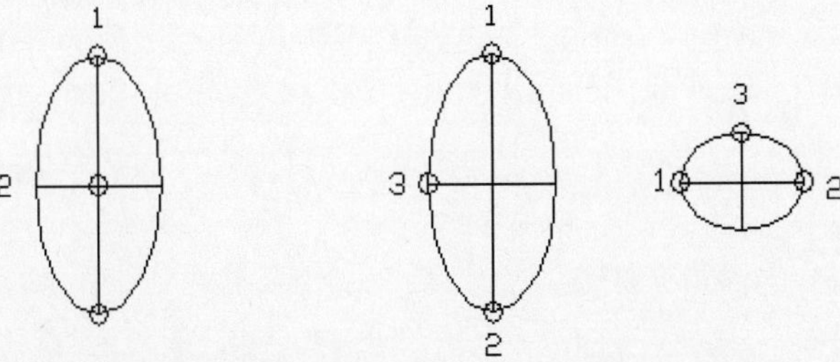

Try It

- Use the Center, Axis, Axis option of the Ellipse command to draw the ellipse shown on the left in Figure 5-3. Use axes in the approximate relative lengths as shown in the figure.
- Draw another ellipse using axes rotated from the horizontal and vertical positions.

If you select the Axis, Eccentricity option, AutoCAD displays the prompt

```
<Axis endpoint 1>/Center:
```

Pick the end of one of the axes. At the prompt

```
Axis endpoint 2:
```

Pick the other end of the same axis. Finally, at the prompt

```
<Other axis distance>/Rotation:
```

pick either end of the other axis.

Try It

- Draw the two remaining two ellipses shown in Figure 5-3.
- Draw other ellipses using the Axis, Eccentricity option by orienting the axis in a variety of directions.

Adding Point Symbols to Your Drawing

Unlike the reference points that you pick when you are executing some commands, drawn points are real objects in a drawing. To issue the Point command, choose Point from the Draw pull-down menu. AutoCAD displays the

```
Point:
```

prompt, and you pick a location for the drawn point. The point is invisible, however, until you set two values needed to make it visible.

There are two settings associated with points—PDMODE and PDSIZE—that you can change by selecting them from the POINT screen menu. PDMODE selects the symbol for the point, and PDSIZE sets the size of the point symbol. The default setting for PDMODE, 1, makes the points invisible. The default value for PDSIZE is zero. If you change these settings, all previously drawn points are converted to the latest settings at the next regeneration of the drawing.

Choosing the symbol for and size of your points is especially easy with AutoCAD Release 12. If you pick POINT from the screen menu and then select TYPE and SIZE, the Point Style dialog box shown in Figure 5-4 appears. You can select the symbol for your points at the top of the dialog box. You can change the size by entering a different number in the Point Size box. You can set the size in absolute units or as a percentage of the screen area. If you select absolute units, the size of the symbol changes when you change the screen display. If you make the size relative to the screen, the point appears unchanged as the screen display is changed. When you are satisfied with your selections, click on OK.

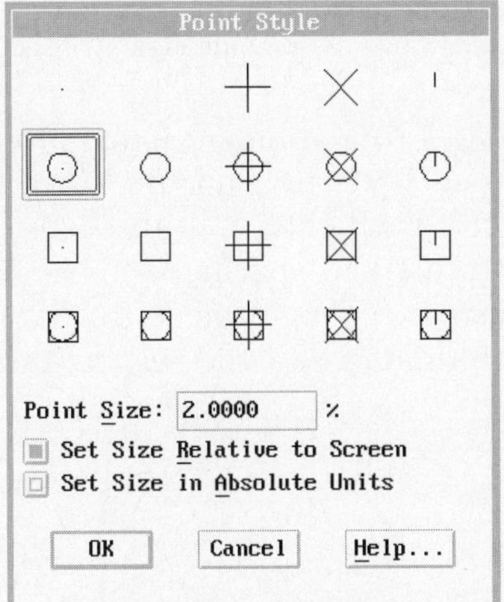

Figure 5-4
Point Style Dialog Box

Try It

- Draw points with a variety of styles and sizes.
- Change the scale from relative to absolute.
- Use the Zoom command to experiment with the effects of relative and absolute sizes.

Using Hatch Patterns to Clarify Interior Details

The Hatch command enables you to use a hatch pattern—one of any number of line or fill patterns—to set aside an area of your drawing. The most common use of hatch patterns in engineering drawings is to clarify the interior geometric details of a part in a sectional view. The hatch pattern may also indicate the material used in manufacturing the part.

Figure 5-5 shows a plate drawn in front, right side, and sectional views. As you can see, the hatched sectional view clarifies the interior detail more easily than hidden lines would. The hidden lines in the right side view of the plate show that the hole penetrates entirely through the plate. At times, however, the interior details of the part are not so obvious. To expose the interior details, the part is cut by an imaginary plane and the material in front of that plane is removed to produce a sectional view. In sectional views, the areas of the object that were intersected by the cutting plane are normally hatched. The cutting plane is shown in the front view as the vertical line through the center. The arrows pointing to the left show that the viewer is looking in that direction.

Figure 5-5
Using a Hatch Pattern in a Sectional Drawing

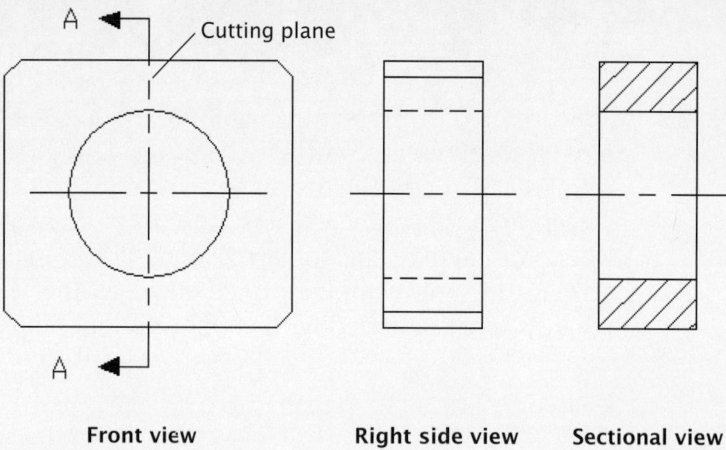

Figure 5-6 illustrates four common hatch patterns. The upper two patterns are user-defined patterns, and the lower two are from AutoCAD's set of stored patterns. Each pattern in the figure is labeled with the name of the pattern, the scale and spacing, and the angle of the pattern. It is good practice to place hatch patterns on a separate layer. The layer can be frozen to remove its data from the regeneration that takes place from time to time.

Figure 5-6
Common Hatch Patterns

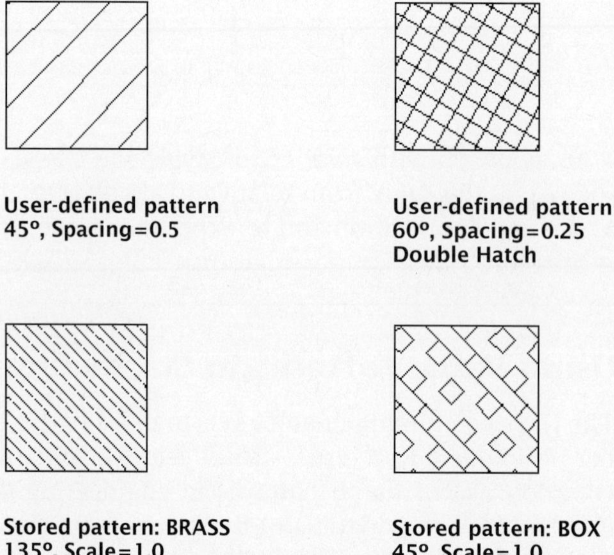

To start the Hatch command, select Hatch from the Draw pull-down menu. The Boundary Hatch dialog box shown in Figure 5-7 appears. You use this dialog box to select the hatch option, define the area to be hatched, preview your selections, and, if you are satisfied with the results, apply the hatch pattern to the drawing.

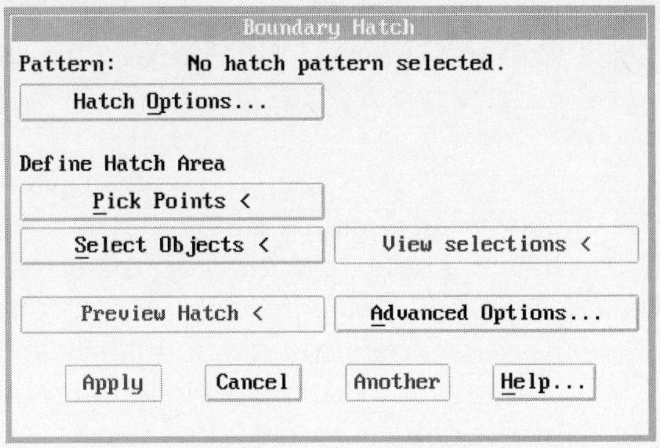

Figure 5-7
Boundary Hatch Dialog Box

Boundary Hatch
Pattern: No hatch pattern selected.
Hatch Options...
Define Hatch Area
Pick Points <
Select Objects <
View selections <
Preview Hatch <
Advanced Options...
Apply
Cancel
Another
Help...

Click on the Hatch Options box to reveal the Hatch Options dialog box shown in Figure 5-8. You use this dialog box either to create a user-defined pattern or to select one of AutoCAD's standard patterns. To create a user-defined pattern, click on the User-Defined Pattern (U) button. Then choose the scale, angle, and spacing of the hatch lines by clicking on the appropriate box and typing the desired value. You can also choose to *double hatch* the area, adding another set of lines at a 90-degree angle to the first set by clicking on the Double hatch button. When you have completed your pattern definition, you return to the Boundary Hatch dialog box by clicking on OK.

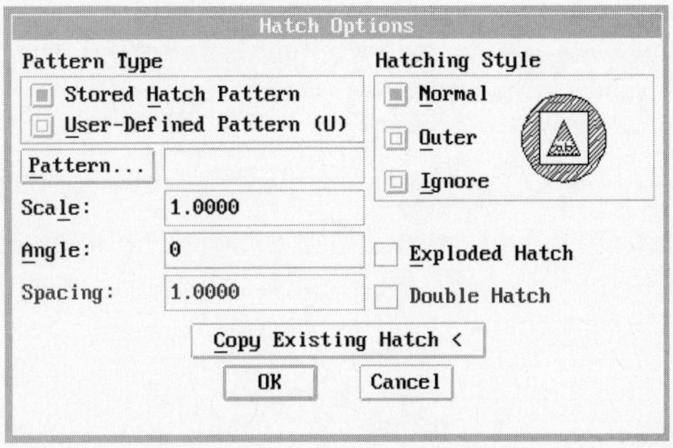

Figure 5-8
Hatch Options Dialog Box

Hatch Options
Pattern Type
Stored Hatch Pattern
User-Defined Pattern (U)
Pattern...
Scale: 1.0000
Angle: 0
Spacing: 1.0000
Hatching Style
Normal
Outer
Ignore
Exploded Hatch
Double Hatch
Copy Existing Hatch <
OK
Cancel

AutoCAD has an extensive list of stored hatch patterns that you can use just as easily as a user-defined pattern. Click on the Stored Hatch Pattern button in the Hatch Options dialog box. You then enter the name of the pattern you want in the Pattern box. To see a list of the AutoCAD patterns, leave the dialog box by clicking on Cancel. Type `Hatch` and then press ENTER. AutoCAD displays the prompt

```
Pattern (? or name/U,Style):
```

Type ? and press ENTER. At the prompt

```
Pattern(s) to list <*>:
```

press ENTER. The text screen appears, listing 53 different patterns by name. Reactivate the Hatch Options dialog box and type the name of the pattern in the Pattern box. Click on the Scale box to choose a scale. Normally, you use the default scale of 1, but if the pattern is too large or too small, you can adjust the scale after you preview the hatch pattern. (Previewing is discussed in a moment.)

When you have completed your pattern selection, click on OK to return to the Boundary Hatch dialog box.

Now you are ready to define the boundaries of the hatched area, which must be a closed area. Click on the Pick Points box in the Boundary Hatch dialog box. The prompt

```
Select internal point
```

appears. Pick a point anywhere within a closed boundary. The message

```
Analyzing internal point
```

appears while AutoCAD locates the boundary. The prompt

```
Select internal point
```

reappears so you can define another boundary. Press ENTER to return to the Boundary Hatch dialog box.

You have selected a pattern and defined the boundary of the area to be hatched. Before you add the hatch pattern to the drawing, you can click on the Preview Hatch box to preview the result. At the prompt

```
Press RETURN to continue.
```

press ENTER. If you are satisfied with the results of your selections, click on the Apply box. If you are not satisfied, return to the Hatch Options dialog box and change your selections.

Try It

- Use the Hatch command to create the user-defined hatch patterns shown in the upper two squares in Figure 5-6.
- Draw two overlapping circles, and hatch the three separate areas with three different combinations of angles and spacing.

Try It

- Use the Hatch command to use the stored hatch patterns shown in the lower two squares in Figure 5-6. Use the BRASS and BOX patterns. Experiment by increasing and decreasing the scale of the pattern.
- Use the Hatch command to view the list of standard AutoCAD patterns. Write down the name of one of the patterns.
- Draw two overlapping circles and use the selected pattern to hatch the three separate areas with three different combinations of angle and scale.

So far you have applied hatch patterns to single closed boundaries. Figure 5-9 illustrates a situation in which you need to hatch the spaces between *nested boundaries.* The Hatch Options dialog box provides three hatching styles: Normal, Outer, and Ignore. The Normal option hatches the areas between alternate sets of nested boundaries. The Outer option hatches only the area between the outer boundary and the next inner boundary. The Ignore option hatches the entire area defined by the outer boundary, ignoring all other internal boundaries. Select the hatching style by clicking on one of the three Hatching Style buttons in the Hatch Options dialog box. The icon in the upper-right corner of the dialog box changes to illustrate the effect of your choice.

To hatch within nested boundaries, you use the Pick Points option from the Boundary Hatch dialog box. For example, pick the points 1, 2, and 3 in order, as shown in the figure. Be careful, however, to pick points near the individual boundaries. For example, if you pick point 2 too close to the circle, AutoCAD looks inward and notes that you have already selected that boundary.

Figure 5-9
Hatching with Nested Boundaries

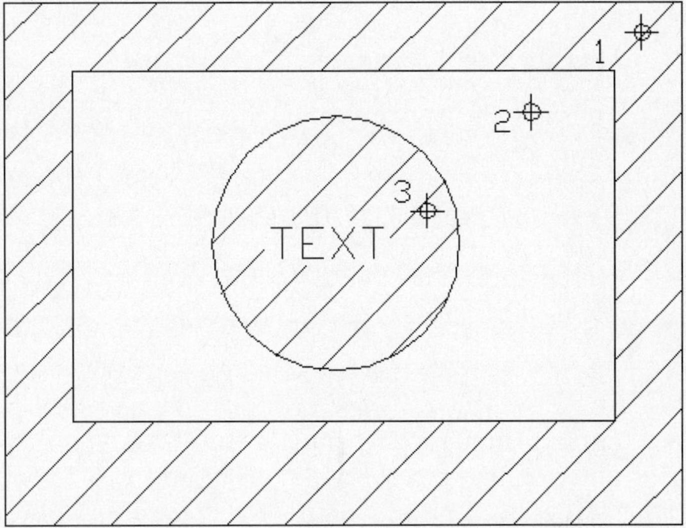

You can also have the hatch pattern skip around any text within the boundary. Before you select any of the boundaries using the Pick Points box in the Boundary Hatch dialog box, click on the Select Objects box, and then click on the text you want to skip. The text is identified as a boundary and is skipped if you are using the Normal style.

Try It

- Draw a set of nested boundaries similar to those shown in Figure 5-9. Include some text in the drawing.
- Use the Hatch command to create the hatch pattern shown in the figure, using the Normal style.
- Experiment with the other two hatching styles.

5-2 ENTERING POINTS ON AN OBJECT

The Measure and Divide commands enter points equally spaced along a line or a curve. These points are nodes that will be useful in later editing problems. The Measure command starts from one end of the object and marks off equal distances along the object. Any leftover segment less than the specified segment length is found at the other end of the object. The Divide command divides an object into a specified number of equal-length segments and inserts points at the division points. Figure 5-10 compares identical arcs with points inserted using the Measure and Divide commands.

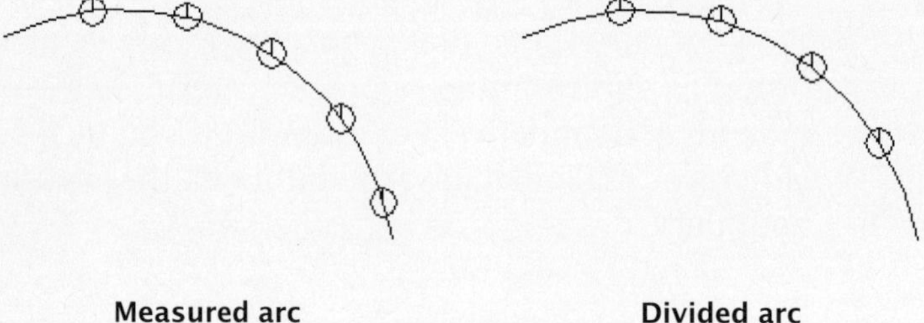

Figure 5-10
Comparing Measure and Divide

Using the Measure Command

To issue the Measure command, choose Measure from the Construct pull-down menu. At the prompt

```
Select object to measure:
```

pick a single object near the end from which the measuring is to begin. At the next prompt

```
&lt;Segment length&gt;/Block:
```

enter a numerical distance. AutoCAD enters point symbols along the object using the current PDMODE and PDSIZE settings.

The Block option allows you to use a symbol of your own creation to mark the points. You will learn about blocks later in this chapter.

Try It

- Draw two identical arcs, similar to those shown in Figure 5-10.
- Use the Measure command to enter points along the arcs. Measure the arcs from different ends.
- Draw lines of different lengths and measure the lines using different segment lengths.

Using the Divide Command

To start the Divide command, choose Divide from the Construct pull-down menu. At the prompt

```
Select object to divide.
```

Pick a single object. At the prompt

```
<Number of segments>/Block:
```

enter the integer that represents the number segments you want the object divided into. Again, the Block option allows you to use a symbol of your own creation to mark the points.

Try It

- Draw a line and a circle.
- Divide the line into eight segments. Notice that the Divide command does not draw a point at the ends of the objects.
- Divide the circle into five segments. Notice that a point is always entered on the right end of the horizontal diameter.
- Draw an arc and divide it into seven equal parts. Change the point style and size and regenerate the drawing by using the Zoom All command that you learned in Chapter 2.

5-3 COPYING OBJECTS USING THE ARRAY COMMAND

The Array command is really a fancy copy command. It makes multiple copies of objects that can be arranged in a *rectangular array* or in a *polar array*. The *rectangular array* shown in Figure 5-11 includes copies of a small rectangle. The copies are arranged in rows and columns. You specify the number of rows and columns and the distances between the copies during the course of the Array command.

Figure 5-11
Rectangular Array of Rectangles

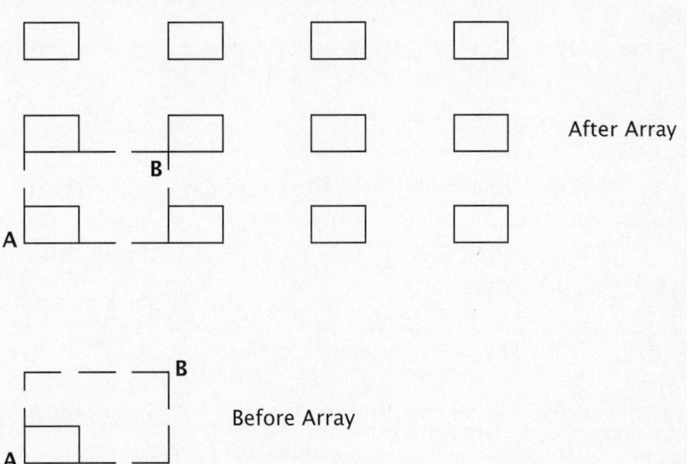

The *polar array* shown in Figure 5-12 includes copies of the same small rectangle as Figure 5-11, but now the copies are arranged around the perimeter of an imaginary circle. The number of copies and the fraction of the circle occupied by the copies are specified during the command. The copies in Figure 5-12 occupy a 180-degree portion of the imaginary circle. The dashed line in Figure 5-12 is shown to clarify the relationship between the object and the center point.

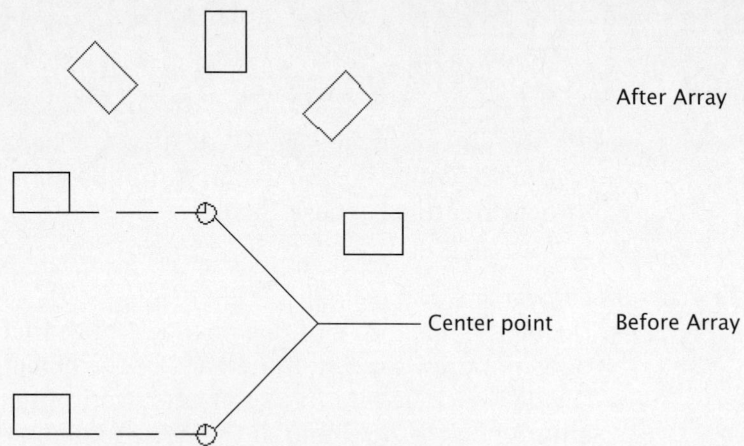

Figure 5-12
Polar Array of Rectangles

To issue the Array command, choose Array from the Construct pull-down menu. To create a rectangular array, pick the objects to be arrayed at the prompt

```
Select objects:
```

At the prompt

```
Rectangular or Polar array (R/P):
```

type R to choose the Rectangular option. At the prompt

```
Number of rows(---) <1>:
```

type the number of rows. At the prompt

```
Number of columns (|||) <1>:
```

enter the number of columns. At the prompt

```
Unit cell or distance between rows (---):
```

enter the vertical distance between corresponding points on the copies. At the prompt

```
Distance between columns (|||):
```

enter the horizontal distance between corresponding points on the copies. AutoCAD makes the copies and terminates the command.

The distances entered may have positive or negative values. If you enter positive values, the copies are made to the right and above the original object. Negative distances cause the objects to be copied to the left and below the original. You can use any combination of signs to arrange the copies in the right location.

Try It

- Draw a small circle in the center of your screen.
- Use the Array command to make copies of the circle. Arrange the copies along five columns and four rows. Space the circles at twice the diameter of the circle.
- Repeat the command, this time using a negative value for one of the distances.
- Use Undo to remove the last array. Use the Array command to make the copies of the circles tangent to each other.

To use the Unit cell option to set the distances, pick a point at the prompt

```
Unit cell or distance between rows (---):
```

At the prompt

```
Other corner:
```

pick another point. AutoCAD calculates the vertical and horizontal components of the line connecting the two points and uses them for the distances between rows and columns. For example, in Figure 5-11 the points A and B can be used as the two points. The dashed lines are shown to define the actual distances used by the Unit cell option.

Try It

- Draw a small circle near the center of the screen. Draw an inclined line down to the right from the center of the circle.
- Draw a rectangular array of circles using Unit cell option and the endpoints of the line.

To create a polar array, choose Array from the Construct pull-down menu. At the prompt

```
Select objects:
```

pick the objects to be arrayed. At the prompt

```
Rectangular or Polar array (R/P):
```

type *P* for Polar array. At the prompt

```
Center point of array:
```

pick a point as the center of the imaginary circle. At the prompt

```
Number of items:
```

enter the number of final copies to be displayed. At the prompt

```
Angle to fill(+=ccw, -=cw) <360>:
```

enter an angle representing that portion of the imaginary circle to be filled. If you enter a negative angle, AutoCAD copies the objects in a clockwise direction about the center point. The magnitude of the angle determines the part of the circle that is to be filled. At the prompt

```
Rotate objects as they are copied? <Y>:
```

type Y (for yes) to rotate the copies so that they have the same orientation to the center point as the original. Type N (for no) to have the copies maintain the same orientation with the coordinate axis as the original. Figure 5-13 illustrates the effect of the rotation response.

Figure 5-13
Comparing Polar Arrays

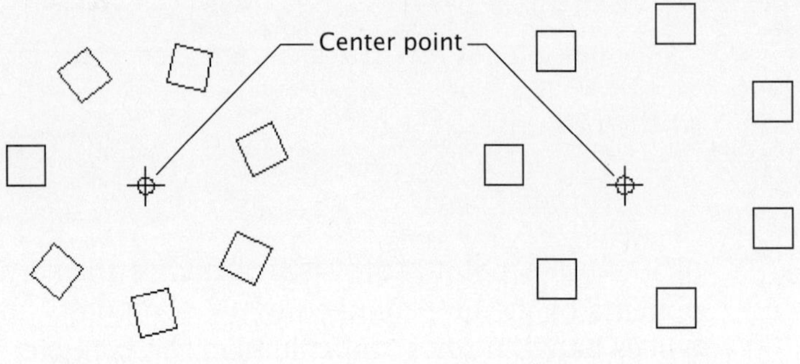

Try It

- Draw a small square near the center of the screen.
- Make five copies of the square about a point located to the left of the square. Fill a 270-degree clockwise angle. Rotate the objects as they are copied.
- Try using a counterclockwise angle and do not rotate the objects.
- Experiment with angles of less than 180 degrees.

5-4 USING BLOCKS TO CREATE SYMBOL LIBRARIES

In Chapter 4 you drew the elements of a circuit diagram separately and then copied them to the proper location on the diagram and rotated them as necessary. You also placed the elements on a separate layer that could be turned off when you were finished. This strategy is a primitive way of building a *symbol library*. The library is stored on the CIRCUIT prototype drawing and is available only if you use that prototype. However, you can use this symbol library only with that prototype. Furthermore, the symbols are made up of individual objects, and you must take care to select all of the components as you copy them.

Often it is easier to store all of the objects in the symbol as a group. In AutoCAD such symbols are called *blocks*. You can reuse a block in a drawing without using the Copy and Rotate commands. Windows, bolt heads, and symbols for trees and other plantings are examples of items frequently made into blocks.

Once a group of objects is made into a block and inserted into a drawing, it acts as a single object. Any editing command changes the entire group. The only way to separate the objects for individual editing is to explode the block, as discussed later in this chapter.

In Figure 5-14, for example, the drawing of the floor plan of an office suite includes a reception area, an executive office, a conference room, and a variety of furniture, including tables, chairs, desks, file cabinets, and book cases. Each item was created separately as a block. Each block was then inserted into the floor plan. The location, size, and orientation of the items were set while the block was being inserted.

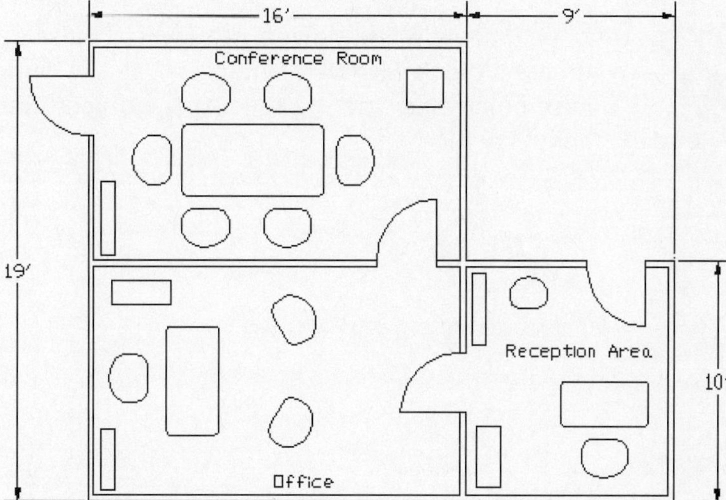

Figure 5-14
Interior Design of an Office Suite

Creating Blocks

You create a block by using the Block or Wblock command to group objects together. Blocks are stored in the current drawing file, and *WBlocks* are stored in a separate external file. (You will learn how to create Wblocks later in this section.) Later you can use the Insert command to retrieve the blocks and place them in a drawing.

When you issue the Block command, you are asked to assign a name to the block, select the objects to be included, and pick a base point. The base point for a block is similar to the base point in the Copy command: It is the point that locates the position of the block when it is copied into the drawing.

To issue the Block command, choose Block from the Construct pull-down menu. At the prompt

```
Block name (or ?):
```

enter the name of the new block, or enter ? to see a list of existing blocks. At the prompt

```
Insertion base point:
```

pick a point to serve as the base point when the block is inserted later. This point is also the point about which rotations take place during the insert step. Finally, at the prompt

```
Select objects:
```

select the objects to be included in the block.

When you have completed the selection, the information is added to the drawing file and the objects disappear from the screen. If you need some or all of the objects for further work in the drawing, you can recover them by typing OOPS.

Try It

- Draw the circle and polygon shown in Figure 5-15.
- Create a block with these objects. Use the center of the circle as the base point. Use OOPS to recover the objects. Save the file to use for the next "Try It!"

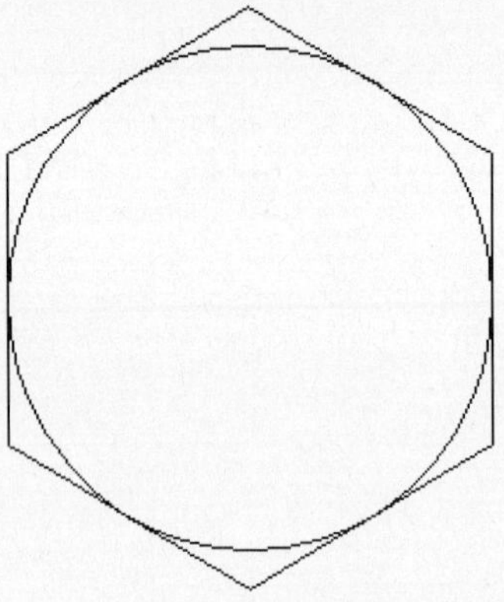

Figure 5-15
Bolt Head

The Block command places the block in the drawing file, where it is accessible only from the drawing in which it was created. If you want to be able to use the block in other drawings, you must use the Wblock command. You initiate the Wblock command by selecting Wblock from Blocks the screen menu during a drawing session. The Create Drawing File dialog box shown in Figure 5-16 appears. This dialog box is essentially the same as the Open File dialog box. To name the Wblock, type the name in the File box. Select the directory or drive for the Wblock file by scrolling up or down the Directories column until the name comes into view and clicking on the desired directory. Click on OK to leave the dialog box. At the next prompt

```
Block name:
```

press ENTER to use the file name you typed in the File box of the dialog box as the block name. The block is written to the file with the .DWG extension.

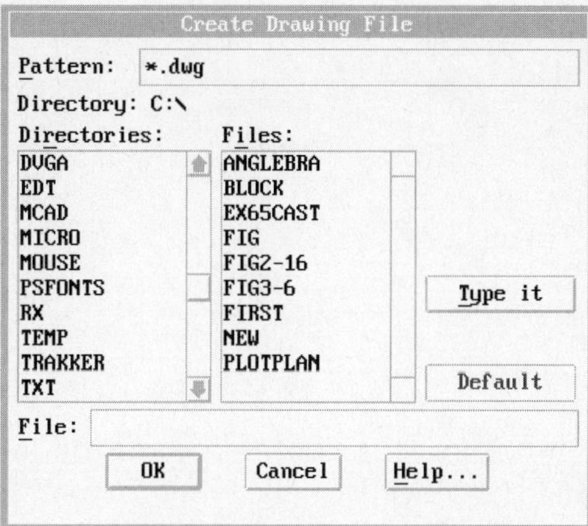

Figure 5-16
Create Drawing File Dialog Box

Try It

- Open the file that you created in the last "Try It!" Create a Wblock using the polygon and circle as objects. Type A:\BOLT as the filename.
- Close the current file and open a new file. The name BOLT should be displayed among the files on the A drive.

Inserting Block into a Drawing

The Insert command allows you to copy a block into a drawing, scale it in both the horizontal and vertical directions, and rotate it, all in one step.

To initiate the Insert command, choose Insert from the Draw pull-down menu. AutoCAD displays the Insert dialog box shown in Figure 5-17. If you are inserting a block that is local to the current drawing, simply enter the block name in the space adjacent to the Block box. If you are inserting a Wblock, enter the file name in the space to the right of the File box. Include the path (the drive name and directories) with the file name. The name of the block appears in the space to the right of the Block box.

Next, if you know them from information in the drawing, you can specify the coordinates of the insertion point, the scale factors, and the angle. Make certain the Specify Parameters on Screen box does not contain an X (if it does, click on the box to remove the X). You can change any or all of the data in the parameter boxes by clicking on the box and typing the new data. When you finish entering the parameters, click on OK and the command terminates.

Figure 5-17
Insert Dialog Box

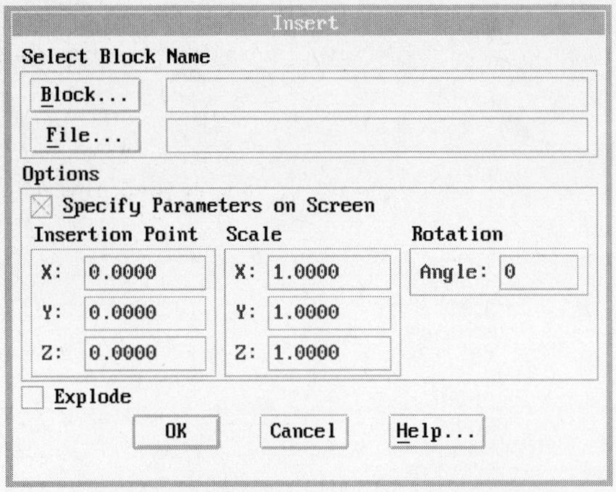

If you do not know the coordinates of the insertion point in advance, you can insert the block by specifying the parameters on the screen and then moving the block as needed. Click on the Specify Parameters on Screen box to place an X there if none is displayed. Click on OK, and a sequence of prompts appears. At the first prompt

```
Insertion point:
```

pick a point where the base point is to be inserted. Moving the crosshairs moves the image of the block on the screen. AutoCAD displays the prompt

```
X scale factor <1>/Corner/XYZ:
```

The XYZ option allows you to change all three scales of three-dimensional blocks. The corner option is beyond the scope of this text. For two-dimensional blocks, you can either press (ENTER) to accept the default X scale factor of 1 or enter a different X scale factor. At the prompt

```
Y scale factor (default = X):
```

you can either press (ENTER) to accept the default value or enter a different Y scale factor. At the last prompt

```
Rotation angle <0>:
```

you can either press (ENTER) to accept the default value or enter a different value. A negative angle rotates the image counterclockwise about the insertion point.

Try It

- Draw the circle and square shown in the upper-left corner of Figure 5-18. Create a block using the center of the circle as the base point.
- Insert the block back into the drawing using the Insert dialog box. Change the X and Y scales to 2, and set the rotation angle to zero.
- Insert the block again using a Y scale equal to twice the X scale and a rotation angle equal to 45 degrees. The result should be similar to the lower image in Figure 5-18.
- Insert the WBlock, BOLT, that you created earlier.

Figure 5-18
Insert Exercise

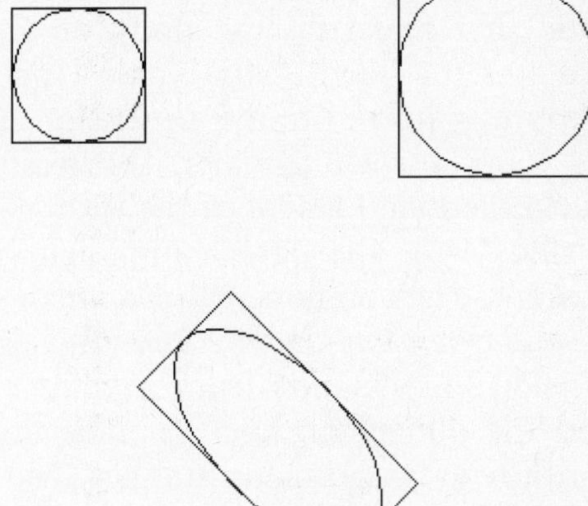

Using the Explode Command to Edit Blocks

After you have made a group of objects into a block and inserted it into a drawing, you cannot edit individual objects in the group. For example, you cannot erase one line of a group of lines in a block. If you need to do so, you must first use the Explode command to *explode*, or separate, the objects. Then you can edit the individual objects easily. You can use the Explode command on other objects that act as blocks, such as polygons and the components of dimensions, which will be discussed next.

To issue the Explode command, choose Explode from the Modify pull-down menu. At the prompt

```
Select objects:
```

select the objects to be exploded using any selection technique. As you select the objects notice that their appearance changes. When you have completed the selection, the objects are ready for editing.

Try It

- Try to erase any of the blocks that you inserted in the last "Try It!"
- Explode the block and try erasing, moving, or copying any one of the original objects.

5-5 ADDING DIMENSIONS TO YOUR DRAWINGS

Dimensions are an essential part of most engineering drawings. While some of the schematic drawings that you have seen so far have not required dimensions, drawings of objects or devices that are going to be manufactured must be completely dimensioned. You use dimensions to show the length of lines, the radius of arcs and circles, and the angles between lines. While most dimensions use only numerical values, some dimensions combine text with numerical data. It is good practice to place dimensions on a separate layer in a contrasting color so they are easy to identify.

The AutoCAD Dimension command automatically draws the lines, arcs, and arrowheads that make up the body of a dimension. In addition, AutoCAD calculates the lengths and angles that are being dimensioned and adds the appropriate text to the dimension. The AutoCAD Dimension command lets you control dimension features, such as the arrowhead style and the alignment and height of the text.

Figure 5-19 illustrates the basic components of standard linear and angular dimensions. The components of a *linear dimension* consist of the *dimension line*, the *extension line*, the *dimension arrow*, and the *dimension text*. The extension line extends from a point on the object to a point slightly beyond the dimension line. *Angular dimensions* have the same components but use arcs as dimension lines. The extension lines are lines which radiate from the origin of the angle being measured.

Figure 5-19
Basic Dimensioning Components

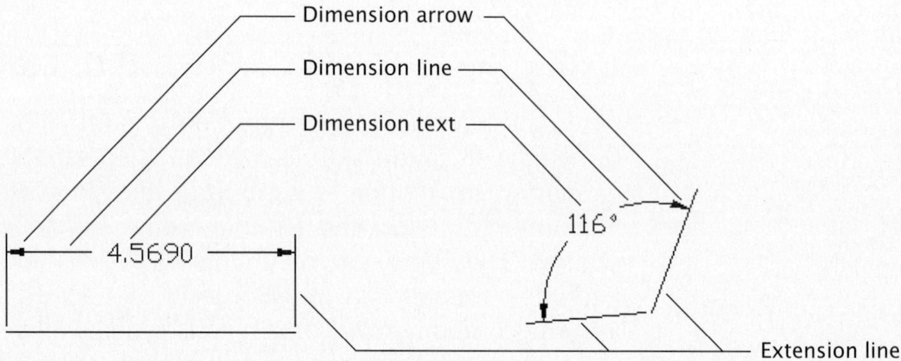

In general, to add dimensions you first select the type of dimension, points on the object, and the location of the dimension line and text. AutoCAD then calculates the distance involved and enters the text along with the components of the dimension.

When you select Dimension from the Draw pull-down menu, five dimensioning options are displayed on the next cascading submenu. When you choose an option from the first submenu, another submenu is displayed. From here you select the final option and AutoCAD prompts you to supply information that will be used to complete the dimension. Once you supply all of the information for the dimension, the command ends. Figure 2-20 illustrates the pull-down menus for the Linear dimensioning option. The basic dimensioning options of Linear, Angular, and Radial are discussed in this section.

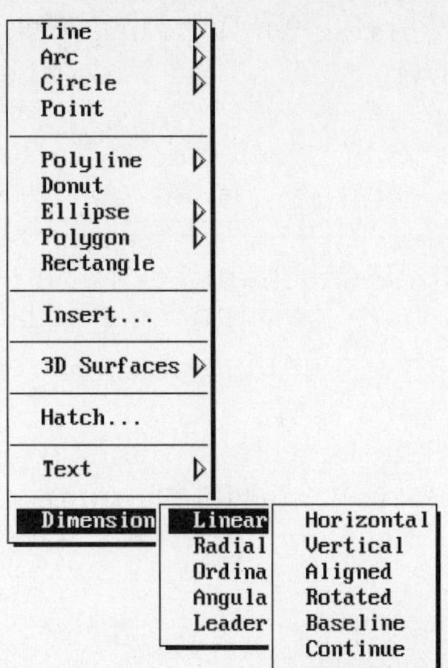

Figure 5-20
Cascading Dimension Menus

Using Linear Dimensions

The Linear option includes horizontal, vertical, aligned, and rotated dimensions, which are illustrated in Figure 5-21. Horizontal and vertical dimensions are illustrated on the left side of the figure. The aligned dimension measures the true length of the line and is parallel to the line. The rotated dimension measures the length of the line, projected in a direction that is not perpendicular to the line. The 1.00 dimension in the figure is the distance between the ends of the vertical line, projected at an angle of 45 degrees from the horizontal axis.

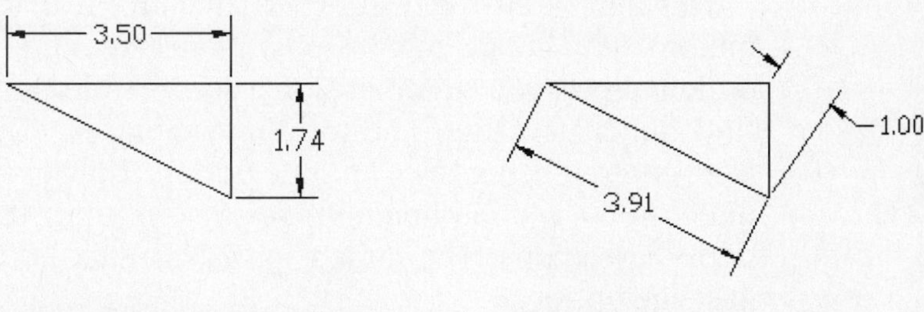

Figure 5-21
Linear Dimension Options

Horizontal and vertical linear dimensions

Aligned and rotated linear dimensions

The prompts and responses for three of the Linear options—Horizontal, Vertical, and Aligned—are identical. You are prompted for the origins of the extension lines, the location of the dimension line, and the dimension text. Choose Linear from the Dimension pull-down menu, and then select Horizontal, Vertical, or Aligned. At the prompt

```
First extension line origin or RETURN to select:
```

pick a point at one end of the line you are dimensioning. At the prompt

```
Second extension line origin:
```

pick the other end of the line. At the prompt

```
Dimension line location (Text/Angle):
```

pick a point to locate the dimension line. The dimension and the text move as you move the crosshairs to help you position the dimension line. At the final prompt

```
Dimension text <value>:
```

press (ENTER) to accept the dimension text. The default dimension text is the length of the line. You can modify the text or substitute different text if necessary, as discussed later in the chapter. The command ends when you accept the text.

When you choose Dimension from the Draw pull-down menu, choose Linear, and then choose the Rotated option, AutoCAD presents the prompt

```
Dimension line angle <0>:
```

Enter the angle the dimension line is to make with the +X axis. The zero angle is the equivalent to measuring the horizontal distance between the length of the lines. A response of 90 degrees measures the vertical length of the line. After you enter the angle, the remaining prompts and responses are the same as for the previous linear dimensions.

Try It

- Draw a triangle similar to the one shown in Figure 5-21.
- Use each of the four linear dimension options to dimension the sides of the triangle.

The menu shown in Figure 5-20 includes two additional commonly used options for linear dimensions: Continue and Baseline. The Continue option allows you to dimension a second line that is a continuation of the first dimension line. The top dimensions in Figure 5-22, 1.50 and 2.50, were entered using the Continue option. The Baseline option allows you to dimension a second line but uses the origin of the first extension line for both dimensions. The dimensions 2.00 and 4.00 were entered using the Baseline option.

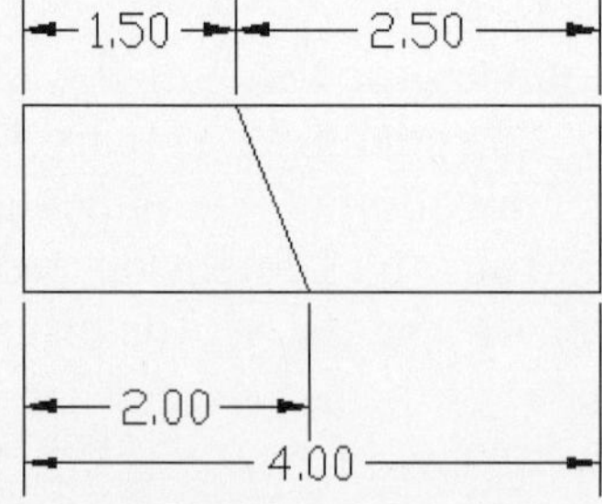

Figure 5-22
Continue and Baseline Options

Initiate the Horizontal command to complete the first of two linear dimensions. Then initiate the Linear command, but instead of picking Horizontal from the menu, pick either Baseline or Continue. At the prompt

```
Second extension line origin or RETURN to select:
```

pick the location of the second extension line. AutoCAD uses a prior extension line as the first extension line and completes the dimension. The location of the second dimension line is determined by AutoCAD based on the option being used.

Try It

- Draw a rectangle with a line connecting two sides, similar to the one shown in Figure 5-22.
- Dimension the horizontal line segments using the Continue and Baseline options.
- Draw a six-sided polygon. Use the Continue option to dimension the horizontal distances between the corners of the polygon. Use the Baseline option to dimension the vertical distances.

Using Angular Dimensions

The Angular option in the Draw, Dimension menu measures the angle between two nonparallel lines and displays the value in degrees. Dimensioning angles is just as easy as dimensioning linear objects. The dimension line component of an angular dimension consists of an arc. Generally you will be dimensioning an angle defined by two lines in a drawing. However, the Angular option will dimension the angle defined by the endpoints of an arc or by two points that you select on a circle. After you choose the method for defining the angle, you select one of four locations for the dimension arc. Two of these locations are illustrated by the dimensions at point B in Figure 5-23. Each of the angles is possible depending on where you choose to place the dimension arc. Finally, you select the point where the dimension text is to be entered. If the point you choose causes the arc to intersect the text, the arc is broken.

Figure 5-23
Angular Dimensions

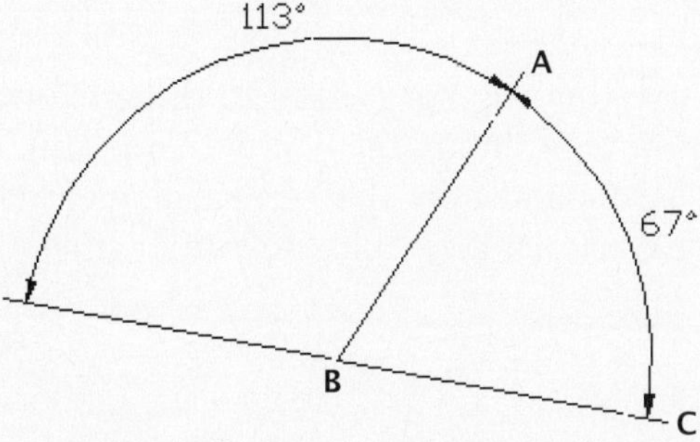

Here are the prompts and responses for angular dimensions. Pick Angular from the Draw, Dimension pull-down menu. The first prompt is

```
Select arc, circle, line, or RETURN:
```

Pick the first line that defines the angle. At the prompt

```
Second line:
```

pick the second line. The prompt

```
Dimension arc line location (Text/Angle):
```

appears. AutoCAD shows you the dimension arc and the text. You drag the dimension arc and text as you move the crosshairs. When you are satisfied with the location, pick the point. The dimension vanishes, and you are prompted for

```
Dimension text <measured value>:
```

Press ENTER to accept the given angle. At the prompt

```
Enter text location(or RETURN):
```

move the text to a location away from the center of the arc, or press ENTER to place the text in the middle of the arc.

If you select the RETURN option at the prompt

```
Select arc, circle, line, or RETURN:
```

you can select the intersection of the two lines that contain the angle. You are not required to select the two lines separately. After that the command proceeds as before.

Try It

- Draw a triangle with different length sides.
- Dimension the three interior angles.
- Dimension the same three angles, but place the dimension arcs outside the triangle.
- Experiment with the alternate method for choosing the intersecting lines.

You can use the Angular option to dimension the central angle defined by the endpoints of an arc or by any two points on the perimeter of a circle. Figure 5-24 illustrates the central angles defined by an arc and two points on a circle. Notice that no radial lines are needed to define the angle.

Figure 5-24 **Dimensioning Central Angles**

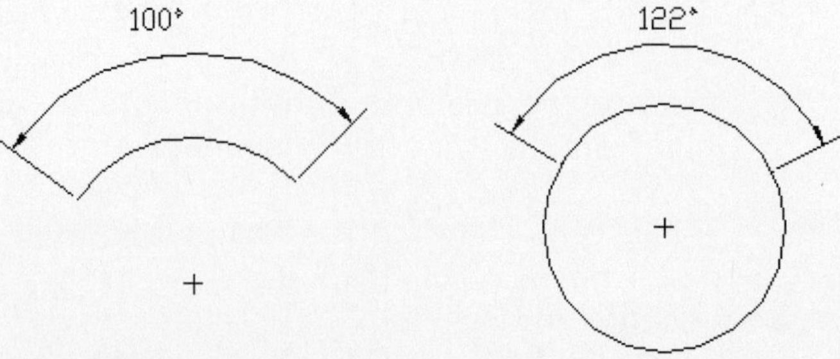

If you pick an arc at the prompt,

```
Select arc, circle, line, or Return:
```

AutoCAD displays the prompt

```
Dimension arc line location (Text/Angle):
```

All you have to do is select the location for the dimension arc and proceed as before. When you pick a point on the circumference of a circle, the prompt

```
Second angle point:
```

appears. Pick another point on the circle and the usual prompts appear until the dimension is complete. The center of the arc or circle is the origin of the lines defining the angle. In the case of the arc, the angle is defined by the center of the arc and the ends of the arc. In the case of the circle, the center and the two points on the perimeter define the angle. Again, the command proceeds as before after the angle has been defined.

Try It

- Draw a circle and arc similar to the arcs shown in Figure 5-24. Draw the arc with a known angle so that you can check the results.
- Dimension the central angle of the arc.
- Dimension an angle defined by any two points on the circle.

Using Radial Dimensions

You use the Radial option in the Draw, Dimension menu to enter *radial dimensions:* the radius and the diameter of an arc or circle. The results of the Diameter and Radius options of the Radial command are illustrated in Figure 5-25. Use the Diameter option to dimension circles, and use the Radius option for both arcs and circles. Both options require you to select the arc or circle. The dimension line or leader is a radial line through the point that you pick on the circumference of the arc or circle. AutoCAD calculates the radius or diameter and enters it on the dimension line. The dimension is placed outside, and a leader is extended to the text. A circle symbol is added to diameter dimensions, and R is added to radius dimensions. Center marks are added to the figure by default.

Figure 5-25
Radial Dimensions

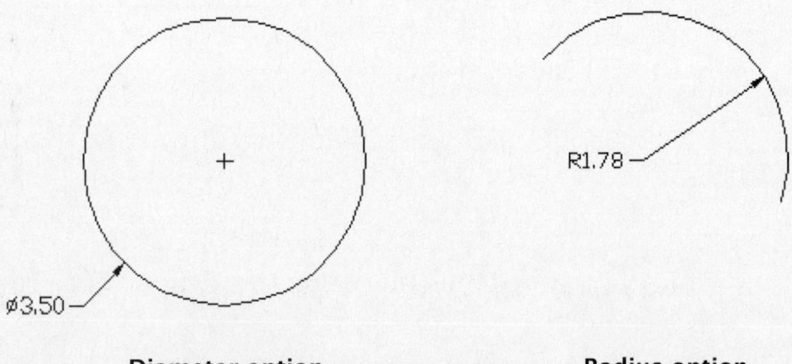

Picking Dimension from the Draw pull-down menu and then choosing Radial displays the three options Diameter, Radius, and Center Mark.

The Center Mark option marks the center of the arc or circle without adding any dimension. If you pick Diameter, the prompt

```
Select arc or circle:
```

appears. Select an arc or circle and the prompt

```
Dimension text <diameter>:
```

appears. The number within angle brackets is the actual diameter of the circle. Press ENTER to accept the text. At the prompt

```
Enter leader length for text:
```

pick a point just outside the circle. When you move the crosshairs, the dimension and the leader move about to help you pick the point. The dimension is entered with a pair of lines pointing to the circle. These lines make up the leader.

The prompts for the Radius option are nearly identical to those for Diameter.

Try It

- Draw some arcs and circles. Use 2.875 as the diameter of one of the circles and 1.500 as the radius of one of the arcs so that you can verify the results of your trial.
- Use the Center Mark option to mark the centers.
- Dimension the circles and the arcs.

Using Leaders

The *leader* is a very useful dimensioning tool that allows you to point to an object and describe it with a note. The Radius and Diameter options use leaders automatically. You can also initiate the command by selecting Dimension from the Draw pull-down menu and choosing Leader. First you are prompted to draw the lines that make up the leader. The first line segment is at an angle from the object and displays an arrow pointing to the start point. The second line is a short horizontal segment. After drawing the lines, you are prompted for the text. The default text is the text that was last entered in a dimension.

When you start the Leader command, the first prompt is

```
Leader start:
```

Pick a point near where you want the arrow to appear. At the prompt

```
To point:
```

pick a point at the end of the first leader line. The prompt

```
To point:
```

continues to appear until you press ENTER without picking a point. At the next prompt

```
Dimension text <>:
```

type the note.

Try It

- Make a drawing similar to the one shown in Figure 5-26.
- Use the Leader option to draw a leader from the midpoint of the baseline and add the text "Base line."

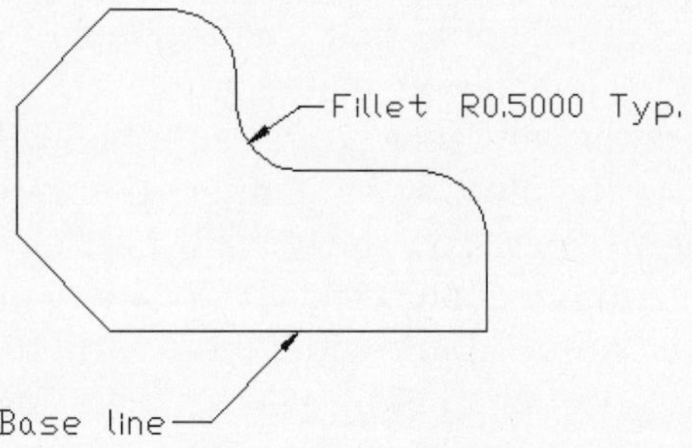

Figure 5-26
Using Leaders and Appending Text

Appending Text to Dimensions

At times you will want to append text of your own to the default dimension text. For example, you may want to indicate that a certain dimension is typical of others on the drawing. You can add the note "Typical" before the contents of the default text by typing, `Typical <>` at the

```
Dimension text <>:
```

prompt that AutoCAD displays during the course of any dimensioning command. In fact, you can enter notes before and after the default dimension text by typing the first part of the note, typing <>, and then typing the second part. Typing the text in this order places the default dimension text between the two parts of the note. This technique was used to enter the dimension and note "Fillet R0.5000 Typ." shown in Figure 5-26.

Try It

- Dimension the fillet arc in Figure 5-26 with the Radius option.
- Add the message, "All fillets =" before the dimension text.

Editing Dimension Text

You may want to modify dimensions after you add them to a drawing. The components of the dimension are created as a combined entity, similar to a block. Therefore, you must explode the dimension before you can modify any portion of it.

Try It

- Make a simple drawing and add dimensions to it.
- Try to erase the text portion of one of the dimensions.
- Explode one of the dimensions and remove its text portion.

5-6 USING THE PLOT COMMAND

You can make copies of your drawings by plotting them with a pen plotter or by using your printer as a plotter. This discussion will be limited to plotting drawings with a printer. We will assume you have a printer attached to your computer and the correct driver (a software program) for your printer is installed so that it is available to AutoCAD. Normally you install the driver when you install AutoCAD. If you need help with the installation see the reference guides supplied with the AutoCAD program.

You must set the plotting parameters before you plot the drawing on a sheet of printer paper. You select what portion of the total drawing is to be plotted. In addition, you select the location, orientation, and size of the plotted image. AutoCAD provides you with the chance to preview the results of the selections before you send the plot to the printer. Release 12 makes these tasks quite simple with a series of dialog boxes.

Using the Plot Configuration Dialog Box

Initiate the Plot command from the File pull-down menu. The Plot Configuration dialog box shown in Figure 5-27 is displayed.

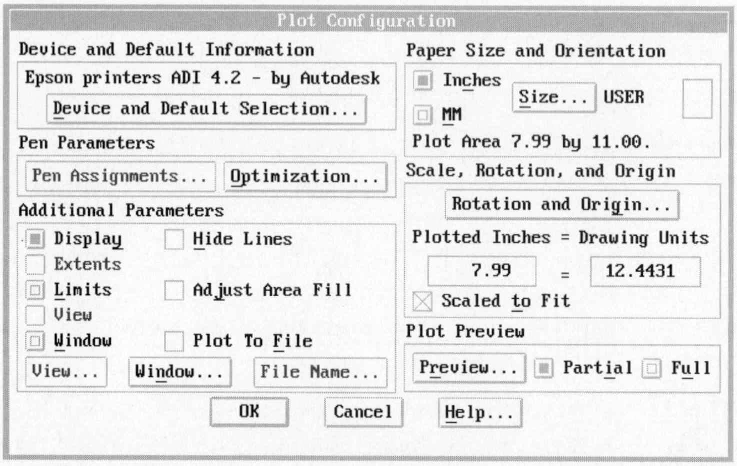

Figure 5-27
Plot Configuration Dialog Box

The dialog box is divided into six sections, each controlling a set of plotting parameters. The two sections, Devices and Default Information and Pen Parameters are beyond the scope of this discussion. The section on Additional Parameters provides aids for selecting the portion of the drawing to be plotted. The section on Paper Size and Orientation allows you to choose a paper size and units. You use the Scale, Rotation, and Origin section to set the ratio of the size of the actual object to the size of the drawn object, the orientation of the plot, and the location of the origin.

After you choose these settings you use the Preview section to see the results of your choices before you send the drawing to the plotter.

Previewing a Plot Before we discuss the selection of the plot parameters, it is useful to learn how to preview a plot using the parameters that have been preset by AutoCAD. You should preview the plot, before sending the plot to the printer, to see how each setting affects the results. The Preview section gives you the choice of seeing only the outline of the effective plotting area or seeing the actual details of the drawing. Click on the Partial button and then on the Preview box. The Plot Effective Plotting Area dialog box in Figure 5-28 appears showing the outline of the paper, in red, and the outline of the drawing area, in blue. Information about the paper size and the effective area is shown in the box. AutoCAD checks the plot for potential problems. If any are found, a warning is shown in the Warnings box. Click on OK to return to the Plot Configuration dialog box. If you want to preview the plot in detail, click on Full before clicking on Preview. A similar dialog box appears showing the actual drawing instead of the blue outline. You can examine the drawing more closely by using the Pan and Zoom option. This option is outside the scope of this text. If you are satisfied with the looks of the plot, click on End Preview to return to the Plot Configuration Dialog box.

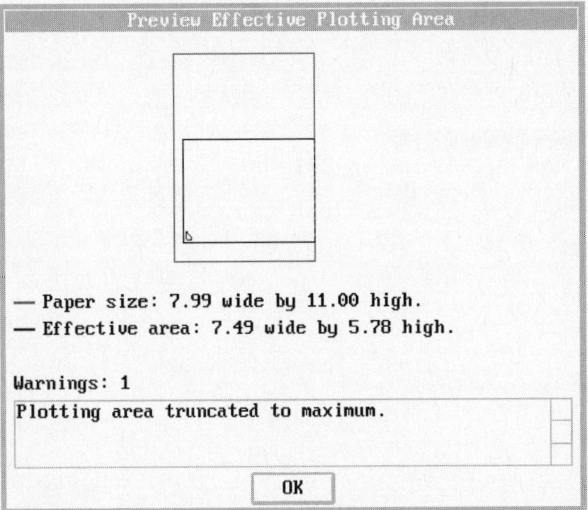

Figure 5-28
Preview Effective Plotting Area Dialog Box

Try It

- Make a simple drawing consisting of lines and circles.
- Initiate the Plot command to display the Plot Configuration dialog box.
- If the Extents button in the Additional Parameters is not on, click on it now.
- Preview the plot using the Partial option.
- Preview the plot using the Full option.
- Return to the previous dialog box.
- Click on Cancel to return to the drawing screen.

Using Paper Size and Orientation This section is used to select the paper size and orientation of the plot. The size is either in inches or millimeters. The default units are inches and this is the setting that you want to use. If you need to specify the paper size in millimeters, click on MM. The orientation is fixed if you are using a printer as the plotting device. You will learn how to rotate the plot in a moment.

The size of the paper to be used for the plot must be selected before you choose any of the additional plot parameters. The outline of the paper appears on the preview dialog box. This outline represents the standard paper size used with printers, approximately 8 by 11 inches. If you click on Size in the Paper size and Orientation section, the Paper Size dialog box, shown in Figure 5-29 appears. The actual sizes that appear in the dialog box on your screen may be different from those shown here. The settings depend on the actual plotting devices that are connected to the computer. The standard size, named USER, is listed in the left column. Its dimensions are shown in the boxes on the right. You can set different paper sizes to be used with the printer by typing the dimensions in the Width and Height boxes. These dimensions must be less than the maximum dimensions of the printer paper. The additional size will be listed in the column at the left with the name, USER1. You select the new paper size by highlighting the name in the left column and Clicking on OK and returning to the Plot Configuration dialog box.

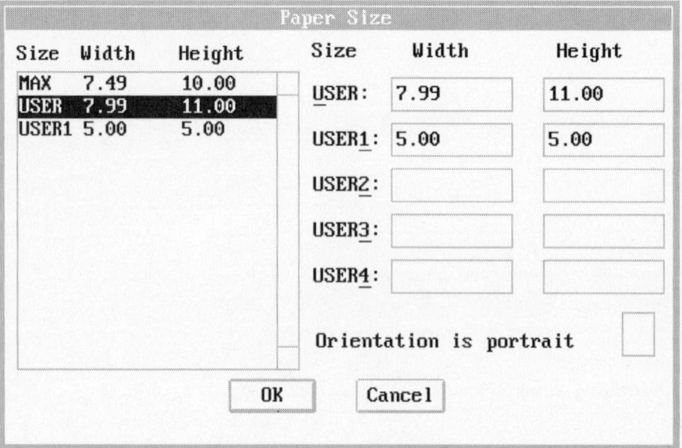

Figure 5-29
Paper Size Dialog Box

Try It

- Click on Size to activate the Paper size dialog box.
- Create a new paper size 5 inches by 5 inches.
- Select the new paper size and click on OK.
- Preview the result.
- Reset the paper size to 8-1/2.

Using the Additional Parameters The Additional Parameters section has five settings that determine how much of the drawing is included in the plot. One of these, View, will not be discussed. Each of the other four, Display, Extents, Limits, and Window is used to select what portion of the drawing or screen is included in the plot. Display selects the current image on the drawing screen. Limits selects only that portion of the drawing within the Limits that you selected at the beginning of your drawing session. Extents selects the entire drawing, including objects currently off the screen. Window selects only that portion of the drawing within a window. You select any of the first three options by clicking on the appropriate button. If you want to use the Window option, click on Window... and the Window Selection dialog box, shown in Figure 5-30, appears. You will draw a window similar to other selection windows that you have used many times earlier in the text. You can select the coordinates of the corners of the selection window by typing new values in the First corner and Second corner boxes. It is easier, however, to select the window directly on the drawing screen. Click on the Pick box. The dialog box disappears and the prompt

```
First corner:
```

appears. Pick a point to define a window around the portion of the drawing to be plotted. At the

```
Second point:
```

prompt pick another point to complete the window. The dialog box will reappear and you can preview your selection.

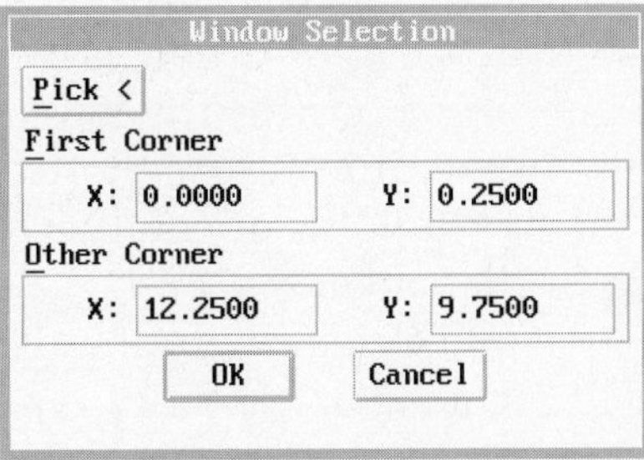

Figure 5-30
Window Selection Dialog Box

Try It

- Use the Zoom command to enlarge your drawing image so that it extends beyond the screen area.
- Initiate Plot command.
- Click on the Display button and do a full preview.
- Repeat the preview with the Limits button on.
- Click on the Windows... box and select a portion of the drawing to preview.
- Return to the drawing screen and do a Zoom with the All option to restore the original drawing.

Using Scale, Rotation, and Origin The scale of the plot is the ratio of a plotted dimension to the actual dimension of the drawn object. For example, using a scale of 1/2 to plot a drawing means that a line with the length of 10 units in the drawing will be plotted to a length of 5 inches on the paper. This scale is defined as 1 inch equals 2 units, or 1=2. Commonly used scales are 1=2, 1=4, 1=5, 1=8, 1=10, and 1=100. You must calculate the scale to be used for your plot. The calculation is quite simple.

First determine the maximum horizontal dimension of your drawing, including any text. Divide that number by the horizontal dimension of the paper. Repeat the step using the vertical dimension of the drawing and the paper. Use the larger of these two ratios as the scale and select the standard scale nearest the calculated value.

The Scale for the plot is set in the section on Scale, Rotation, and Origin. This scale is set by typing 1 in the Plotted Inches box and the related scale value in the drawing Units box. If it is not important to use a precise scale for the plot, you can let AutoCAD compute the scale factor for you. Click on the Scale to Fit box and the settings will be adjusted automatically. Furthermore, the new settings will appear in the Plotted Inches and Drawing Units boxes.

Try It

- Click on the Scale to Fit box and note the scale settings.
- Preview the plot.
- Enter scale settings to Plotted Inches = 1 and Drawing Units = 5.
- Preview the plot.
- Enter scale settings to Plotted Inches = 5 and Drawing Units = 1.
- Preview the plot.

You can change the orientation of the plot and control where the drawing origin coordinate point, (0,0), is located on the paper. The default orientation is vertical, that the Y-direction is vertical on the paper. The default location of the origin is near the lower-left corner of the paper. The remaining points in the drawing are plotted relative to that point on the paper. You can change both the orientation and the location of the origin to make the plot fit the paper.

Click on the Rotation and Origin... box and the Plot Rotation and Origin dialog box, shown in Figure 5-31, appears. There are four rotation settings, 0, 90, 180, and 270 degrees. Click on the appropriate button to choose the rotation setting to use. You move the plot origin by typing a new value in the X Origin and Y Origin boxes. Increasing the X value moves the image to the right on the paper and increasing the Y value moves the image up the paper. Click on the OK box to accept the changes and leave the dialog box.

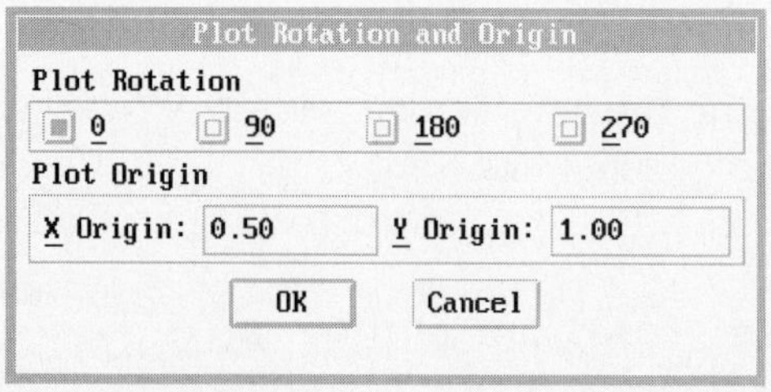

Figure 5-31
Plot Rotation and Origin Dialog Box

Plot Rotation and Origin
Plot Rotation
0 90 180 270
Plot Origin
X Origin: 0.50 Y Origin: 1.00
OK Cancel

Try It

- Set the rotation angle to 90 degrees and use Full to preview the result.
- Move the origin 6 units to the right and 4 units upward and preview the result.
- Place the origin at X = 0.5 and Y = 1.5 and preview the results.

Sending the Plot to the Printer After you are satisfied with the plot parameters, click on OK in the Plot Configuration dialog box. The message:

```
Position paper in plotter
Press (RETURN) to continue or S for hardware setup.
```

appears. You can make adjustments in the printer setup or press (ENTER) to start the plot. AutoCAD begins the plotting process and various messages appear in the command area while plotting information is sent to the printer. If you need to interrupt the plot, type (CTRL)-C to cancel the process. The plot continues for a short time while the printer processes the information that is stored in its buffer.

Application 1: DESIGN OF A HIGH-PERFORMANCE BICYCLE WHEEL

Mechanical and Materials Engineering

The design of a high-performance bicycle wheel involves choosing the materials as well as the geometric shape. These two factors are related. If you use a material with a high strength-to-weight ratio, you can reduce the size of the components without sacrificing strength. The number and shape of the spokes influence the comfort and aerodynamic properties of the wheel. Using a composite skin over a foam core makes it possible to mold a spoke with an excellent aerodynamic profile.

You can now use the five-step problem-solving process to draw the bicycle wheel.

1. Identify the Object and Its Function

The object is a three-spoke high-performance bicycle wheel. The wheel is to be formed using a composite skin over a foam core. The wheel is to be compatible with standard bicycle frames.

2. Research Models and Determine Dimensions

The research that supports the design of a high-performance bicycle wheel involves investigating different materials and geometries. You can find data on the materials in the product information distributed by material suppliers. If necessary, you can acquire more detailed information directly from the company engineers. The design of the profile of the spokes involves a numerical analysis of the proposed shape to determine its strength. You could also have the aerodynamic characteristics analyzed by a computer. After a preliminary design is complete, prototype models are made and tested extensively in the laboratory. Finally, engineering drawings are made.

3. Draw a Rough Sketch

The drawings in Figure 5-32 and Figure 5-33 serve as the rough sketch. Figure 5-32 shows the overall size of the wheel and its major details. Figure 5-33 shows an enlarged view of the detail of the valve inlet for the inflatable tire. This detail is too small to be clear in the drawing of the entire wheel. Figure 5-33 also shows the shape of the spoke. Plan the order in which you will create the drawing. It is efficient to draw temporary center lines to locate the center of the circles. Draw the circles and the outline of one spoke. After finishing the details of one spoke, array it to form the remaining spokes. Finish the details and dimension the wheel.

Figure 5-32
Three-Spoke Bicycle Wheel

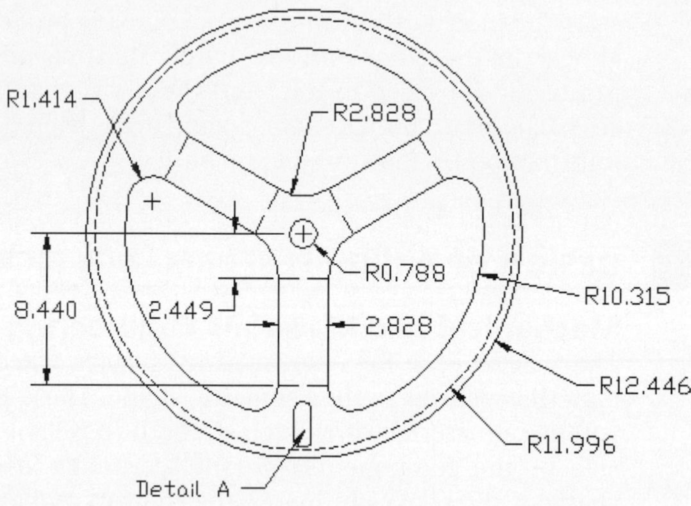

Figure 5-33
Detail A

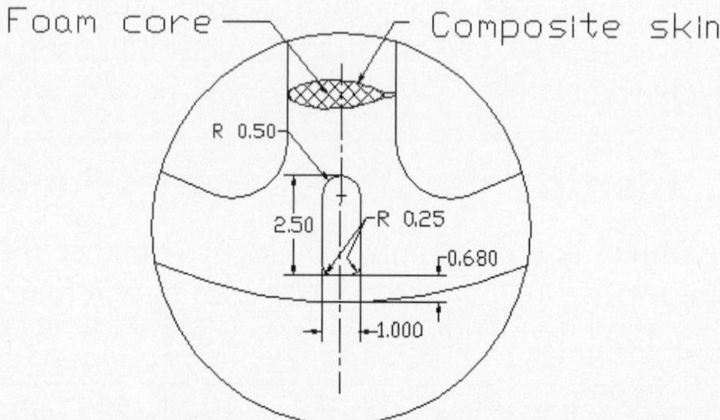

4. Make Proper Screen Adjustments

Set up another prototype drawing. Set the limits so that the drawing of the wheel and the detail fit on the screen. Use decimal units with three decimal places. Set up separate layers for the continuous and hidden lines. Set up a layer for the dimensions and notes. Use a contrasting color for the dimension layer.

5. Draw, Print, and Save the File

A suggested order in which to draw the components of the wheel was outlined in step 3. You should plan the location of the dimensions so that they are clear. You also need to develop a plan for drawing the detail shown in Figure 5-33, both as an enlarged drawing and on the wheel drawing. Save the drawing as WHEEL.

What If

What if the wheel had four spokes? Would this require any major change in the drawing process?

What if you knew the thickness of the spoke? Could you use the thickness and the width of the spoke and draw an approximation to the section shown in Figure 5-33? Could you use a combination of an ellipse and several arcs to draw the approximation?

SUMMARY

In this chapter you learned to use the drawing commands Polygon, Ellipse, Point, and Hatch. You learned how to use the Measure and Divide commands to enter points along objects. You discovered how to use the Array command to make multiple copies of objects on a regular pattern. You found out how to combine objects into a block that can be treated as a single object. You also learned how to insert blocks into a drawing, manipulating them as you do so. You learned about the Explode command that lets you separate blocks and dimensions into their component parts for editing. You can now add dimensions to your drawings, providing information that is essential to the successful completion of any project. Finally, you can plot your drawing using your printer as a plotting device.

Key Words

angular dimension
block
dimension line
dimension text
double hatch
ellipse
explode
extension line
hatch pattern
leader
linear dimension
major axis
minor axis
nested boundaries
polar array
radial dimensions
rectangular array
symbol library
Wblock

Exercises

Draw the objects shown in the following exercises. Use the dimensions where given. Draw the schematic approximately to scale. Add dimensions and notes where they are supplied.

Exercise 5-1
Schematic for Producing Solid CO2

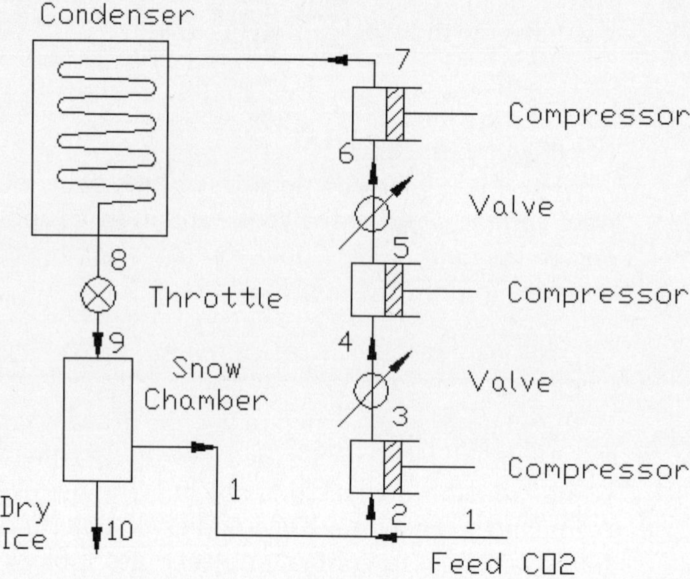

Draw the compressor and valves as blocks. Use the Leader option to draw the lines with arrows.

Exercise 5-2
Angle Bracket

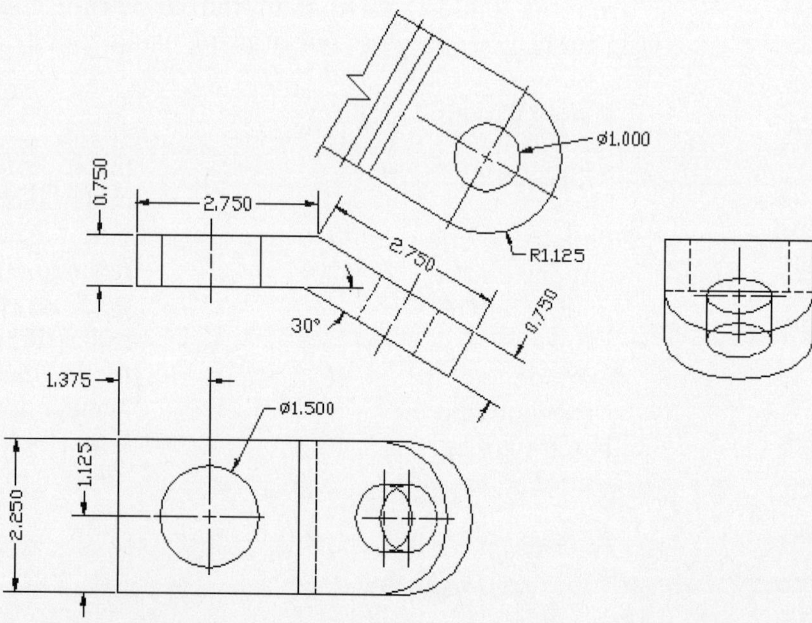

Draw the four views of the bracket. Note the use of ellipses to represent the circles as they appear in the right and lower views.

Exercise 5-3
Wide Flange Column Base Plate

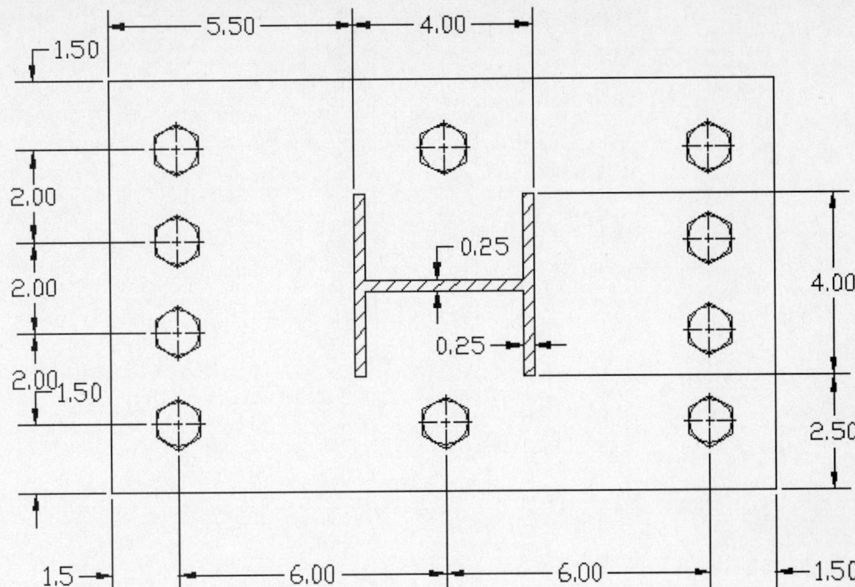

Use the block of the hexagonal bolt head. Array the bolt heads and erase the extra ones.

Exercise 5-4
Casting

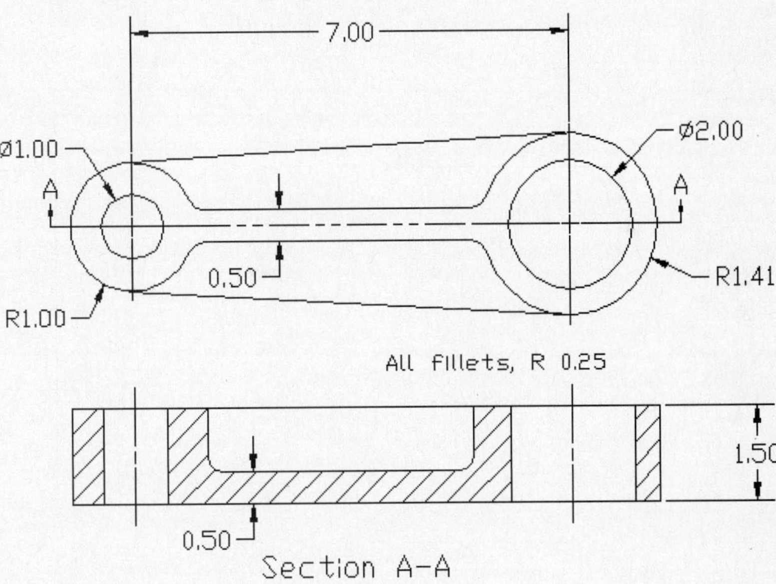

Exercise 5-5A
Gear

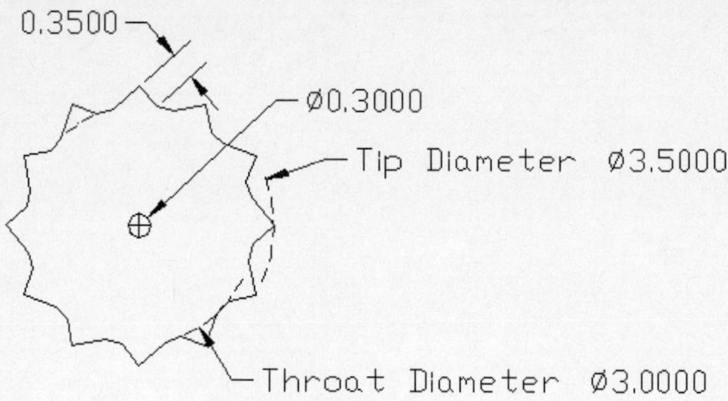

Exercise 5-5B
Tooth Detail

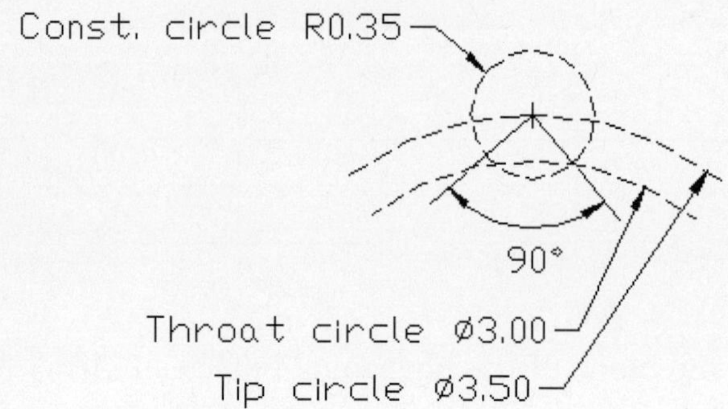

Draw one tooth using the dimensions shown in the detail. Use the Array command to complete the gear.

Exercise 5-6
Fin Plate

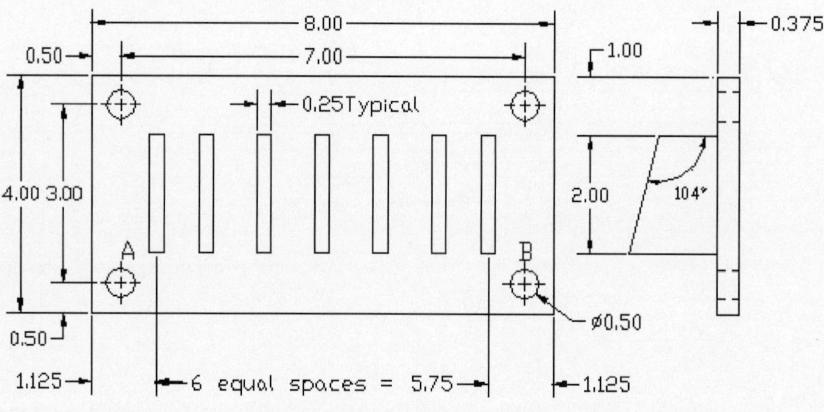

Exercise 5-7
Circuit Diagram

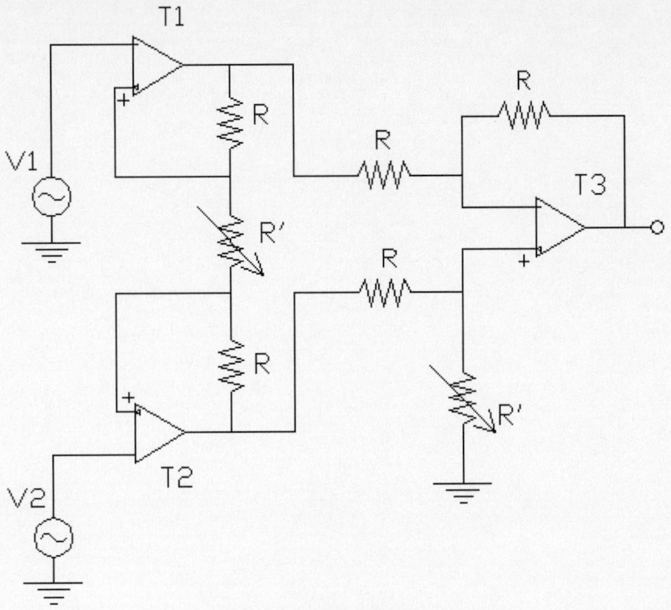

Exercise 5-8
Landscape Design

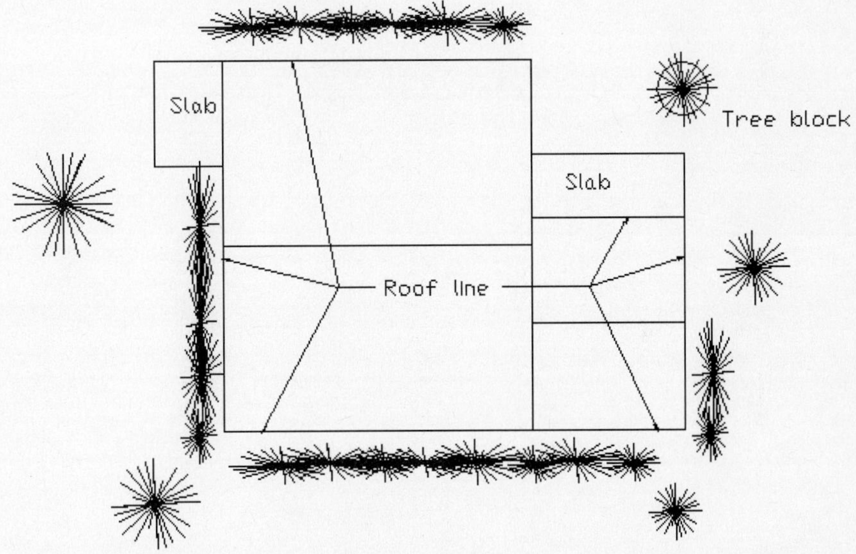

Open the drawing of the Foundation Plan you created in Chapter 3, Exercise 3-6. Draw the roof lines two feet beyond the foundation walls. Draw a tree symbol using radial lines emanating from the center of a circle, similar to the Tree block shown. Make a block, without the circle, and insert it into the drawing to simulate trees and the plantings along the building.

6 Making Three-Dimensional Drawings

Finite Element Analysis

Engineers use curved surfaces in a great variety of modern structures. Radio telescopes, modern aircraft bodies, curved roofs, and high-performance bicycle wheels are all examples of curved surfaces. To analyze the surfaces of such complex objects engineers use a numerical technique called finite element analysis, replacing the actual surface by a network of small plane-geometric shapes, or elements. Finite element analysis yields very accurate data about the structural behavior of the actual curved surface. CAD systems are used to make the 3D models of the surface. The results—the geometry and arrangement of the elements—are then used in the numerical analysis. In this chapter, you will draw a roof structure that consists of a hyperbolic paraboloid—a means of constructing "curved" surfaces from plane shapes.

INTRODUCTION

All of the drawings in the previous chapters have been two dimensional—that is, the Z coordinate of each point is zero. This chapter introduces two techniques for drawing *three-dimensional* (*3D*) objects, objects that have *thickness* in the Z direction. The first technique is to add thickness to a two-dimensional object. For example, adding thickness to a circle produces a cylinder. The 3D drawing that results is called an *extruded object.* Once you've learned to create extruded objects, you learn how to view the drawings so the objects appear in three dimensions. The second technique for drawing 3D objects is to draw the outlines of the object using Z coordinates along with X and Y coordinates. These 3D drawings are called *wireframe models*, or simply *wireframes.* As you draw wireframes, you learn how to create and use custom coordinate systems. So far you have been drawing in the default or World Coordinate System. You must be able to create custom or User Coordinate Systems to edit successfully in three dimensions. At the end of this chapter, you learn how to combine views of the 3D drawing into a set of orthographic views that are suitable for engineering purposes.

6-1 CREATING EXTRUDED 3D OBJECTS

You are already familiar with everyday items that can be drawn easily as extruded objects. The side of a soda can is a cylinder formed by moving a circle along a line perpendicular to the plane of the circle. A rectangular box, or prism, is formed by moving a rectangle along a line perpendicular to the plane of the rectangle. Figure 6-1 illustrates the extruded 3D objects formed by moving a circle, a rectangle, and an ellipse along a line.

Figure 6-1
Examples of Extruded Objects

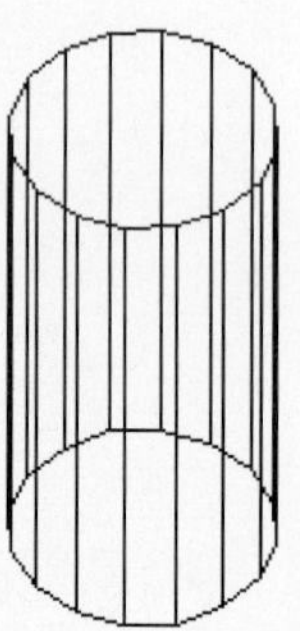

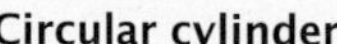

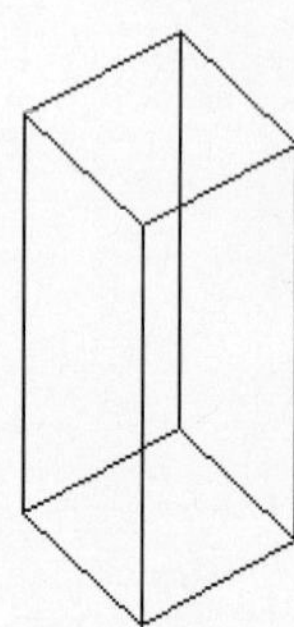

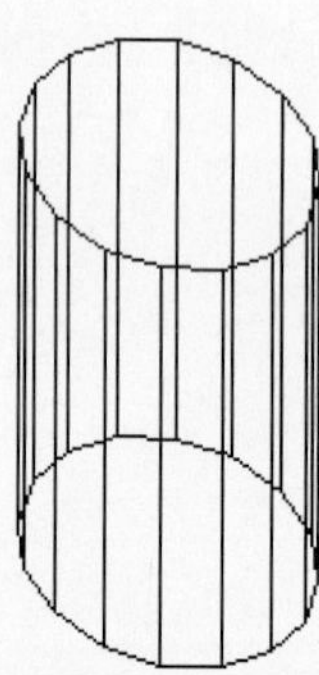

Earlier chapters described two commands, Change and Chprop, that let you add thickness to existing two-dimensional objects. You can also use the Change command to change the *elevation* of an object. The elevation of objects drawn in the XY plane is zero. Changing the elevation is the equivalent of moving the object to a plane parallel to the XY plane. You do not need to change the elevations of objects to create simple extruded shapes, but you might need to do so when combining two extruded objects, as described a bit later in the chapter. The shapes shown in Figure 6-1 illustrate what you can do by changing the thickness of simple objects. First you draw each object in the XY plane. Then you add thickness to the objects. Finally, you change the viewpoint so the 3D images are visible. (Although objects with thickness are actually 3D, this will not be apparent from your current viewpoint.) These steps are used to draw and view all extruded 3D objects.

The Change command is reviewed briefly before you create extruded objects. When the Change command presents the prompt

```
Select objects:
```

pick the objects to be changed. At the prompt

```
Properties/<Change point>:
```

type P and press ENTER to select the Properties option. At the prompt

```
Change what property (Color/Elev/LAyer/Ltype/Thickness)?
```

type T and press ENTER to change the thickness of the selected objects.

The prompt

```
New thickness <0.0000>:
```

appears, indicating that the default thickness is zero. Enter a new thickness and press ENTER twice to end the command.

If you are changing the elevation (the location above or below the XY plane) of an object, type E and press ENTER at the

```
Change what property (Color,Elev,LAyer,Ltype,Thickness)?
```

prompt. The prompt

```
New elevation <0.0000>:
```

appears. Enter the new elevation. If you enter a positive value, the Z coordinates will be positive. If you enter a negative value, the Z coordinates will be negative. The X and Y coordinates will not be changed.

Try It

- Draw a number of objects like those shown in Figure 6-1. Include a circle, an ellipse, a polygon, a rectangle, and a point.
- Change their elevations and thicknesses, noting that from the current viewpoint they do not appear to be in 3D.
- Save the drawing as 3D1 so you can use it later.

6-2 USING THE VPOINT COMMAND TO SEE IN 3D

As mentioned, just adding thickness to objects does not make them appear to be three dimensional. AutoCAD has several options for displaying objects in three dimensions. We will look at only one, the Vpoint command, which allows you to change the viewpoint—orientation of the XYZ coordinate system relative to the viewer. In the current orientation of the axes, you (the viewer) are looking along the Z axis down on to the XY plane; your point of view is 90 degrees to the XY plane. The Vpoint command enables you to rotate the direction of the XY axes and also to change the direction from which you view the XY plane. Figure 6-2 illustrates the use of the Vpoint command. The rectangle on the left was drawn in the XY plane using the default viewpoint. The image on the right is that same rectangle viewed by rotating the XY plane 315 degrees and viewing the XY plane from 30 degrees rather than 90 degrees.

Figure 6-2
Comparing Viewpoints

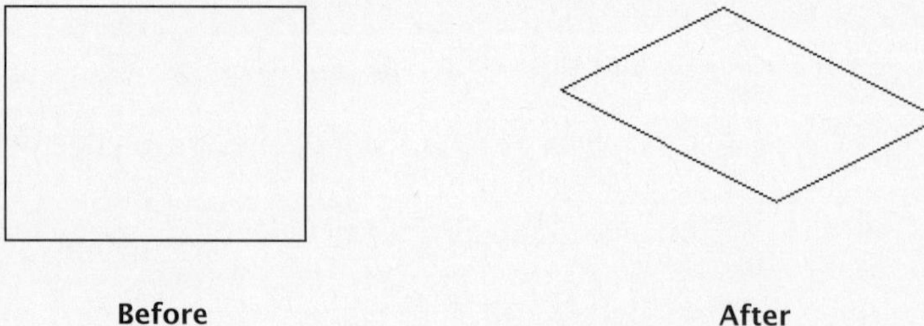

Before **After**

To change your viewpoint, choose Set View from the View pull-down menu, choose Viewpoints, and then choose Presets. AutoCAD displays the Viewpoint Presets dialog box shown in Figure 6-3. Here you can select the two angles that define your new point of view. Initially, the angle from the X axis is 270 degrees and the angle from the XY plane is 90 degrees. This information is shown in the X Axis and XY plane boxes as well as by the positions of the markers in the diagrams in the upper portion of the dialog box. You can change the angles to the marked preset values by clicking on the space between the angle markers in the diagrams. To select some intermediate value for either angle, type the actual value in the X axis or XY plane box.

Figure 6-3
Viewpoint Presets Dialog Box

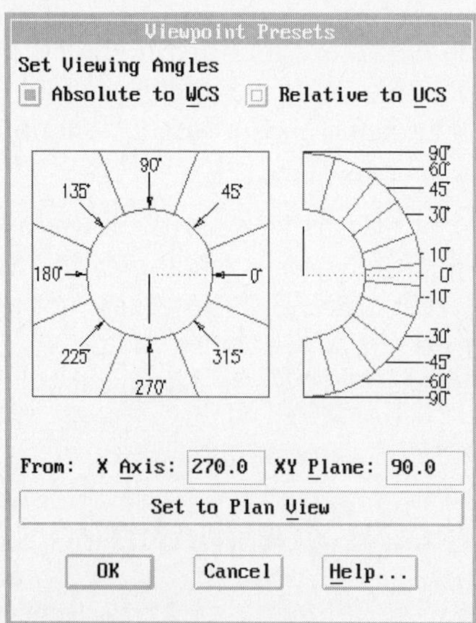

After you select the angles to define a new viewpoint, you will want to save the settings so you can use them later. You can name and save the viewpoint settings by choosing Set Views from the View pull-down menu and choosing Named Views. AutoCAD will display the View Control dialog box shown in Figure 6-4.

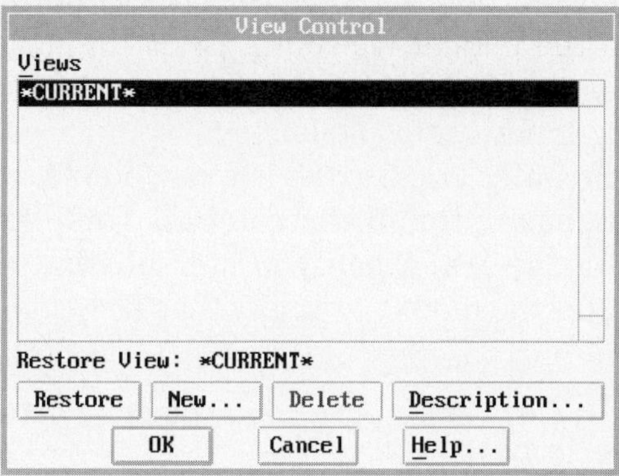

Figure 6-4
View Control Dialog Box

To name the current view setting, click on New. The Define New View dialog box shown in Figure 6-5 appears. Type the name of the view in the New Name box and click on OK. The View Control dialog box reappears, and the name you just typed is listed under Views. Click on OK to leave the dialog box. To return to a named view, retrieve the View Control dialog box, click on the name of the desired view, click on the Restore button, and click on OK.

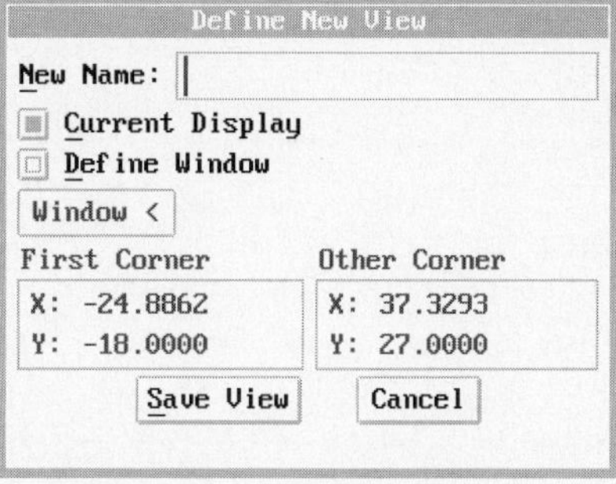

Figure 6-5
Define New View Dialog Box

Try It

- Open the 3D1 drawing.
- Open the Viewpoint Presets dialog box.
- Experiment with various combinations of the X axis and XY plane angles. You may have to use Zoom All to see the entire set of objects. The orientation of the UCS icon in the lower-left corner of the screen shows how the new viewpoint affects the orientation of the X and Y axes.

The Axes option on the View pull-down menu is an alternative technique for selecting a new viewpoint. Issuing this command brings up a display similar to the one shown in Figure 6-6. This *Compass and Axes system* is useful because it permits you to see the position of the X, Y, and Z axes while you select the viewpoint. The concentric circles and the lines are similar to a compass. Moving the crosshairs to the exact center of this compass and picking the point selects the normal, or default, viewpoint. (Remember, the default viewpoint is looking at the XY plane along a line perpendicular to the plane, with the positive X axis pointing to the right.) Points in the inner circle establish viewpoints perpendicular to the Z axis. Points on the outer circle establish viewpoints parallel to the Z axis. Moving the crosshairs around the compass rotates the three axes displayed below and to the left. When you are satisfied with the result, press the pick button on the mouse to select that viewpoint.

Figure 6-6
Compass and Axes System

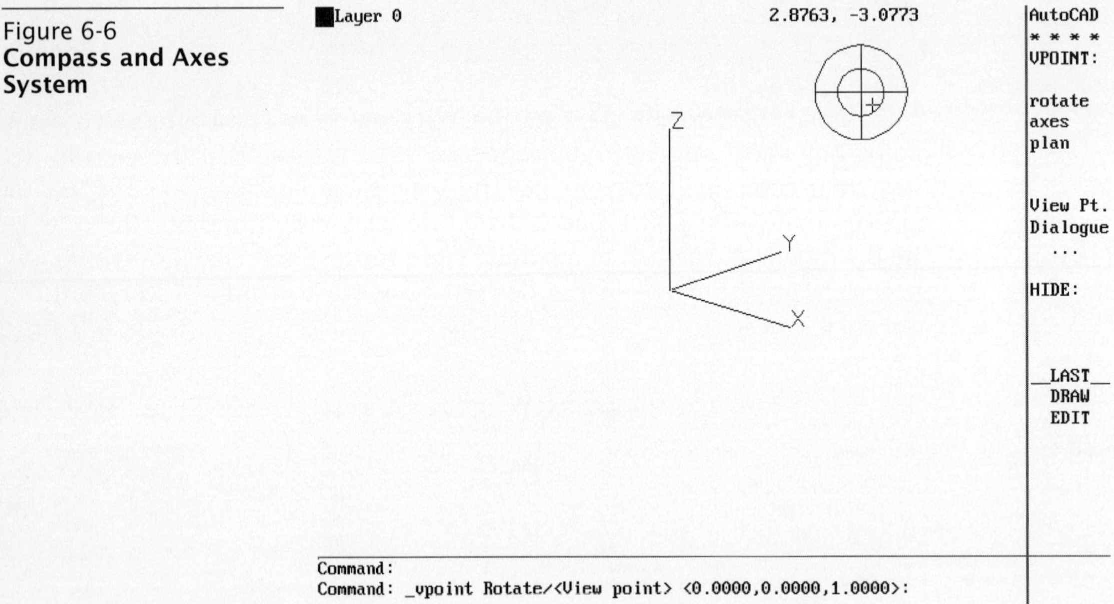

Try It

- Try using the Compass and Axes system to change your point of view.
- Try to return the point of view back to the normal viewpoint.
- Use the View pull-down menu to check the current viewpoint settings.

6-3 COMBINING EXTRUDED OBJECTS

You have learned how to draw individual extruded objects and how to view them in three dimensions. Now you will combine two extruded objects to draw the simple but complete object shown in Figure 6-7. This block with a circular cylinder on top resembles a column on a pedestal. The left image in the figure shows how the object looks from the default point of view. The right image shows how the object appears in three dimensions.

The order of the drawing steps for objects made up of extrusions is quite straightforward:

1. Draw the basic objects in the XY plane.
2. Change the elevation of any object that is not in the XY plane in the final drawing.
3. Change the thicknesses of the objects as needed. The thickness and elevations of the objects must be coordinated. For instance, in Figure 6-7 the thickness of the prism is 2, so the elevation of the cylinder above it should be 2.
4. View the result in three dimensions.

You may discover that it is easier to change your viewpoint after step 1 and then complete the drawing while viewing it in three dimensions.

Figure 6-7
Column-Pedestal Extrusion

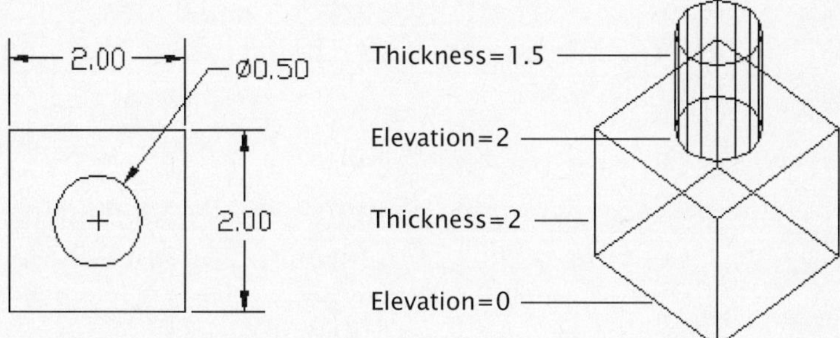

Try It

- Create the object shown in Figure 6-7. After you have completed the drawing, use the Compass and Axes system to experiment with different viewpoints.
- Try changing the thickness of the block to 3 units, keeping the base of the circular cylinder on the top of the block.
- Undo the last step and try making the cylinder appear as a hole through the block.

6-4 ASSEMBLING THE TOOLS FOR WIREFRAME MODELS

The extrusion techniques introduced so far only enable you to add thickness to and change the elevation of plane objects. You cannot, however, draw a device such as the one shown in Figure 6-8 by using an extruded shape. You cannot draw the sloping plane as part of a rectangular prism. Instead, you must draw the device as a wireframe model. (You will draw this device, called an alignment block, later in this chapter.)

Wireframe models, or wireframes, in AutoCAD are similar to the physical models you can construct using wires. You draw lines and curves in three dimensions, connecting them to outline the shape of the object.

One strategy for drawing wireframes is to create a box that contains the device and then remove those pieces that are not part of the finished product. You need to know how to draw the box in three dimensions

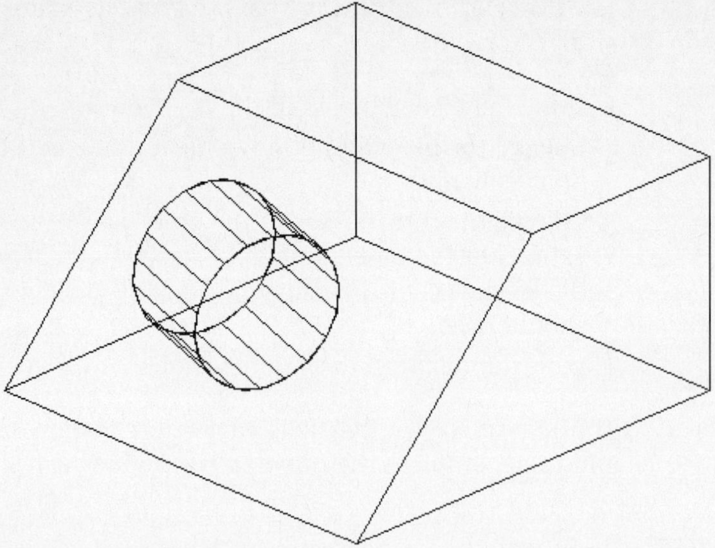

Figure 6-8
An Example of a Wireframe Model

before you can continue. The process of drawing a box involves the following steps:

1. Draw the base rectangle.
2. Change your viewpoint to see the rectangle in three dimensions.
3. Copy the rectangle to form the top of the box. You can use 0,0,0 as the coordinates of the base point. Use 0,0,*h* as the coordinates of the second point, where *h* is the height of the box.
4. Complete the box by connecting the corners of the base rectangle and the top rectangle.

Try It Draw a box similar to the one shown in Figure 6-9. Use angles of 235 degrees for the X axis and 35 degrees for the XY plane for your new viewpoint. Use the Chprop command to create the four dashed lines. You have drawn a simple wireframe model of the box.

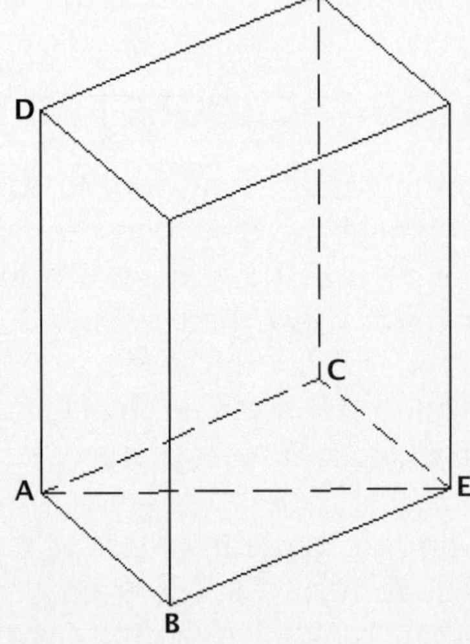

Figure 6-9
3D View with the WCS Icon

When you create more complex wireframe models, you will need to move or turn off and on the screen icon. In addition, it is essential to know something about User Coordinate Systems.

Controlling the Screen Icon

The *screen icon* shows you the location and the direction of the positive X and Y axes, but often it also obscures part of the drawing. When you start a new drawing, the screen icon is located at the 0,0 coordinate point in the lower-left corner of the screen. You turn the icon off by selecting UCS from the Settings pull-down menu, choosing Icon, and then choosing the Off option. You turn it on by clicking on the On option.

When you create a User Coordinate System, you change the location of the origin. However, the icon remains in the lower-left corner of the screen. To move the icon from the lower-left corner to the new origin, choose UCS from the Settings pull-down menu, choose Icon, and then choose the Origin option. To restore the screen icon to the lower-left corner of the screen, use the Off option followed by the On option. You cannot move the icon until you create a User Coordinate System, but you can practice turning the icon off and on.

Try It

Try turning the screen icon off. Turn it back on.

Creating User Coordinate Systems

So far, all of your drawings have used the AutoCAD default coordinate system. The icon in the lower-left corner of the screen is a reminder that the *World Coordinate System (WCS)* is in effect. Even after you change your viewpoint, you have not left the WCS. The change in viewpoint rotates the icon on the screen but leaves it at the 0,0 coordinate point and leaves the X arrow pointing to the positive X coordinate direction.

As you have seen, you can draw in three dimensions while you are in the WCS. However, some editing involves working on planes that are not parallel to the WCS. For example, you cannot offset or trim lines in the inclined plane in Figure 6-8. In these cases, you must create new, custom, coordinate systems in the particular plane where the editing takes place. Custom coordinate systems are called *User Coordinate Systems (UCSs).*

Figure 6-9 shows a wireframe model of a rectangular prism displayed in three dimensions. The WCS icon appears in the lower-left corner of the screen. It is at the origin of the WCS.

Figures 6-10 through 6-13 each illustrate a different User Coordinate System. The UCS icon is at an origin, which you select. The directions of the X and Y coordinate axes, shown by the icon, are also chosen by the user.

You use the UCS command to create the UCS coordinate systems. The command offers several options for locating the origin of a UCS and establishing the directions of the axes. In general, a drawing requires a UCS for each plane in the object. Your particular drawing may require several different systems. The UCS command allows you to name and save the systems and recall them as necessary.

The easiest way to start the UCS command is to type UCS and press (ENTER). The prompt

```
Origin/ZAxis/3point/Entity/View/X/Y/Z/Prev/Restore/Save/
Del/ ?/<World>:
```

appears.

The various UCS options and their results are listed in Table 6-1. As usual, you select an option by typing the capitalized letter in its name.

Table 6-1 UCS Options

Option	Results
Origin	Prompts you for an origin point. The origin of the current coordinate system, WCS or UCS, is moved to the point that you select.
ZAxis	Prompts you for an origin point and a point on the positive portion of the Z axis. The positive X and Y coordinate directions are oriented according to the conventional mathematical coordinate directions.
3point	Prompts you, in order, for an origin point, a point on the positive X axis, and a point on the positive Y axis. The UCS is established according to these three points.
Entity	Prompts you to select an entity to orient the UCS. You pick a line. The origin is placed at the end of the line nearest the point you picked when selecting the line. The positive X axis is directed toward the other end of the line.
View	Creates a UCS parallel to the plane of the screen.
X	Prompts you for a rotation angle about the X axis. The current UCS is rotated about the X axis by the angle that you enter.
Y	Prompts you for a rotation angle about the Y axis. The current UCS is rotated about the Y axis by the angle that you enter.
Z	Prompts you for a rotation angle about the Z axis. The current UCS is rotated about the Z axis by the angle that you enter.
Prev	Restores the last UCS that was used.
Save	Prompts you for a name and saves the current UCS with that name.
Restore	Prompts you for a name and makes the named UCS current.
Del	Prompts you for the names of saved UCSs. Any UCSs that you specify are deleted and cannot be reinstated with the Restore option.
?	Lists the saved UCSs by name.
World	Restores the WCS.

The most commonly used options for creating new UCSs are the 3point option and the X, Y, and Z rotation options. The Save and Restore options are also used frequently to avoid duplication of effort. As you create UCSs, note that the W in the screen icon disappears, but the icon remains in the lower-left corner of the screen unless you turn it off or move it, as described earlier.

To create a UCS using the 3point option, type UCS. The main UCS prompt appears:

```
Origin/ZAxis/3point/Entity/View/X/Y/Z/Prev/Restore/Save/
Del/ ?/<World>:
```

Type 3 and press ENTER. At the prompt

```
Origin point <0,0,0>:
```

pick the origin point. At the prompt

```
Point on the positive portion of the X-
axis<0.0000,0.0000,1.0000>:
```

pick a point to select the direction of the +X axis. At the prompt

```
Point on the positive-Y portion of the UCS X-Y plane
<0.0000,0.0000,1.0000>:
```

pick a point to select the direction of the +Y axis.

Try It

- Create the UCS shown in Figure 6-10. Note the appearance of the UCS icon.
- Move the icon to the origin of the UCS.
- Save the UCS, using the name ABC.

Figure 6-10
Creating a UCS with the 3point Option

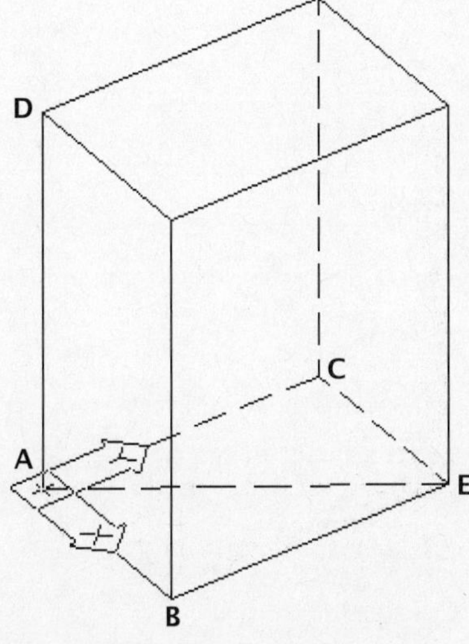

If you select X from the main UCS prompt, the following prompt appears:

```
Rotation angle about the X axis <0>:
```

Enter an angle, and the current UCS system is rotated about the X axis by that amount.

If you select Y from the main UCS prompt, AutoCAD displays the prompt

```
Rotation angle about the Y axis <0>:
```

Again, enter an angle, and the current UCS system is rotated about the Y axis by that amount.

Finally, if you select Z at the main UCS prompt, the prompt

```
Rotation angle about the Z axis <0>:
```

appears. Enter an angle, and the current UCS system is rotated about the Z axis by that amount.

Using the rotation options to change the current UCS into a new UCS may require two rotations. Converting the UCS in Figure 6-10 to the UCS in Figure 6-11 is just such a situation. You must first rotate the UCS about the X axis to orient the Y axis from A to D; then you must rotate the UCS about the Y axis to orient the X axis from A to C.

Figure 6-11
Creating a UCS with the X and Y Options

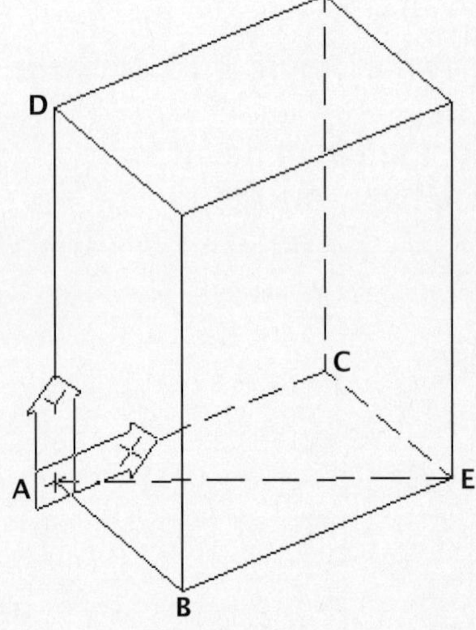

Try It

- Create the UCS shown in Figure 6-11 using the UCS in Figure 6-10.
- Save it with the name ACD.
- Move the screen icon back to the lower-left corner of the screen.
- Make the ABC UCS current with the Restore option.
- Create the UCS shown in Figure 6-12. Save it with the name ABD.
- Experiment with the command by moving the origin of the ABD UCS to point E, and direct the X axis toward B and the Y axis toward C. Move the icon to the origin to verify your results.

The Z axis does not appear with any of the UCS icons. Again, the direction of the Z axis is consistent with what you have learned in mathematics or physics.

Figure 6-12
Creating a UCS with the Z Option

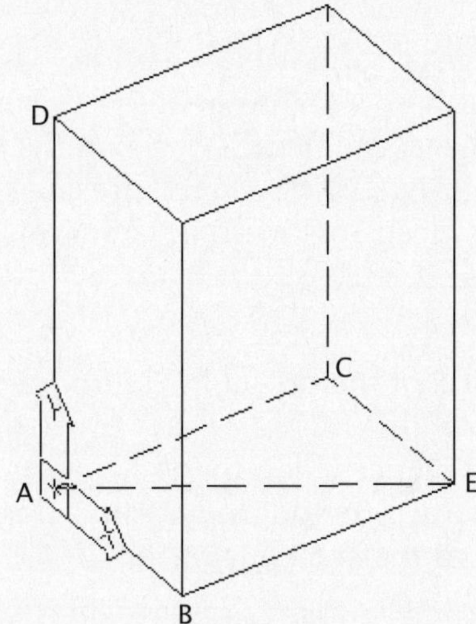

Try It

- Restore the ABD UCS. Rotate the ABD UCS so that the positive Y direction is from A toward B and the positive X direction is downward.
- Use the 3point option to create the UCS in Figure 6-13.
- Save the drawing as UCSWF for use later in the chapter.

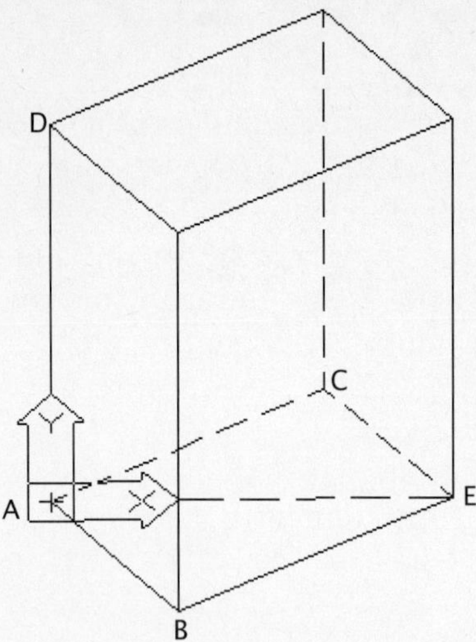

Figure 6-13
Creating a UCS on an Inclined Surface

Later in the chapter you will need to capture views of the 3D drawing as blocks. One of those views is the image as seen with the current viewpoint. To capture a view, you need a UCS parallel to the screen. You create the View UCS simply by typing V and pressing ENTER at the main UCS prompt. There is no need to save this view; you can return to it just by typing V.

Try It

- Create the View UCS of the object in Figure 6-13. Save the UCS with the name VIEW.
- Restore the WCS. Practice using the Prev option to recall the last UCS. Practice using the Restore option. As you change to a different UCS, note any changes to the screen icon.

Using Rulesurf and Surftab to Define Curved Surfaces

You use *ruling lines* to create *ruled surfaces* that are curved in wireframe models. When you create extrusions of curves, AutoCAD adds the ruling lines automatically. When you draw curved surfaces in wireframes, you must add ruling lines to define the surface.

The Rulesurf command uses ruling lines to define ruled surfaces. You need to pick two objects, called *defining curves*, to determine the location and orientation of the ruling lines. (Note that you cannot mix open and closed curves.) After you select the objects AutoCAD divides each object into a set number of intervals and draws lines from the division points on one object to the corresponding division points on the other object. If you select an open curve, AutoCAD counts the division points beginning at the end of the curve nearest the pick point, so the results are affected by the way you select the objects.

To initiate the Rulesurf command, select 3D Surfaces from the Draw pull-down menu and then select Ruled Surface. At the prompt

```
Select first defining curve:
```

pick an object, either a line or an arc. At the prompt

```
Select second defining curve:
```

pick another object. If the objects are open curves, lines, or arcs, the endpoints nearest the selection determine the orientation of the ruling lines.

Figure 6-14 illustrates ruled surfaces using lines as the defining curves. The two sets of lines in the drawing are of the same length and orientation. However, the lines were picked at points A and B in the image on the left, while they were picked at points E and H in the image on the right.

Figure 6-14
Ruled Surfaces Using Lines

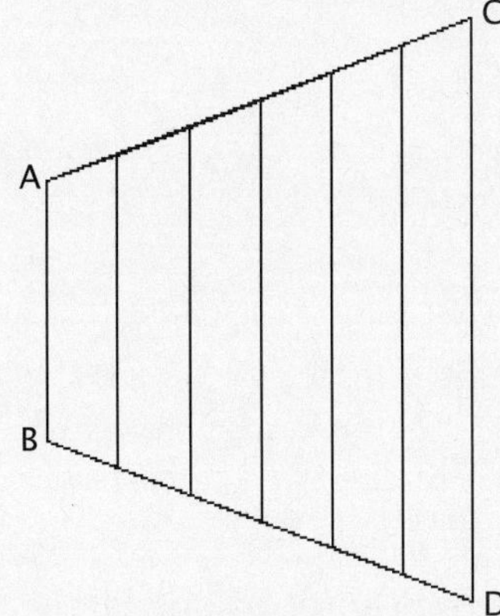

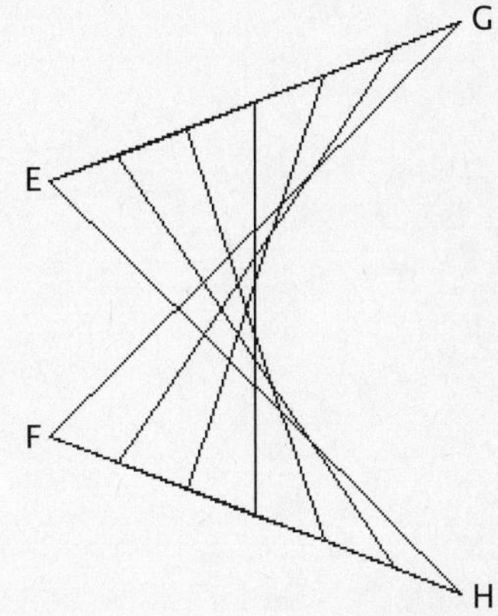

Try It

- Draw the lines AC and BD, as shown in Figure 6-14, and make a copy to create the lines EG and FH.
- Use the Rulesurf command to create the two images shown in Figure 6-14.

You can also use arcs as defining curves for ruled surfaces. As with lines, AutoCAD counts the division points beginning at the end of the arc nearest the pick point. Figure 6-15 illustrates how you can use the same defining curves but achieve different results by picking different portions of the curves.

Figure 6-15
Ruled Surfaces Using Arcs

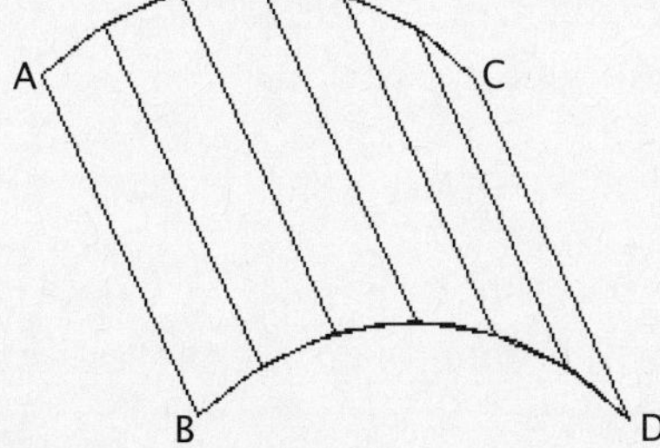

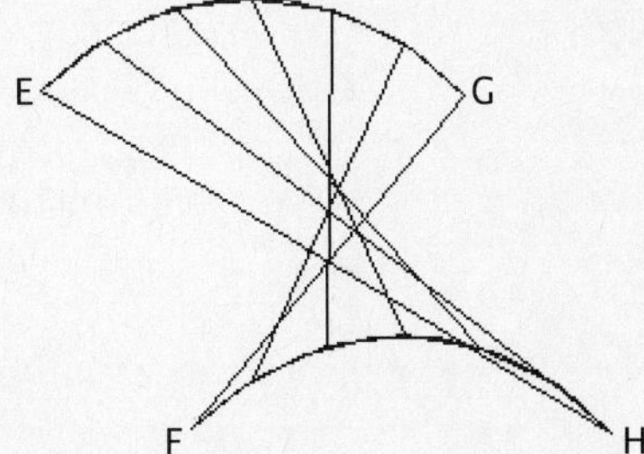

Try It

Draw one arc A–C from Figure 6-15 in the XY plane. Draw the second arc, B–D, using a constant Z coordinate. The arcs must be plane curves.

- Copy the arcs to create the arcs EG and FH, as shown in the figure.
- Use the Rulesurf command to complete the drawing in Figure 6-15.
- Use the Vpoint command to view these surfaces in three dimensions.

The ruled surfaces shown in Figure 6-16 use closed curves as the defining curves. It does not make any difference where you pick the closed curve. The results will always be the same, since the object has no endpoints.

Figure 6-16
Ruled Surfaces Using Closed Curves

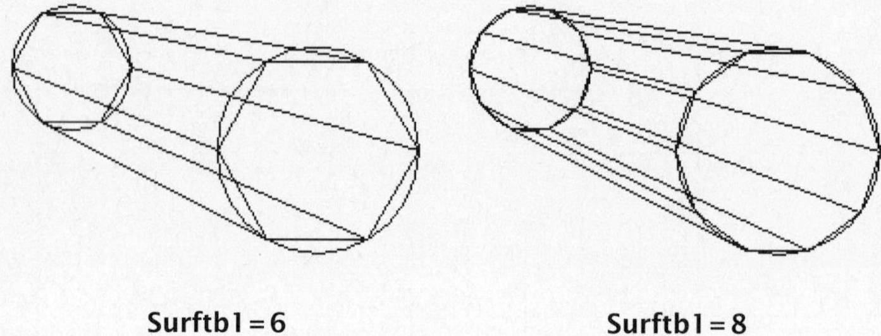

Surftb1 = 6 **Surftb1 = 8**

Try It

- Draw two circles. Place the center of one circle at 4,4,0. Place the center of the other at 6,6,3. Use two different values for the radius. Make a copy of the circles on the right-hand side of your screen.
- Create the ruled surface shown on the left of Figure 6-16.
- View the surface using the Vpoint command.

In the surfaces shown in Figures 6-14 and 6-15 and on the left side of Figure 6-16, AutoCAD used six panels to define the ruled surface. This default number, six, is a reasonable number to represent a surface for most applications. You can increase or decrease the number of panels by changing the value of SURFTB1. Choose 3D Surfaces from the Draw pull-down menu and select Ruled Surface, the screen menu displays all of the options for creating surfaces. The pull-down menus and the screen menus are coordinated. Included on the screen menu is Surftb1. Surftb1 controls the setting for surfaces with a single set of ruling lines. Select Surftb1 from the screen menu and the prompt

```
New value for SURFTAB1 <6>:
```

appears. Enter a new value. Generally, a value between 6 and 12 is best since larger values will create a very dense looking surface.

Try It

- Change the Surftab1 setting to eight and add ruled surfaces to the circles on the right, as shown in Figure 6-16. Notice the differences in the two ruled surfaces. Note that existing surfaces are not updated automatically when you change the Surftbl setting.
- Experiment with a very large Surftbl setting, say 200. Note the result and then use U to erase the surface.
- Experiment to determine the smallest permissible Surftbl setting.

Now you have all of the tools you need to draw the wireframe model shown earlier in Figure 6-8.

6-5 DRAWING A WIREFRAME MODEL

Now you can apply the new skills you have just acquired to draw a wireframe model. While you will not be learning any new drawing or editing commands, you will learn a strategy that can be used for all wireframes. As you learn the strategy, you will learn more about the need for UCSs. You will have the opportunity to experiment with editing commands, such as copy, offset, and trim, while working in three dimensions.

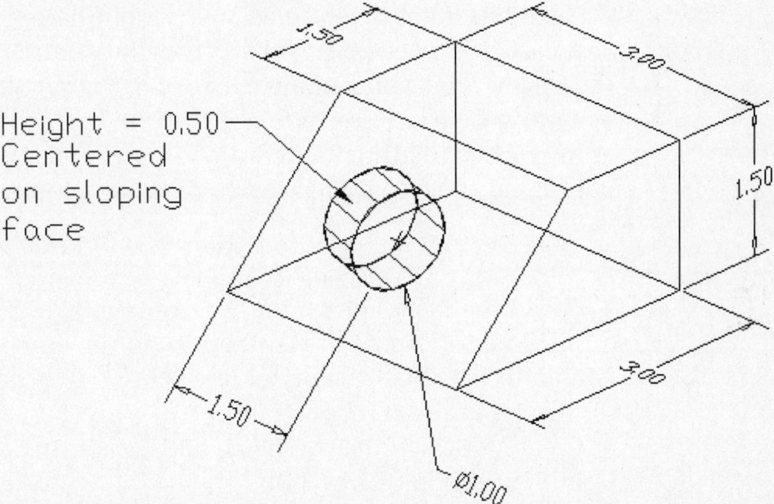

Figure 6-17
Alignment Block

The object that you will draw is the alignment block shown in Figure 6-17. The object is used to align two parts. The cylindrical projection on the inclined surface will match a cylindrical hole in a matching part. As mentioned earlier, you must first draw the outline of a rectangular prism that contains the final object. Then you will edit away those portions that are not part of the final object. The prism that contains this object is shown in Figure 6-18.

Figure 6-18
Outlining Prism

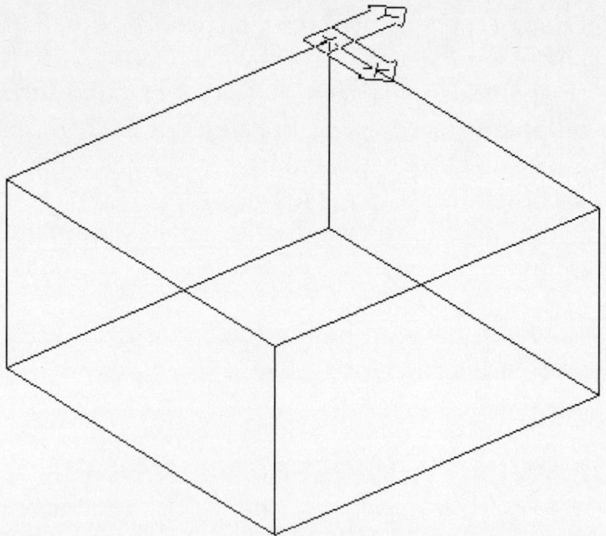

Try It

Draw the prism shown in Figure 6-18. Use the four steps that you used earlier to draw the prisms for the UCS exercises. Use 230 degrees and 30 degree angles to view the prism.

Next you must begin to remove lines that are not part of the object. In this case you need to trim back the lines in the top plane. When you edit on a plane that is not the current one, the results are unpredictable. As a general rule, you want to orient the UCS on the plane on which you will be editing. Drawing the prism did not require the use of a new UCS. However, editing an object with the Trim or Offset commands does require a new UCS.

Try It

- Offset the back line on the top plane in Figure 6-19 by 1.50. Note the message, "Command results may not be obvious" in the command line and observe that the offset line is not in the desired location. Use Undo to reverse the last command.
- Create a UCS in the top plane and locate the icon at the origin of the UCS. Save the UCS as TOP.
- Repeat the Offset command.
- Draw the inclined lines to outline the inclined plane.
- Restore the WCS and try trimming the front part of the lines using the inclined lines as cutting edges. Again note the same message in the command line.
- Create a new UCS in the right plane and save the UCS as RIGHT.
- Trim the lines.
- Erase the extra lines.
- Create a UCS in the front plane. Make the +Y axis upward. Save the UCS as FRONT for use later in the chapter.

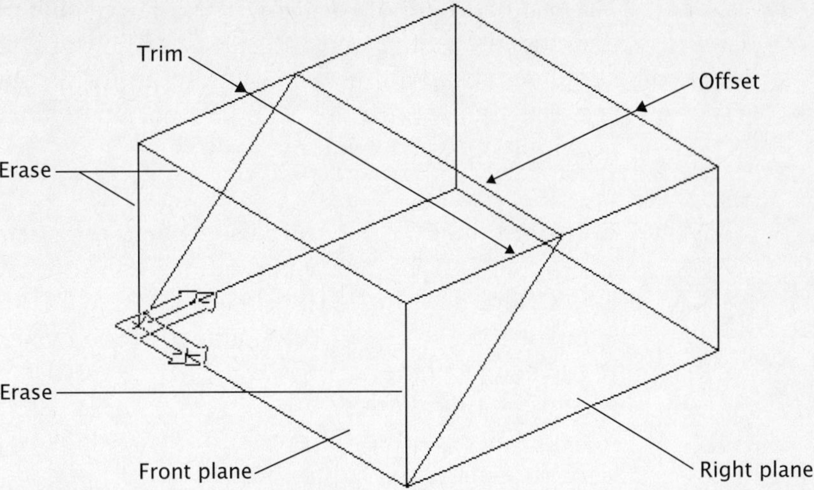

Figure 6-19
Offsetting and Trimming in Three Dimensions

You just saw what can happen if you try to use a simple editing command without using the proper UCS. Drawing objects as simple as circles will produce strange results unless you use a suitable UCS. The outline of the object from Figure 6-17 is complete except for the circular cylinder at the center of the inclined plane.

Try It

- Try drawing a circle with a diameter of 1. Place the center anywhere. Notice that the circle is parallel to the FRONT UCS.
- Restore the TOP UCS and draw another circle. Again, note that it is in a top plane.
- Erase the two circles.
- Create a UCS in the inclined plane. Place the origin at the point shown in Figure 6-20.
- Use the Offset command to draw the center line on the inclined plane, as shown in Figure 6-20. Move the origin to the midpoint of the center line and save the UCS as INCLINE.
- Draw the circle with the center at the midpoint of the line, and erase the line.

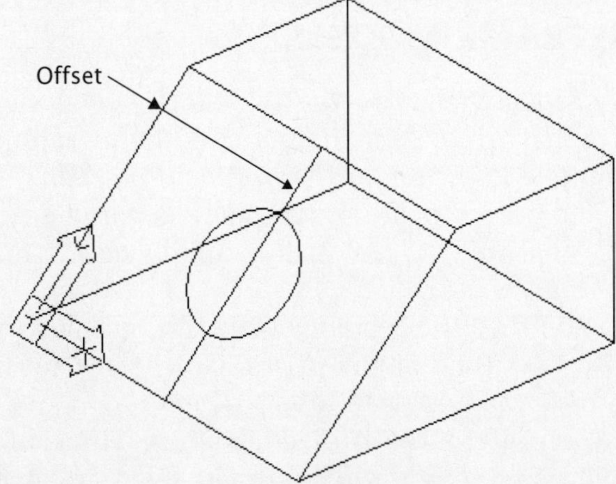

Figure 6-20
Drawing on an Inclined Plane

The final steps in drawing the alignment block are to copy the circle and add the ruling lines. Recall that the Copy command requires you to supply a base point and a second point of displacement. Earlier you were concerned only with the X and Y coordinates of the points. Here you will be supplying a Z coordinate as well.

Try It

- Restore the TOP UCS, and try copying the circle. Observe that the copy is parallel to the top plane.
- Use Undo to remove the circle.
- Restore the INCLINED UCS, and copy the circle 0.5 units above the current XY plane.
- Add the ruling lines.
- Experiment with different Surftab1 settings to produce the ruled surface shown in Figure 6-21.
- Save the drawing as ALIGNBLK.

Figure 6-21
The Completed Wireframe

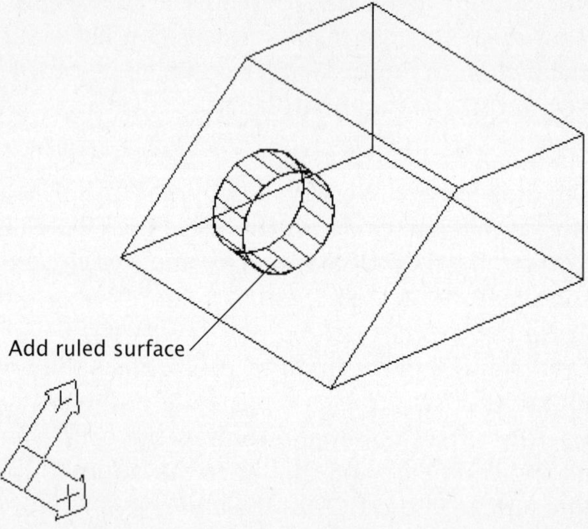

6-6 CREATING ORTHOGRAPHIC VIEWS FROM WIREFRAME MODELS

Orthographic views are the two-dimensional views used in drawings of objects that are to be manufactured. Orthographic views are visualized by a technique known as *orthographic projection*. An image of the object is projected onto a plane. If the plane is parallel to a principal plane in the object, the view is an orthographic view. This idea is illustrated in Figure 6-22.

Imagine that the rectangular prism in Figure 6-22 is placed in a glass box. If the outline of the prism is projected up to the top surface of the glass box, the top view appears in that plane. The dashed lines with arrows represent the projection lines. Three of the six possible orthographic views—front, top, and right side—are arranged on the right of the figure. This is the standard arrangement. The other three views are the bottom, back, and left side views.

Figure 6-22
Illustrating Orthographic Views

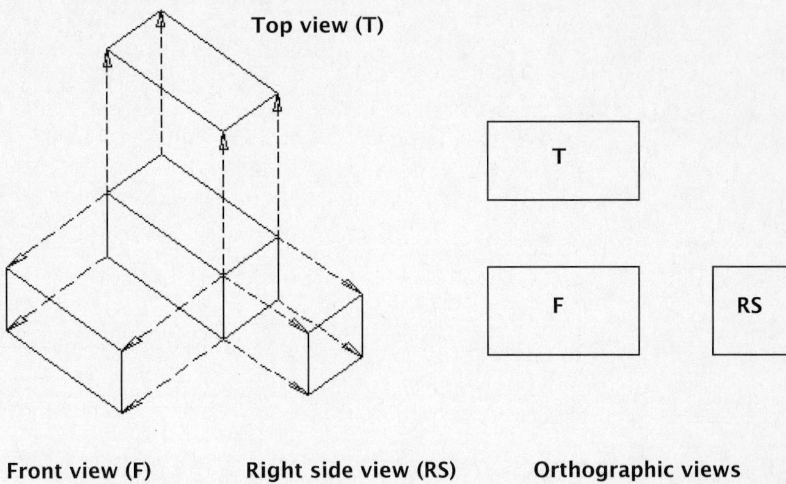

You can easily create standard orthographic views of the wireframe model of the alignment block that you just completed. Formal engineering drawings typically consist of three orthographic views, each showing the device from a different viewpoint. You will create three orthographic views plus a special pictorial view of the alignment block.

To create orthographic views from a wireframe model, you start by making blocks of the object. Recall that the Block command combines any number of drawn objects into a single entity. If you use the Block command on a wireframe model, the image captured is the view of the object projected into the plane of the current UCS. In other words, you can create a block of the top view of the alignment block while the TOP UCS is current. The front and right side views are captured as blocks while the FRONT and RIGHT UCSs, respectively, are current. You can then insert these blocks into a drawing and align them in the standard orthographic positions. You will need to remove the ruled surfaces and add the dimensions to complete the drawing.

Figure 6-23 shows three orthographic views of the alignment block. The 3D image of the wireframe is shown along with the three orthographic views. This image was created as a block using the UCS View option. The image captured by the Block command when the View UCS is current is the actual image of the wireframe on the screen.

Try It

- Open the UCSWF drawing.
- Create blocks with each of the ABC, ABD, and ACD UCSs current, plus a block with the UCS View option current.
- Change to the WCS and make a new layer.
- Insert the blocks back into the drawing on the new layer.

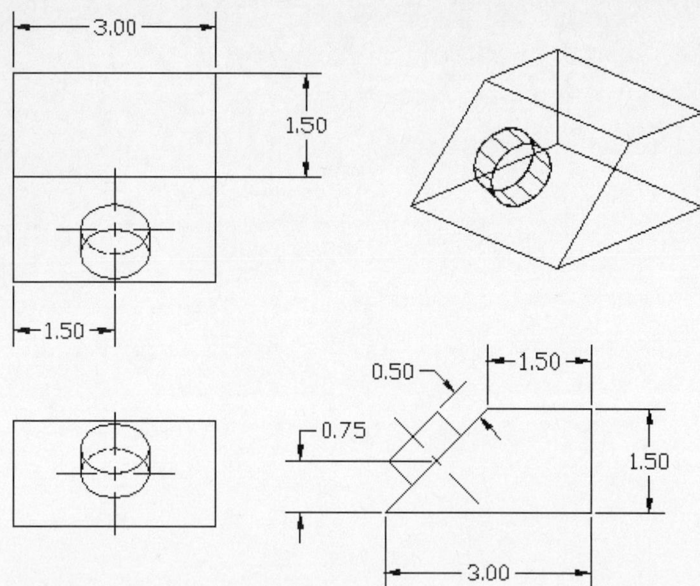

Figure 6-23
Orthographic Views from a Wireframe Model

The general strategy for assembling orthographic views from wireframe drawings is to create the blocks. Remember, using the Wblock command creates drawing files that you can insert into any drawing. After creating the Wblocks, you can insert them into a new drawing. As you insert the orthographic views, it is essential to align them accurately. This task is easier if you select a common base insertion point when you make the separate blocks.

Editing the wireframes presents some new problems. For instance, the cylinder in the right side view shows the ruling lines. You must erase these and replace them with two short lines. Similarly, you should erase the ruling lines in the front and top views. Before you can do any editing you must explode the blocks. The last step in completing the orthographic views is to add dimensions and notes. Refer to Chapter 5 if you need to refresh your memory on these topics.

Application 1: HYPERBOLIC PARABOLOID SHELLS

Civil and Structural Engineering

Hyperbolic paraboloids (hypars) are surfaces defined by the equation $z = kxy$. The surface is saddle shaped, with the center or saddle point at $x = y = 0$. The hypar is often used as a roof structure covering a square plan area. Figure 6-24 shows a hyperbolic paraboloid covering a 40-by-40-foot area. The front edges of the hypar are sloped upwards from the front corner to a point 16 feet above the lower corner. The back edges slope back downward 16 feet. If you use these dimensions, the value for k in the equation is 0.02.

The surface is a ruled surface. The hypar in Figure 6-24 shows the straight line generators very clearly. The same hypar is shown in Figure 6-25, in which the point of view is along a line through to lower corners. In this figure the architectural appeal of the surface is apparent.

Figure 6-24
Hyperbolic Paraboloid Surface

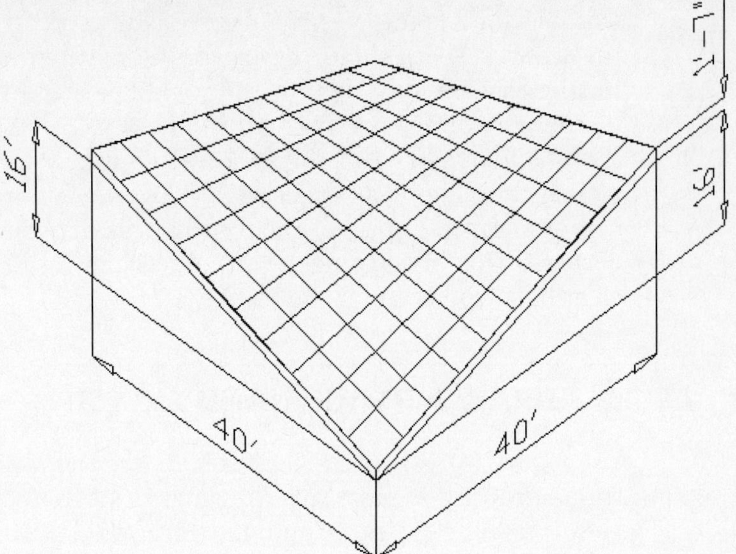

Exercise 6-25
Hyperbolic Paraboloid Surface View Along the Lower Corners

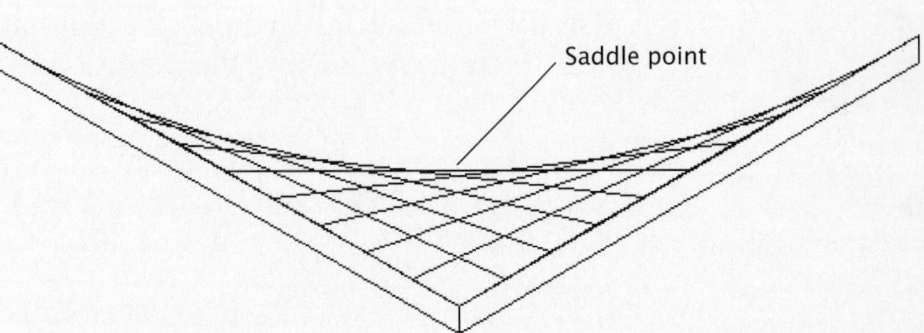

With ideal support conditions, impossible in real structures, the shell can be analyzed as a network of parabolic tension cables acting together with a network of compression arches. Because the ideal conditions are impossible, the shell may be analyzed as set of finite elements: the diamond-like figures formed by the intersecting ruling lines. Structural engineers will use a drawing like the one in Figure 6-25 to verify the geometric shape of the roof and define elements to be used later in the analysis. The drawings in Figures 6-24 and 6-25 may also be used as part of a presentation to an architectural client.

You can now use the five-step problem-solving process to draw the 3D hyperbolic paraboloid.

1. Identify the Object and Its Function

The object is the hyperbolic paraboloid shell. It is to be used as a roof structure. The shell will be supported on beams placed along the boundaries of the shell.

2. Research Models and Determine Dimensions

The choices of the geometry of the roof surface are limited by the area to be covered. Commonly used surfaces include flat plates, domes, barrel shells, folded plates, and the hypar. You will need to research each shape to decide if it is geometrically suitable. For example, a dome may not be suitable for a square area. Other factors to consider are the strength of the various shapes and the ease of construction. The hypar was chosen for the ease of construction and for the visual attractiveness of the shape.

The plan dimensions are set by the area to be covered. The selection of a single hypar to cover the area was chosen. An alternative plan would be to use four identical shells, each covering one quarter of the area. The common central point of the four hypars may be higher than the opposite corners. This arrangement will add visual interest while providing more clear head room under the roof.

3. DRAW A ROUGH HAND SKETCH

Use Figure 6-25 as a sketch. You can use the strategy developed for wire-frame drawing to start this drawing. Draw a 40-by-40-by-16-foot box, and view it using 225-degree and 45-degree angles. Draw the four sloping lines that define the edges of the shell. Figure 6-26 shows the result of this step. Use Offset and Trim to finish the thickened front edges. Erase the extra construction lines. Draw the surface with two sets of ruling lines. Figure 6–27 shows the progress so far.

Figure 6-26
Hyperbolic Paraboloid Layout—Step 1

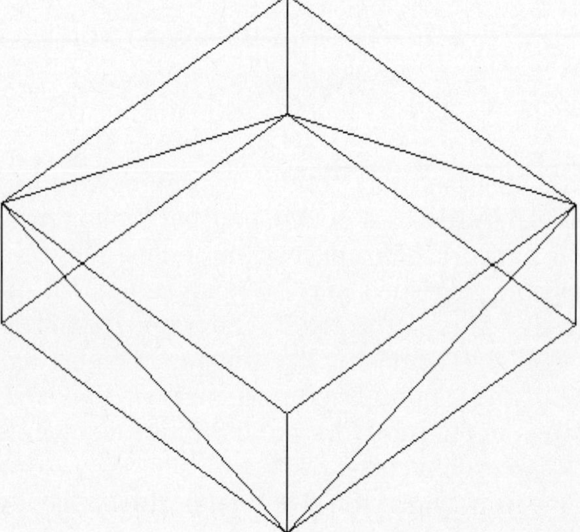

Draw one set of ruling lines using two opposite edges as defining curves. After you have drawn one set of ruling lines, you cannot choose the other pair of edges as defining curves for the second set of ruling lines. The first set of ruling lines creates a mesh, similar to a block. The mesh obscures the edges of the shell. When you try to select an edge as a defining curve, AutoCAD selects the mesh instead. To solve the problem, you must move the first mesh, add the second set of ruling lines, and move the first mesh back again. Figure 6-28 shows the two sets of ruling lines with the first set temporarily moved.

Figure 6-27
Adding Thickened Front Edges

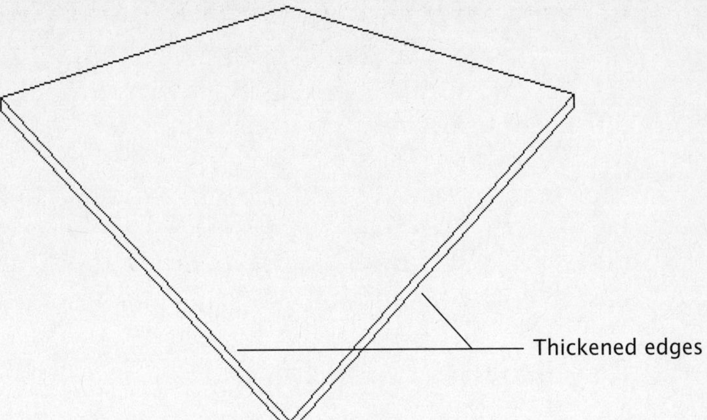

Figure 6-28
Adding the Ruled Surfaces

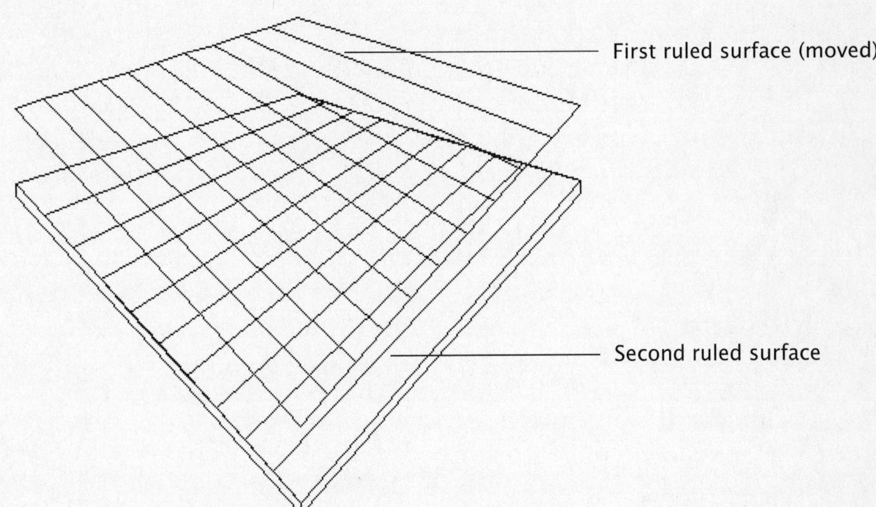

4. Make Proper Screen Adjustments

Use Engineering units with 1 decimal place. Set the limits to 0,0 and 60'45'. Save these settings as a new prototype.

5. Draw, Print, and Save the File.

Draw the hypar as shown in Figure 6-25. Create three Wblocks, one using the UCS View setting, one with angle settings of 225 degrees and 0 degrees, and one with angle settings of 270 degrees and 90 degrees. Insert these blocks into a new drawing, and add text describing the images.

What If

What if the selection of the type of roof to use required four 20-by-20-foot hypars adjacent to one another? The outside points on the hypars are to be at 0-foot elevation and the common center point at 16 feet. How will you modify your approach to draw this new configuration?

SUMMARY

In this chapter you first learned how to draw 3D objects using extrusions. Then you learned how to change your viewpoint to see the object in three dimensions. The next step was to combine individual extruded objects to make a more complex drawing. You learned how to control the screen icon, how to create User Coordinate Systems, and how to draw curved surfaces using the Rulesurf command. You used these tools to draw wireframe models. Finally, you learned what orthographic drawings are and how to create them from wireframe models.

Key Words

Compass and Axes system
defining curve
elevation
extruded object
hyperbolic paraboloid (hypar)
orthographic projection
orthographic view
ruled surface
ruling lines
screen icon
thickness
three-dimensional (3D)
User Coordinate System (UCS)
viewpoint
wireframe model (wireframe)
World Coordinate System (WCS)

Exercises

Exercise 6-1
Tool Jig

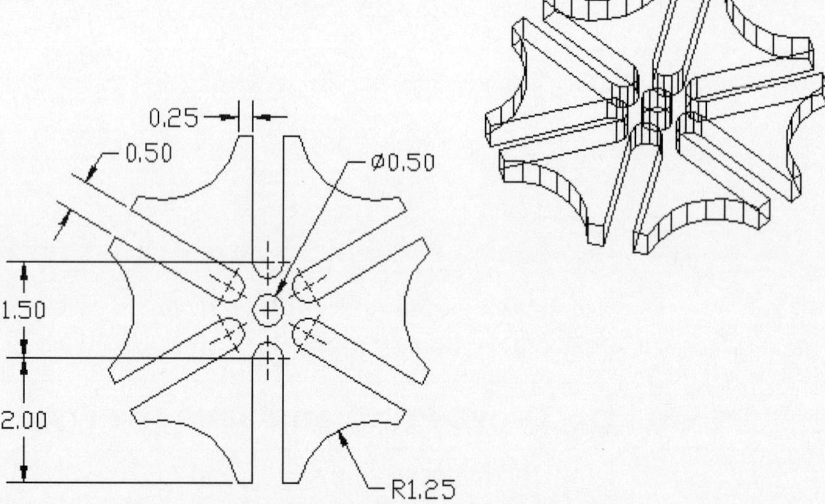

Make an extruded 3D drawing of the tool jig. The thickness is 0.5.

Exercise 6-2
Rocker Mechanism

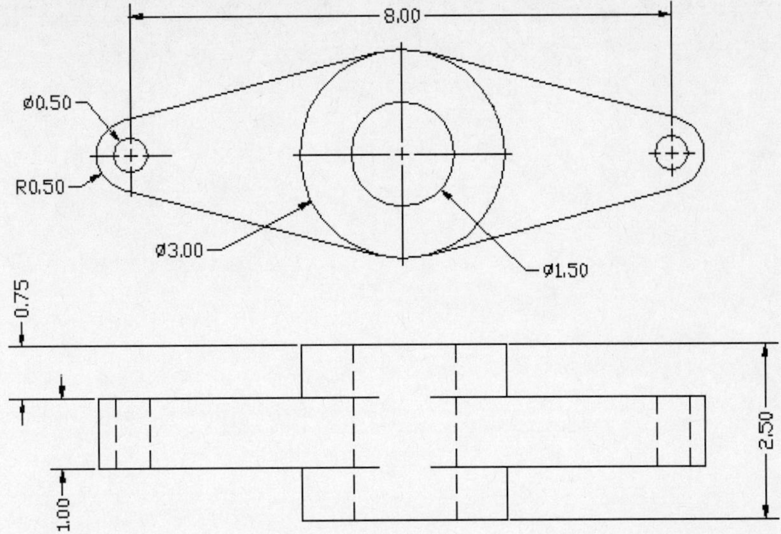

Make an extruded 3D drawing of the rocker mechanism.

Exercise 6-3
Gear

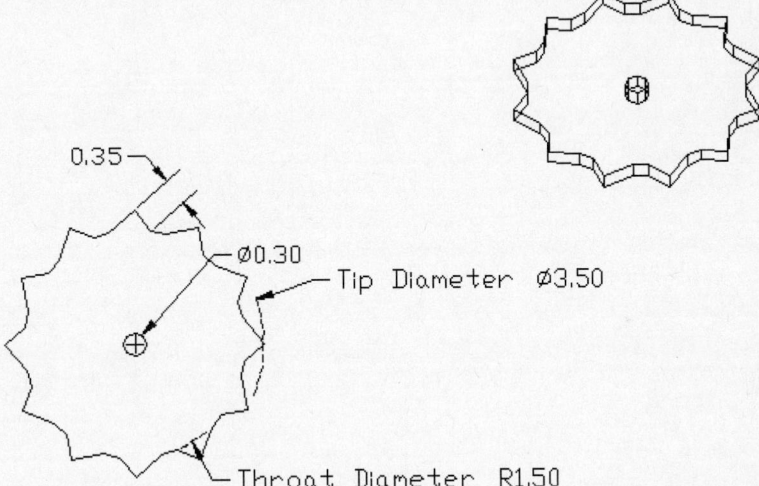

Make an extruded 3D drawing of the gear. The thickness is 0.2.

Exercise 6-4
Tool

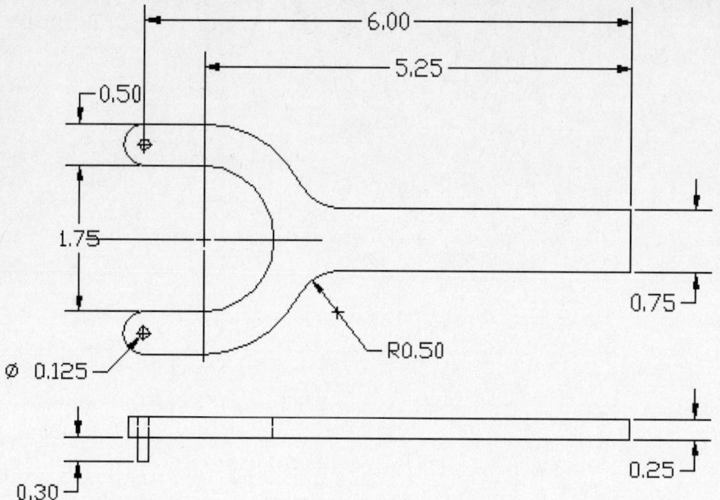

Make an extruded 3D drawing of the tool.

Exercise 6-5
Block

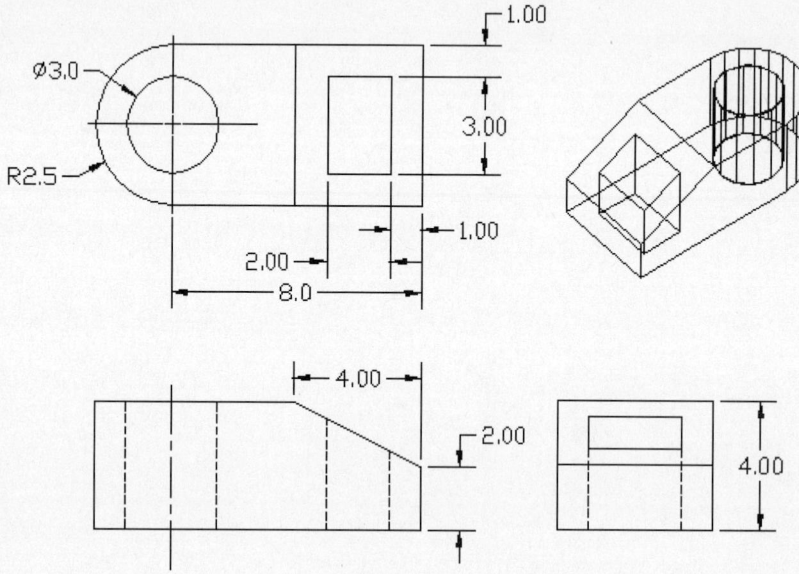

Make wireframe models of the devices in Exercises 6-5 through 6-9. Make orthographic drawings from the wireframe models. Add the dimensions and notes.

Exercise 6-6
Fin Plate

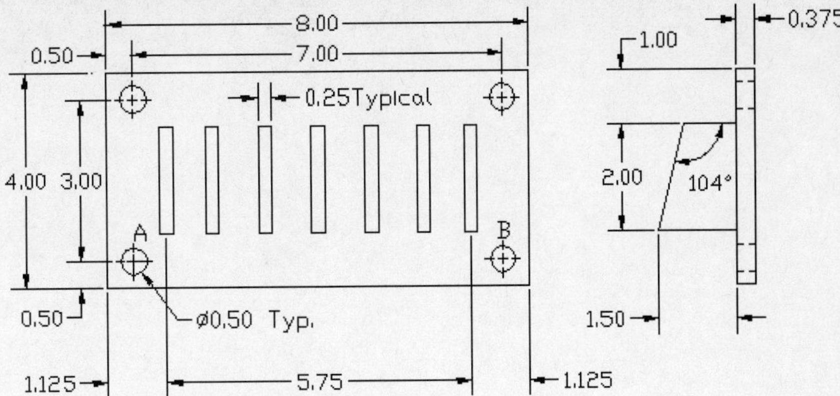

Exercise 6-7
Probe

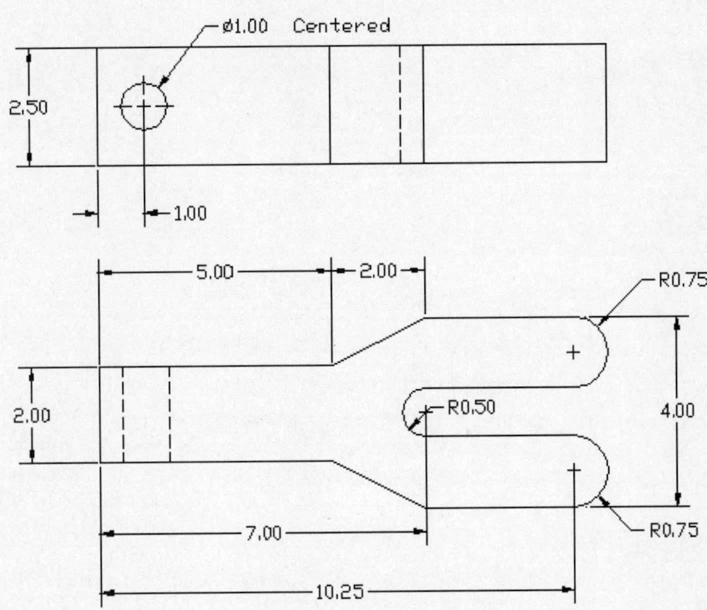

Exercise 6-8
Slide Plate

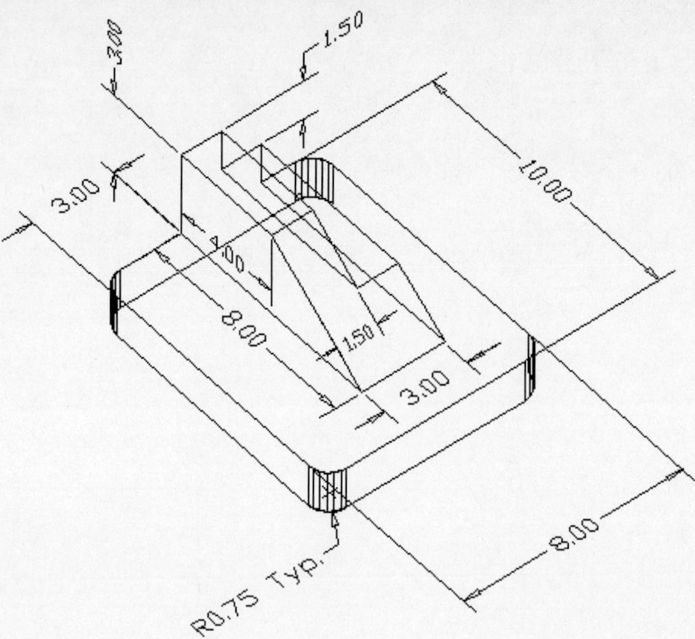

Exercise 6-9
Punch Guide

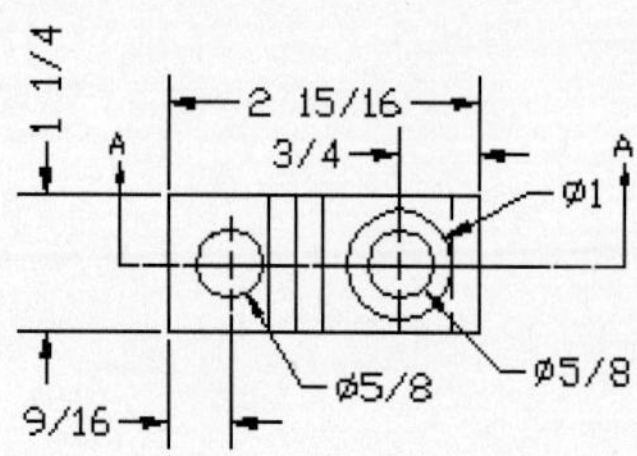

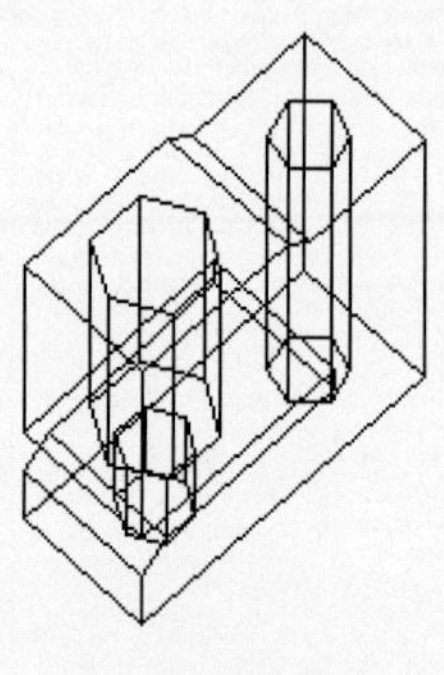

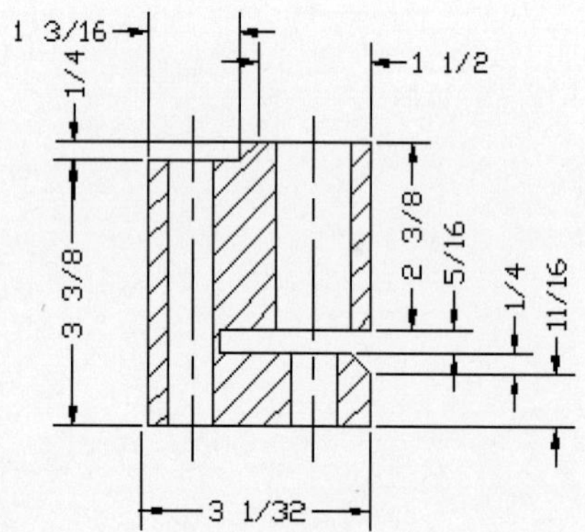

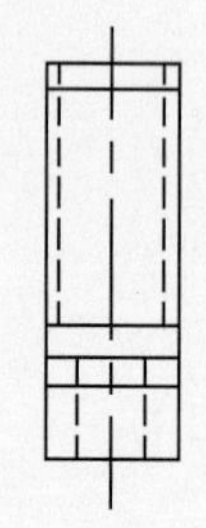

Index

NOTES

NOTES

NOTES

NOTES

NOTES

NOTES